Food Cultures of Mexico

**Recent Titles in
The Global Kitchen**

Food Cultures of the United States: Recipes, Customs, and Issues
Bruce Kraig

Food Cultures of Israel: Recipes, Customs, and Issues
Michael Ashkenazi

Food Cultures of France: Recipes, Customs, and Issues
Maryann Tebben

FOOD CULTURES OF MEXICO
Recipes, Customs, and Issues

R. Hernandez-Rodriguez

The Global Kitchen

BLOOMSBURY ACADEMIC
NEW YORK • LONDON • OXFORD • NEW DELHI • SYDNEY

BLOOMSBURY ACADEMIC
Bloomsbury Publishing Inc
1359 Broadway, New York, NY 10018, USA
50 Bedford Square, London, WC1B 3DP, UK
29 Earlsfort Terrace, Dublin 2, Ireland

BLOOMSBURY, BLOOMSBURY ACADEMIC and the Diana logo
are trademarks of Bloomsbury Publishing Plc

First published in the United States of America by ABC-CLIO 2021
Paperback edition published by Bloomsbury Academic 2025

Copyright © Bloomsbury Publishing Inc, 2025

COVER PHOTOS: Mercado Municipal, San Cristobal de las Casas, Chiapas, Mexico.
(dbimages/Alamy Stock Photo); World flags vectors. (pop_jop/iStockphoto)

All rights reserved. No part of this publication may be reproduced or
transmitted in any form or by any means, electronic or mechanical,
including photocopying, recording, or any information storage or retrieval
system, without prior permission in writing from the publishers.

Bloomsbury Publishing Inc does not have any control over, or responsibility for,
any third-party websites referred to or in this book. All internet addresses given
in this book were correct at the time of going to press. The author and publisher
regret any inconvenience caused if addresses have changed or sites have
ceased to exist, but can accept no responsibility for any such changes.

Library of Congress Cataloging-in-Publication Data
Names: Hernández Rodríguez, Rafael, 1963- author.
Title: Food cultures of Mexico : recipes, customs, and issues /
R. Hernandez-Rodriguez.
Description: Santa Barbara, California : Greenwood, an imprint of ABC-CLIO,
2021. | Series: The global kitchen | Includes bibliographical references
and index.
Identifiers: LCCN 2021009221 (print) | LCCN 2021009222 (ebook) |
ISBN 9781440869235 (cloth) | ISBN 9781440869242 (ebook)
Subjects: LCSH: Food habits—Mexico. | Cooking, Mexican. | Mexico—Social
life and customs.
Classification: LCC GT2853.M6 H49 2021 (print) | LCC GT2853.M6 (ebook) |
DDC 394.1/20972—dc23
LC record available at https://lccn.loc.gov/2021009221
LC ebook record available at https://lccn.loc.gov/2021009222

ISBN: HB: 978-1-4408-6923-5
PB: 979-8-2163-8669-8
ePDF: 978-1-4408-6924-2
eBook: 979-8-2160-8577-5

Series: The Global Kitchen

To find out more about our authors and books visit www.bloomsbury.com
and sign up for our newsletters.

For Rosi, Gaby, and Doña Esther Rodríguez

Contents

Series Foreword		ix
Introduction		xi
Chronology		xv
Chapter One	Food History	1
Chapter Two	Influential Ingredients	19
Chapter Three	Appetizers and Side Dishes	41
Chapter Four	Main Dishes	61
Chapter Five	Desserts	81
Chapter Six	Beverages	101
Chapter Seven	Holy Days and Special Occasions	121
Chapter Eight	Street Food and Snacks	145
Chapter Nine	Dining Out	165
Chapter Ten	Food Issues and Dietary Concerns	189
Glossary		209
Selected Bibliography		217
Index		223

Series Foreword

Imagine a typical American breakfast: bacon, eggs, toast, and home fries from the local diner. Or maybe a protein-packed smoothie, sipped on the go to class or work. In some countries in Europe, breakfast might just be a small cookie and a strong coffee, if anything at all. A South African breakfast might consist of a bowl of corn porridge with milk. In Japan, breakfast might look more like dinner, complete with rice, vegetables, and fish. What we eat varies from country to country, and even region to region. The Global Kitchen series explores the cuisines of different cultures around the world, from the history of food and food staples to main dishes and contemporary issues. Teeming with recipes to try at home, these volumes will delight readers by discovering other cultures through the lens of a treasured topic: food.

Each volume focuses on the culinary heritage of one country or one small group of countries, covering history and contemporary culture. Volumes begin with a chronology of major food-related milestones and events in the area, from prehistory to present. Chapters explore the key foods and meals in the country, covering the following topics:

- Food History;
- Influential Ingredients;
- Appetizers and Side Dishes;
- Main Dishes;
- Desserts;
- Beverages;
- Holidays and Special Occasions;
- Street Food and Snacks;
- Dining Out; and
- Food Issues and Dietary Concerns.

Chapters are textual, and each chapter is accompanied by numerous recipes, adding a hands-on component to the series. Sidebars, a glossary of important terms, and a selected bibliography round out each volume, providing readers with additional information and resources for their personal and scholarly research needs.

Whether readers are looking for recipes to use for classes or at home, or to explore the histories and traditions of world cuisines, the Global Kitchen series will allow readers to fully immerse themselves in other cultures, giving a taste of typical daily life and tradition.

Introduction

Mexican food in the United States has become so ubiquitous that it seems almost impossible to imagine a time when tacos, nachos, *quesadillas*, burritos, or *guacamole* were not a staple of the American diet and regular fare at restaurants and diners across the nation. Mexican restaurants are also part of our everyday life not only in big cities like New York, San Francisco, and Los Angeles but practically in any town in our nation. Mexican food—or Mexican-inspired food, rather—is an intrinsic part of the American culture that not only visually dominates the urban landscape with billboards, restaurant signs, and taco trucks, but it has entered our vernacular in phrases like the "whole enchilada," "holy guacamole," or "Montezuma's revenge." From chain restaurants, to "authentic" eateries, to fine dining establishments, Mexican food seems as American as, well, *pie de manzana*.

Part of the success of this cuisine is its proximity; part of its charm is its exoticism, at least to the average American—it is all those colorful margaritas; the spicy tacos that awake our taste buds; those restaurants covered with sombreros and multicolored piñatas hanging from the ceiling; the walls exhibiting riveting paintings of tiny villages and fields of agave and cactus plants; the smells of grilled meat and corn tortillas floating our way every time a waitress passes by our table with somebody else's order or when a basket of chips and salsa is presented to us as a welcoming offer; it is the loud and festive mariachi music, as well as the fluorescent palm trees. But Mexican food is much more than that. It is a cuisine that can trace its roots thousands of years back; a cuisine that emerged from the encounter of Native American and European cultures and evolved for over five centuries of mixing gastronomies and traditions; a cuisine that helped Mexicans to reaffirm their identity when the nation became independent from Spain; a cuisine that connected deeply with the people and became truly national after a bloody revolution; a cuisine that transformed itself during the twentieth century and transcended its borders to become a world cuisine known in other nations and other continents.

A cuisine that as a crowning achievement boasts being the first one to be recognized by United Nations Educational, Scientific and Cultural Organization (UNESCO) as an intangible cultural heritage of the world, which for some disingenuous people, confirms the importance of Mexican food around the world. This is a monumental achievement, no doubt, but it begs the question, why not Italian, or French, or Peruvian food? After all, Mexican food is neither the most sophisticated in the world nor the most aristocratic or even the most diverse and better tasting. These aspects are all a matter of personal predilection, certainly; however, they help us to point what is essential about Mexican food without disregarding its creativity and its importance for our tastebuds. And this is exactly what UNESCO acknowledged when considering Mexican food as a candidate for cultural world heritage and what convinced them in the end that it was a cuisine worth being preserved: its importance for Mexican cultural identity.

This intimate connection with a people, not only with Mexicans living in the country but the millions more around the world, who see in food a direct link to the life they left behind is central to the preservation of the cuisine. As beloved Mexican poet Ramón López Velarde wrote in his masterful poem "Sweet Motherland," Mexico always offers "a paradise of compotes" to its children and then it gives itself to them in such a way that "on loving tongue they savor / the tang of sesame seeds," so much so that "in the early mornings of the homeland, / on streets like mirrors, overflows / the holy aroma of a bakery." Immigrants always travel with their gastronomy, and Mexicans are no exception. But what is interesting about Mexican immigrants is the active and conscious will they have to preserve a popular cuisine no matter where they are, based on tradition, but aware that it has, and continues to be, adapted to other circumstances and other latitudes, with a conviction, above all, that it matters.

Yet despite its popularity and its importance, the history of Mexican food remains relatively unknown to most people. This book will try to offer a comprehensive, although concise, account of the development of what the author considers Mexican food, from its Mesoamerican and Iberian origins, to its interaction with other cuisines, and to its reinvention in recent decades by imaginative chefs. Along the way, the book will review some of the most important appetizers, main dishes, drinks, and desserts that characterize this gastronomy. The book will also look into ingredients that are the most influential and into what foods are traditional for holidays and special occasions, as well as what sorts of foods people eat on the street or when they go out to celebrate special events in their lives at elegant restaurants, some of which are considered among the best in the world. The text will talk about not only what sort of restaurants people frequent but also what other traditional venues are there when going out in Mexico, such as markets, stands, and popular fairs.

This text will also teach readers how to make traditional dishes, and not just the ones that mothers make at home every day, but exciting, cool foods one could find on the street or at a fancy restaurant. In other words, readers will fully experience a food that cannot be separated from the culture, the history, the traditions, and the people that made it and enjoyed it for centuries. At the same time, the book will look into several issues that are related to food and eating habits; particularly, it will pay attention to how changes in a traditional diet may have contributed recently to a serious obesity epidemic and to an increase in noncommunicable diseases in Mexico. But above all, readers will have the opportunity to look into a cuisine that most think they know, hopefully with new eyes, to discover its past, to experience its present, and to contemplate its future. As noted earlier, Mexican food cannot be separated from the culture, the history, the traditions, and the people of Mexico. However, its recognition as a world heritage also means that this cuisine represents much more than that and that it belongs to all. But above all, it confirms something that everyone already knows: it tastes pretty good.

Chronology

22–20,000 BCE
The first humans arrive in Mesoamerica, probably from Asia.

10,000 BCE
Groups of hunters and gatherers establish themselves in North and South America.

8000 BCE
Humans settle in Mesoamerica; they start domesticating local plants, most notably corn.

1300–400 BCE
The Olmecs, considered the earliest Mesoamerican civilization, appear along the coast of the Gulf of Mexico.

100 BCE–750 CE
The civilization that built the monumental city of Teotihuacan flourishes.

100 BCE–300 CE
The Maya begin to rise as a distinctive civilization.

300–900 CE
This period marks the splendor of the Maya civilization in what archeologists considered the classic period.

900–1168 CE
The Toltecs flourish in central Mexico.

1325–1521 CE
The Aztecs establish and flourish in what is today Mexico City.

1519
Hernán Cortés arrives on the coast of the Gulf of Mexico and founds the village of Veracruz, marking the beginning of the conquest of Mexico.

1521
Tenochtitlan, the proud capital of the Aztec Empire, falls to the Spaniards after years of war, consolidating the conquest of Mexico.

1511
King Ferdinand orders Spanish explorers to bring turkeys to Spain, five females and five males.

1528
Cortés returns to Spain after conquering Mexico and brings chocolate and probably tomatoes to Europe.

1535
The viceroyalty of New Spain is established including what is today Mexico, the Southwest United States, California, and Texas, as well as parts of Central America.

1541
Charles V gives permission to Alonso de Herrera to produce beer in New Spain.

1606
Chocolate is brought to Italy from Spain by Antonio Carletti, starting its dissemination through the rest of Europe.

1615
Spanish princess Anne of Austria gives her future husband, Louis XIII, a present of chocolate as an engagement gift, thus starting its popularity outside of Spain.

1785–1786
The Hunger Year, called this because of a widespread famine in New Spain caused by early frosts and droughts.

1795
José Cuervo gets permission from the Crown of Spain to produce tequila.

1810
New Spain declares its independence from Spain. A ten-year war follows.

1821
New Spain gains its independence from Spain and becomes Mexico.

1821–1822
Agustín de Iturbide is proclaimed emperor of Mexico in what is known as the First Mexican Empire.

1824–1835
The first republic is established in Mexico, with Guadalupe Victoria as the first president.

1833–1844
Santa Anna governs Mexico as a dictator.

Chronology

1836
Texas separates from Mexico.

1838–1839
France invades Mexico in what is known as the Pastry War or First French Invasion

1846–1848
Mexican-American War. Mexico loses almost half of its territory.

1861
Napoleon III invades Mexico in what is known as the Second French Invasion.

1864
Maximilian of Habsburg arrives in Mexico to take over the government of the Mexican Empire. That year also the first European bakery, El Globo, opens its doors.

1864–1867
Maximilian and his wife, Charlotte of Belgium, establish a European-like court in Mexico City, with an army of chefs, cooks, and pastry chefs brought from Austria, France, and Italy.

1867
Benito Juárez, elected president of Mexico, expels the French and marks an end to Maximilian's empire. On June 19, Maximilian of Habsburg is executed by firing squad in the Cerro de las Campanas.

1867–1876
Restoration of the Republic.

1876–1911
Dictator Porfirio Díaz becomes president and remains in power for over 30 years.

1888
Nuevo Cocinero Mexicano, the first cookbook of Mexican food, is published in Paris.

1910–1921
The Mexican Revolution starts a violent war against Dictator Díaz.

1921
An exhibition of popular arts, the first of its kind in Mexico, and a *Noche Mexicana* are organized in September to celebrate the popular culture and food of Mexico.

1938
Mexico nationalizes its oil industry.

1940s–1950s
Period of modernization and industrialization with the first civilian presidents since Juárez.

1968
Mexico is the first Latin American country to organize the Summer Olympics; the government wants to project an image of peace and prosperity to attract tourism. Weeks before the event, there is a massacre of students demanding more participation in the public life and more opportunities.

1970
Mexico organizes the Soccer World Cup and attracts thousands of foreign tourists.

1974
Tequila becomes the first non-European spirit to be given a denomination of origin.

1976
Huge reserves of oil are discovered in the Gulf of Mexico, making Mexico an important exporter of oil.

1980s
Periods of economic crisis show a decline in the standard of living; foreign liquors, spirits, and other foods are considered luxury items. The consumption of national products is encouraged instead.

1985
On September 19, an 8.1 earthquake on the Richter Scale with its epicenter in the state of Oaxaca devastates Mexico City and other cities nearby, killing thousands.

1986
Mexico organizes the Soccer World Cup for a second time, giving a boost to its tourism industry.

1994
The North America Free Trade Agreement (NAFTA) goes into effect.

2000
The governing party since the revolution is defeated. President Vicente Fox of the conservative party PAN becomes president. Pujol, the restaurant considered the best in Mexico and one of the best in the world, opens.

2002
First Starbucks opens in Mexico.

2010
On November 16 Mexican food is declared an Intangible Heritage of Humanity by UNESCO.

2018
Andrés Manuel López Obrador becomes the first left-wing president of Mexico.

2020
On March 27 a new law for labeling processed food that requires large, frontal warning symbols that products are high in sugar, saturated fats, and salt becomes official.

CHAPTER ONE

Food History

The Indigenous Civilizations

The history of Mexican food is long and interesting. It is a history that involves a variety of ingredients indigenous to the Americas, as well as techniques developed by pre-Columbian civilizations, some of which disappeared from history, leaving no record or a few clues as to their way of life. This history also includes the overlapping of traditions, cultures, and practices of Native American civilizations first, and later, of European ones, with the arrival of the Spaniards. The history of Mexican food is indeed millenary, considering that it begins with the foods of the ancient cultures of Mesoamerica—a name given by specialists to the middle part of the continent, including the central and southern parts of Mexico and all of Central America—where some of the most advanced civilizations in the continent settled and prospered and where their cuisine later blended with another equally millenary cuisine, that of the Iberian Peninsula. The food the Spaniards brought to Mexico was already a combination of the food of different cultures such as Phoenician, Greek, Roman, Carthaginian, Jewish, and, above all, Moorish. Even though Mexican food, strictly speaking, is the food resulting from the combination of Iberian and Mesoamerican cuisines, it is fair to consider the latest the more distinctive of the two.

Roughly speaking, archeologists think that the first inhabitants of Mesoamerica arrived in the area some 20,000 years before Christ. According to Mexican archeologist José Luis Lorenzo, the finding in the 1960s of two hearths and bones of Pleistocene animals that had been roasted and consumed in Tlapacoya, an archeological site near Mexico City, confirmed the presence of humans "at that place some twenty-two to twenty-one thousand years before our era" (103). Some 10,000 years later, semi-nomadic groups of hunter-gatherers were already established in most of North and South America. These peoples, for the most part, ate the roots and plants collected nearby and some local animals they managed to kill. Some archeologists think the animals they killed included large species like bears, deer, and even mammoth, but others think that, considering the rudimentary tools they had, most likely they specialized in small game, although it is possible they took advantage of large animals trapped in mud or scavenged those killed by wolves, big cats, and other predators. It was not until about 6000 to 5000 BC, however, that Mesoamericans started cultivating native plants, most notably corn, which allowed them to transition into sedentary communities that grew to become important civilizations.

The first known civilization in Mesoamerica, and the one that is considered the predecessor of other civilizations like the Maya and the Aztecs, is the Olmec, a civilization active some 3,000 years ago, which thrived on the coast of the Gulf of Mexico. Simultaneously, in neighboring regions, other Olmec-like cultures developed, expanding the influence of the Olmecs to a large portion of Mesoamerica. What made the advancement of this civilization possible was the development of agriculture and the invention of cultivation techniques. The three main crops of Mesoamerican cultures were corn, a plant of the grass family that was domesticated some 10,000 years ago; beans; and chili peppers—these crops were the basis for a rather balanced diet, a diet complemented by other domesticated plants, like squash and sweet potatoes, but also wild fruits, plants, grains, roots, and animals such as deer and boar. They also had domesticated birds, most notably duck and turkey.

Fishing in the rivers and lakes of central and southern Mexico, although in a lesser degree, was also an important dietary source, as well as the collection of honey. The splendor of the Olmec civilization lasted until 400 BCE. Unfortunately, not much is known about this ancient people, as wonderful as the remains of their civilization that survived are, since they did not leave any written records of their existence. What is known has been put together by archeological excavations and the analysis and interpretation of monuments, stone sculptures, and a few organic remains. Regrettably, practically no human remains have survived that could give us an idea of their physical characteristics or genetic information; their lack of writing or any way of keeping records has made it impossible to learn much about their language, religion, social organization, commerce, art, poetry, or philosophy. The decline of the Olmecs coincided with the rise of the other great ancient Mesoamerican civilization—the Maya.

Approximately 2,000 years ago, the Maya developed the first great civilization of Mesoamerica, a civilization with a complex social organization and with an advanced understanding of mathematics, astronomy, architecture, and the arts. Like the Olmecs, the Maya depended on agriculture to survive, and their crops were the same as the Olmecs, with the addition of other products more adapted to their torrid climate like cacao, pineapple, and other tropical delights. Corn, beans, and chili peppers nonetheless remained the main crops for the Maya, just like they were fundamental for all the other Mesoamerican civilizations. Unlike the Olmecs, the ancient Maya created a writing system and were meticulous about keeping records of their lives, religion, history, philosophy, art, and everyday affairs, and therefore were able to preserve detailed information about their civilization, making it a lot easier for future generations to value and understand their achievements. The development of the Maya civilization is divided in three periods. The first one is called Protoclassic and goes from 100 BCE to 300 CE. This period is known for the emergence of elaborate urban centers with a distinctive architecture.

However, the Maya civilization that is admired and recognized all over the world because of its advances in art, science, and technology; the one that created a very precise calendar; the one that left impressive temples and pyramids that conquered the jungles of southern Mexico, is the one that flourished during a period that encompasses roughly six centuries, from 300 to 900 CE. It is during this period that Maya civilization reaches its peak and develops a highly advanced writing system. Because of this distinctive characteristic, more information about the Maya than any other ancient American civilization has reached us, providing precious knowledge about their social system, as well as their cosmovision, but also about their eating habits. After the splendor of the Maya, around 900 CE, this civilization rapidly came to an end. The Maya had never erected a centralized empire, but rather like the Greeks, they were a civilization based on independent city-states.

The precise reason for the collapse of the Maya civilization is still a mystery, but most archeologists and historians agree that something forced the people to abandon their cities, and for many, that "something" may have been a famine. Based on the records and the archeological remains that survived to today, it is known that the population had grown so large that it simply became harder to feed all the people. Under these circumstances, any unforeseen event could have spelled disaster, and that is precisely what most experts think happened—that a disaster occurred in the form of a drought. Other experts think that it was rather the progressive yet constant struggle for controlling the available resources between the several city-states that precipitated the decline of the civilization. Whatever the reason, the Maya dispersed throughout the jungles of Central America and the plateau of the Yucatán Peninsula by the end of the first millennium. By the time the Spaniards got to Mexico in 1519, they found isolated communities in the region. Inga Clendinnen gives us an indication of the first steps of amalgamation of the two cuisines when she writes how Indians brought to the Spaniards corn tortillas, fruits, honey, ducks, and turkeys, which the Europeans called chickens, "as offerings of peace as they approached certain towns," adding that the Spaniards saw these gifts "as food first, tokens of submission second, and as evidence of native agricultural techniques or modes of production not at all" (Clendinnen, *Ambivalent Conquest*, 24).

Parallel to the rise of the Maya, there was another civilization that dominated the central valley of Mexico. This civilization's epicenter was an urban complex called Teotihuacan, considered the most impressive city of pre-Columbian America. Since very little information exists about this civilization, and since the name of the people that built it is unknown, they are called Teotihuacans. The city was so impressive already in the view of the Aztecs that they thought the city had been built by the gods. The name "Teotihuacan" actually means City of the Gods in *Nahuatl*, the language of the Aztecs. By the time the Aztecs appeared as a civilization, the Teotihuacans had already vanished and, like the Olmecs, left no trace of their existence, except for a monumental empty city. This civilization expanded from 100 BCE to 750 CE, and information about the civilization is based on archeological findings and the magnificence of their city. This city stands still, glorious and defiant, just outside of Mexico City. The beautiful palaces, the mural paintings still visible in many of them, and the two imposing pyramids reveal a sophistication without parallel and explain the name given by the Aztecs to the city centuries after it had been abandoned.

Although a mystery in many ways, Teotihuacan shares many cultural aspects with other Mesoamerican cultures, like the Olmecs, the Toltecs, the Maya, and the Aztecs. One of them is, of course, food. Some of the same crops and techniques that distinguish these cultures were also found in the archeological excavations of Teotihuacan. Like in the case of the Maya, many archeologists have suggested that the fall of Teotihuacan was related to its splendor; that the city had grown so large that it became impossible to feed its populations. Experts think that its decline was due to an unbalanced relationship with the environment. Maya and Teotihuacans overlapped in their development, and recent discoveries showed that they interacted with each other, so it is possible that they also fought for resources. The interaction and exchanges between Mesoamerican cultures, from the early settlements to the arrival of the Europeans, is now considered a fact by most archeologists. This is what allows us also to talk about them as Mesoamericans, a conglomerate of related civilizations, sharing traditions, culture, and most certainly eating habits. Among these Mesoamerican civilizations, the Toltec have a capital importance. The Toltec flourished in central Mexico around the first millennium CE, and it was considered by the Aztecs their mother culture. In fact, for the Aztecs, Toltec, as an adjective, often meant civilized, as opposed to *chichimeca*, or barbarian, a word used to refer to the semi-nomadic peoples from northern Mexico and the southwestern United States.

Gastronomically speaking, all these civilizations shared similar foods and cooking techniques, shaping a common cuisine based on maize processed and cooked with lime and ashes (a technique called "nixtamalization") to make it edible; ground it; and then made it into tortillas, *tamales*, and other cakes or diluted in water with spices, fruits, or honey to make traditional drinks. By the time of the arrival of the Europeans, Mesoamerica had already developed highly advanced civilizations with distinctive cultural traits and a common cuisine that included some of the same ingredients, techniques, and utensils. Because these civilizations established commercial routes, they made it easier to share these techniques and ingredients, expanding their culinary exposure by consuming not only what was natural to their environment but also incorporating other crops from distant lands into their diets. The appearance of maritime motifs in the temples of Teotihuacan, for example, a city hundreds of miles away from the ocean, seems to corroborate this. Also, Moctezuma, the Aztec emperor, had fish available to him daily, brought fresh from the Gulf of Mexico by an elaborate system of relay races.

Of all the Mesoamerican civilizations, it is the Aztec that is the most well known. Not only is it the civilization that came in direct contact with the Europeans at its pick but also the one that conquered its neighbors, consolidating an empire and establishing commercial and tributary exchanges with them. They kept accurate records of their way of life in codices that allowed us to take a look into their particular view of the world. Since they came into direct contact with the Europeans, information about the Aztec appears in chronicles, histories, translations, and other writings compiled by the conquistadores. When the Spaniards arrived in Mexico in 1519, they encountered a very sophisticated empire that amazed them not only because of its richness and social organization but also because of the bounty and diversity of crops and foods available in the land. The Spaniards that first colonized Mexico talked again and again about the marvelous spectacle of the markets, which were many according to Fray Bartolomé de las Casas, where all sorts of edible things, raw and cooked, were sold, including many vegetables, different varieties of fruits—some similar to the ones known in Spain and some very different—and countless roots and herbs, as well as fish, all kinds of birds, rabbits, hares, deer, and, to de Las Casas's amazement, salt. The same account is given by Bernal Díaz, a soldier who could not help it but write in awe at the sight of the main market in the Aztec capital. He remarks that the market was very organized and one could find women selling cooked foods, including "small cakes made from a sort of ooze which they get out of the great lake" that tasted like cheese (Díaz, 73). He was so overwhelmed in amazement at what he saw, that in frustration he exclaims: "But why do I waste so many words in recounting what they sell in that great market, for I shall never finish if I tell it all in detail" (Díaz, 72).

The bounty and diversity of foods sold in markets surprised the Europeans because of their variety but also because of their novelty, forcing them to make sense of it all. Their struggle was particularly evident in their attempts to catalogue, organize, and interpret, according to their own views, this new information. The cooking techniques and the table etiquette of the Aztecs were equally surprising, such that Cortés makes a point to describe in detail the eating habits of Moctezuma to the king of Spain: how the meals were served by hundreds of youths and how the dishes were so numerous "that the king ate or drank every manner of dish served to him, whether it were meat, fish, fruit, or herbs of whatever kind was found in the land. Since the climate is cold every plate and dish had under it a little brazier filled with lighted coals that it might not get cold" (96). After the emperor had eaten and smoked tobacco, the house servants and the emperor's guard would eat from the leftover food. The Aztecs were a highly stratified society; however, the basic organizing principle was the family, and most land was communal, so each family grew their own food, which they could consume, store, or trade for goods. The situation of the ordinary people was very different from that of the nobility and poverty existed in the Aztec capital, just like in Europe at the time; in fact, "Cortés took it as a final proof of Indian civility that the poor begged from the rich in city streets in Mexico, just as they did in Spain" (Clendinnen, *Ambivalent Conquest*, 38).

With time, Spaniards became ambivalent about this food. If they had accepted it at first, it was because they needed it to survive, but once Mexico became New Spain, grains, herbs, and livestock were brought from Europe. Once settled, the Europeans favored wheat, dairy products, and meat as their main diet, while indigenous people continued to rely heavily on traditional Mesoamerican products. Soon, however, they developed a taste for each other's foods. Ingredients and techniques started to mix, creating a new cuisine. Besides cattle, pork, wheat, and cheese, fruits like lemons, oranges, figs, quince, plums, and pomegranates were brought to America, while native ingredients were taken to the Old World and incorporated into the European diet. Tomatoes, for example, are today more associated with Italian food than with Mexican food, and chocolate is considered quintessentially Swiss, even though the Aztecs and Maya deemed it a delicacy given to them by the gods. Beef, pork, cheese, and cream became staples of the colonial diet flavored with local spices, chili peppers, and herbs and cooked in ways similar to the ways the Aztecs and Maya cooked.

Colonial Mexico

For over 300 years of colonial dominance, New Spain developed traditional dishes and foods that reflected this amalgamation of European and American cuisines. The traditional Mesoamerican diet was now seasoned with pork lard, cheese, butter, or cream. Even though American dishes like *mole* and tomato stews were common among all classes and ethnicities, chili peppers, beans, and corn remained for the most part the food favored by the masses. Over the centuries, following the political and social trends of the colony, food continue to evolve and developed into an authentic American cuisine, where corn, squash, chilies, and beans continued to reign supreme across the colonies, combined with foods and products brought from Spain. The traditional cuisine of the Iberian Peninsula by the time the Spaniards came to Mexico was already a blend of local products and those brought by the Romans and the Moors. Fruits, plants, spices, and even animals typical of Middle Eastern cuisine became part of the traditional Spanish diet. Nevertheless, in a region at constant war with Muslims, which had also maintained an ambivalent attitude towards Jewish communities since early on, food for the Iberians became an obvious indicator of identity. Eating pork, for example, was more than just a dietary preference for them and was turned into a political statement, since both Islam and Judaism forbid eating pork. This preference for pork and pork products was brought to Mexico and prevails even today in the use of lard and in the classic combination, typically Mexican, of pork and beans or pork in tomatillo sauces.

Once Mexico became New Spain, palaces, convents, and Christian churches were built all over on top of indigenous temples and pyramids, using the same stones and materials of the pagan edifices. A new culture was literally imposed over the old one, creating a society that had no precedent in the world. This peculiarity was evident in practically all aspects of colonial life, such as religion, politics, social organization, art, and food. Of all of them, food is perhaps the most interesting one, simply because it is at the center of life. The mixing of ingredients from the Old and the New Worlds continued and created a new variety of dishes and food traditions. It is this combination of ingredients, techniques, and traditions that is collectively called Mexican food, and it started early on but continues to evolve through time. Even though ambivalent at first, Europeans not only adopted some of the Indian foods but also praised them for their nutritious value and curative properties as well as taste. And despite the resistance of the indigenous people to completely adopt the European diet, as López de Gómara comments, surprised that the Indians preferred their traditional foods when they had access to bread, meat, and wine, both foods coexisted and combined in harmony. A nun from the seventeenth century testifies to this when she writes that in her house tortillas were made every day "to put on the table, for it is custom, in the country on the haciendas, to serve both bread and tortillas together" (Myers, 71).

Independent Mexico

After Mexico became independent from Spain, the food did not change much or that dramatically from the food consumed during the colonial era. It did change, however, in the same way that any other cuisine changes—as the result of its interaction with different culinary fashions. Migration within the country and from other countries, the political and social environment, and the presence and importance of certain nations that interacted with the new nation all played a role in the evolution of Mexican food. But the core of what is considered Mexican food—that mix of European and American ingredients and techniques—had already been established and remained unchanged. According to many historians, New Spain was already looking towards the future at the end of the eighteenth century, rejecting the Baroque and embracing the Enlightenment, and with it, its own identity. With independence came a sense of pride in the richness and fertility of the land and in the heritage of the native cultures.

However, political problems made it difficult for the young nation to live up to its potential. The decades after independence saw a plague of civil wars, international conflicts, invasions, and wars with the United States and France, culminating with Mexico losing large parts of its territory and the imposition of a European emperor, Maximilian of Habsburg. Successive interactions with nations like Spain, Italy, and Austria continued to alter Mexican food. French cuisine in particular became important for Mexicans early on, in part because France invaded the country twice in less than 30 years. The first invasion (1838–1839), in fact, is known as *Guerra de los Pasteles* (Pastry War), and it was provoked by a group of French pastry chefs complaining of the looting of their shops by Mexican forces during one of the civil wars between liberals and conservatives. The second war (1862–1867) was a response by Napoleon III to a two-year moratorium imposed by President Benito Juarez on the Mexican foreign debt. France saw this as an opportunity to expand its influence in America and openly supported Maximilian of Austria when he was offered and accepted the crown of the Mexican Empire (1864–1867). The emperor arrived in Mexico, bringing with him cooks, bakers, and other servants that made sure he and his wife, Princess Charlotte of Belgium, had the sort of luxurious foods they were used to. However, as Empress Charlotte wrote to friends in Europe, they started to adopt some local ingredients and adapt them to their dishes. The end of the imperial dream of Maximilian, a few years after his arrival in Mexico, signaled the beginning of the Mexican Republic, and it was accompanied by a patriotic fervor that was evident in every aspect of the life and culture of Mexico, including the food.

It became harder and harder to distinguish one social or ethnic group from another based solely on what they ate at home. Due to the constant civil wars, the war with the United States that cost Mexico half of its territory, and the French invasions, the production of food suffered enormously, since many haciendas and farms were burnt to the ground by the invaders, forcing the population to rely on family gardens and the food produced in the traditional communal agricultural lands. Home cooking was again based on the traditional food of the country: corn, beans, and chilies. Once Mexico became more stable, the aristocracy and the emergent middle class were presented with the opportunity to eat European-like foods at the cafés and restaurants that many invaders-turned-cooks opened in the cities. For most Mexicans at the time, dining out meant eating French food. People nonetheless continued to transform Mexican food by incorporating these foreign influences into the foods they consumed at home, often served side by side on the table.

Several indirect sources, mostly literary and travel diaries, confirm this coexistence of food, drinks, and techniques. One of the most evident is Guillermo Prieto, the most popular poet of the nineteenth century, who was also a politician of the Liberal Party. His volume of popular poems, *Musa Callejera (Street Muse)*, aims at revealing a true national culture, already there but in need of articulation. In many of his poems, food is not only mentioned but is the main theme—often jokingly—revealing a unique Mexican culture. He mocks, for example, pretentious poor girls who claim

"Not to know what tortillas or lentils are," and eat only "*Beefsteak*, salmon, and *roast beef*" (Prieto, 89). And he describes a dinner where "Quickly the slices of / Lamb disappear / While in a pond of sauce / A *chile relleno* sticks out" (Prieto, 105). He mentions bread, vegetables, sausages, fruits, and sweets, as well as traditional dishes like *mole verde* and *tamales*. But perhaps the verses that give us a better idea of the coexistence of drinks and foods of both traditions are the ones where he describes a picnic, where bottles of champagne are next to the pots with pineapple *pulque*, and the *mole* and sausages appeared side by side with radishes and French fries (Prieto, 119).

Modern Mexico

While most of the people regularly ate a combination of traditional Mexican and European foods, restaurants and elegant dinners were dominated by French cuisine until at least the revolution. This trend of imitating French culture during the nineteenth century was similar everywhere in the world; however, after years of civil wars and foreign interventions, Mexico finally was able to have peace, albeit at a very high price. In 1877 Porfirio Díaz, a hero of the war against France, became president and remained in power until 1910, ruling with a strong arm and, ironically, a refinement he imagined as French. Being a pragmatist, Díaz managed to increase the economy and to industrialize the country while establishing relations and modern policies toward countries like the United States, France, Spain, England, Germany, and even Japan. There is no doubt that the Porfiriato brought a period of peace and prosperity to the middle and upper classes, while at the same time it abused the masses and fomented a lack of democracy and representation, which created the conflicts that culminated with a revolution in 1910.

Considered the first social revolution of the twentieth century, the Mexican Revolution overthrew the dictatorship of Porfirio Díaz. The changes brought by the revolution extended to all areas of culture and society, but with a particular emphasis on the vindication of the people. Its social agenda also made it possible to look at popular culture differently. In many ways, the revolution was also an attempt to return to the unresolved issue of access to food for all. The motto of the revolution was *Tierra y Libertad* (Land and Liberty), which points to the discontent of the masses with the lack of access to land and to the ability to produce their own food, an activity that was in the hands of a few landowners that operated haciendas and monopolized the agricultural system. Similarly, in the north of the country the revolution represented the possibility of democratizing and modernizing farms and the production of meat, milk, and dairy products. The revolution was an agrarian revolt as much as a fight for democracy. In 1921 the revolution was declared triumphant, and a new constitution, written in 1917, was implemented. Eleven years of fighting had ended up with a more democratic and just nation.

The revolution was a popular uprising, and as such, it yielded a series of propositions and cultural practices that tended to idealize the life of the people, particularly of the masses from the countryside and the growing number of factory workers in urban centers. Furthermore, the revolution contributed to the mobility of populations all around the country, bringing in contact for the first time masses of individuals from the most distinct parts of the country and diverse backgrounds, helping to create a consciousness of being a unified people with similar traditions, culture, language, religion, and ideals. The progressive position of the new government included all the citizens of the country, but favored those most vulnerable—factory workers, farmers, children, and women. After the revolution, all the sectors of society—government workers, intellectuals, artists, proletarians, pro-women rights groups, and indigenous communities—saw the opportunity to organize and work together. Government officials recruited artists and intellectuals to create and develop a national culture that would include and promote all forms of popular traditions, including gastronomy. The most significant example of this is the so-called *Noche Mexicana*, or Mexican Night, a popular festival organized by the painter Adolfo Best Maugard.

Best Maugard was also the minister of culture and the organizer of the festivities of the Centennial of the Mexican Independence, which happened during the revolution. His idea was to put together an exhibition of popular art to vindicate and exalt the artistic sensibility of the people and to showcase Mexican talent from all corners of the country. His idea was so radical that when he reached out to the governors of all the states, asking them to send examples of the crafts and traditional arts of their regions—clay pots, wood toys, cooking implements, sarapes, leather bags, glass ornaments—they did not understand why he wanted those primitive artifacts. It took a little convincing for them to finally send handmade crafts. Best Maugard also wanted to include foods from different parts of the country. So in addition to the exhibition of popular arts, he organized a festival he called *Noche Mexicana*, at Chapultepec Park, where musicians played on platforms distributed through the woods, while stands decorated with the national colors offered typical dishes, until then associated mostly with the lower classes, but served by ladies of the aristocracy, who "sold popular food and beverages—*pollo asado, enchiladas, tamales, buñuelos, atole*, and hot chocolate—served on ceramics from Guadalajara and Texcoco" (López, "The Noche," 26).

This event was so popular that it was embraced by the people, and even today many families and friends gather in houses to improvise their own *Noche Mexicana*, dressed in traditional attire and eating traditional foods, in September to celebrate Independence Day. It is thanks to the revolution that Mexican popular culture was appreciated and valued nationwide as a sign of national identity. Such recognition of popular culture as *the culture* of Mexico was reflected in the new appreciation for traditional and popular dishes, both elaborate and modest ones. This vindication of Mexican food allows for its gastronomy to evolve and gradually become the favorite food of all Mexicans, rich and poor, from the north and from the south, from the coast, the mountains, or cities. The early decades of the twentieth century marked that moment of reaffirmation of the eminently popular essence of Mexican culture. Since then, Mexican food has become more fashionable, and all classes and ethnicities proudly adopt Mexican food and its main ingredients as their main food.

Mexico's commercial relations with Germany, Italy, and Japan grew, and in 1930 the United States saw it as a threat. The American government therefore "considered gaining Mexicans' favor a top priority for American national security" (Moreno, 45). Even though Mexico continued trading with European countries, it also saw a friendlier political attitude from and towards the United States, resulting in more trade between the two nations, as well as more balanced economic and cultural exchanges. The modernization of the country, the increasing contact with other countries, and Mexico's interest in attracting tourism contributed to a professionalization of the food industry in the country, as well as to the professionalization of restaurant workers. Along with this professionalization of the food and restaurant industries emerged a new generation of professional chefs interested in taking seriously, for the first time, the flavors, techniques, and ingredients of traditional Mexican cuisine. This professional valorization of Mexican traditional food was accompanied by an interest in documenting and preserving a cuisine that was considered so important for the identity and history of the country. Many cookbooks started to appear, helping to unify the national gastronomy.

Simultaneously, there was a movement in Mexico of digging deeper into the history of the cuisine, looking for traditional recipes and ingredients and experimenting with them; this movement gave birth to new generations of chefs dedicated to updating and promoting Mexican food, adapting it to a more contemporary taste without losing its essence. Mexican restaurateurs started to take advantage of this interest and started to open restaurants in Mexico and abroad, even in countries more familiar with Mexican food via Hollywood, attempting to bring the "real thing" to the world. From New York to Chicago, Boston, Lima, or São Paulo to Madrid, London, Berlin, and Amsterdam, Mexican restaurants have proliferated all over the world, and many Mexican chefs have had the opportunity to train and display their abilities internationally. The crowning achievement of these efforts and trends was the inspired decision to present Mexican food as a candidate for the title of intangible cultural heritage of the world. To convince the world that Mexican food was an accomplishment of human inventiveness that could be shared with the world and deserved recognition seemed like a monumental task. However, the decision of including Mexican food in the list of intangible heritage of the world in 2010, the first one approved by the United Nations Educational, Scientific and Cultural Organization (UNESCO), seems to confirm that there is something about Mexican food that cannot be separated from the culture, the history, the traditions, the people, and the identity of Mexico.

Tortillas Caseras (Homemade Tortillas)

Yield: Makes 8 tortillas

1 cup masa harina
1 cup warm water

Equipment: mixing bowl, plastic wrap, tortilla press, measuring cups, *comal* or griddle

1. Mix masa harina and water until well mixed. Let rest for a few minutes.
2. Work dough with your hands until it is smooth and malleable. You may need a little more water or masa harina to obtain the desired consistency.
3. Make 8 balls with the dough that are the same size, more or less.
4. Place the ball in between 2 sheets of plastic wrap and press them in the tortilla press. If you do not have a tortilla press, you can use 2 plates or flat cutting boards. Place the balls of dough in between the plates or cutting boards and press hard and firmly until the tortillas are formed. Or you can use a rolling pin to roll the balls of dough to the desired thickness.
5. Remove the tortilla from the sheets of plastic and cook on a *comal* or griddle for about a minute on each side or until done.

Serve the tortilla with any stew, beans, melted cheese, or any other Mexican dish.

Salsa de Molcajete

Yield: Serves 6 to 8

2 large tomatoes or 3 medium tomatoes
¼ medium white onion
1 clove garlic
2 serrano or jalapeño peppers
Salt to taste

Equipment: a *comal* or a cast iron griddle, a *molcajete* or mortar

1. Roast the tomatoes, peppers, garlic, and onion either in a *comal* or a cast iron griddle.
2. Once the vegetables are soft and charred in some spots, flip them until they are done on all sides.
3. Place a pinch of salt and the garlic in the *molcajete*; grind until it forms a paste.
4. Add onion and grind it well; add peppers, grinding and incorporating them into the paste.
5. Add the tomatoes, crushing them with the pestle until the desired consistency is reached.
6. Mix all the ingredients well and season with salt to taste.

To serve, place the molcajete at the center of the table so people can help themselves. It goes well with grilled meats or tacos; it can also be served over eggs, beans, or soups.

Frijoles de La Olla (Beans in a Pot)

Yield: Serves 6

1 pound beans, flor de mayo, pinto, or bayo
½ medium white onion
2 tablespoons lard, optional
6 cups water

Equipment: large pot, mixing spoon, measuring cups and spoons

1. Clean the beans, removing any debris or spoiled beans.
2. Place beans, onion, and lard, if using, in a large pot. Add the water and bring to a boil.
3. Lower the heat, cover, and simmer the beans for a couple of hours or until tender. Season with salt to taste. You can use black beans as well, in which case, add 1 or 2 springs of epazote with all the other ingredients.

Serve the beans in a serving bowl as a side dish or use them for other dishes like refried beans or bean soup.

Chiles Curados (Pickled Chili Peppers)

Yield: Serves 3 to 4

½ pound of jalapeño or serrano chili peppers
3 tablespoons of vegetable oil
1 medium white onion sliced
5 cloves of whole garlic
1 medium carrot, peeled and cut in sticks the size of the peppers
6 cauliflower florets, optional
6 green beans cut in half, optional
2 cups of water
2 cups of apple cider vinegar
2 sprigs of thyme, fresh
2 sprigs of oregano, fresh
2 sprigs of marjoram, fresh
2 bay leaves
6 black peppercorns
3 allspice berries
Salt to taste

Equipment: large pot, measuring cups, mixing spoon, glass jar with lid

1. Slice chili peppers either lengthwise or across in round slices the size of a quarter. You can also use the chili peppers whole—just pierce the peppers with a sharp knife a few times.
2. Heat vegetable oil in a large pot, add onions and sauté for a few minutes; add the garlic and cook until aromatic; add the chili peppers and continue to cook the vegetables for a few more minutes.
3. Add water, vinegar, thyme, oregano, marjoram, bay leaves, peppercorns, and allspice berries; cook for a few minutes; add carrots and other vegetables if using. Bring to a boil and simmer for a few minutes. Add salt to taste.
4. Remove from heat and let cool completely.

To serve, place the chili peppers and vegetables in a small bowl with enough juice on the table so people can help themselves. Keep in the fridge for about a week.

Ensalada de Nopalitos (Cactus Salad)

Yield: Serves 8

8 medium *nopales*, cleaned
4 medium tomatoes
½ large white onion
3 jalapeño or serrano peppers
½ cup chopped cilantro
1 teaspoon dry oregano
The juice of one medium lime
½ cup vegetable oil
Salt to taste

Equipment: large pot, salad bowl, mixing spoon, measuring cup

1. Cut the *nopales* in thin strips of about 2 to 3 inches in length; place them in a large pot and cook with salt in low heat until they are done.
2. Rinse *nopales* a few times under running water, strain, set aside, and let them cool.
3. Meanwhile, chop tomatoes, onion, and chili peppers.
4. Once the *nopales* are cool, place them in a salad bowl with the tomatoes, onions, and peppers; carefully mix all vegetables well.
5. Dress with the lime juice and oil; sprinkle the oregano and salt, and mix again to coat all the vegetables with oil and juice. Add the cilantro on top just before serving.

To serve, place the salad on the table for people to serve themselves. It can be served as a side dish or as an appetizer with corn tortillas.

CHAPTER TWO

Influential Ingredients

The main ingredients of Mexican cuisine are those cultivated by the Mesoamerican peoples, going back thousands of years, as well as the ingredients brought to America by the Europeans, mostly ingredients native to the Iberian Peninsula. Modern Spain emerged just as Columbus was seeking support for his expeditions to India and China, when Ferdinand of Aragon and Isabella of Castile unified the Iberian kingdoms and together expelled the Moors from Europe, the same year of the discovery of America—1492. Mexican food as it is known today inherited both traditions and created something new. The ingredients in this chapter reflect that double heritage. Included here are ingredients that are still common in the Mexican diet, excluding foods that were popular in Mesoamerican times that are no longer consumed or are not common foods.

Vegetables

Considering that Mesoamericans did not have domesticated animals, or very few, it is not surprising that most of the traditional pre-Columbian staples are vegetables, with the exception of turkey. Contemporary Mexican cuisine, however, incorporates vegetables native to America as well as those brought from Europe. One of the most popular vegetables in Mexican cooking is avocado, which is used as a vegetable, although in reality it is a fruit. In Mexican cuisine, avocado is used in guacamole and other salsas, as well as salads, or simply sliced as a side dish. It is sometimes cut in small pieces and used to top soups, sandwiches, *tostadas*, *sopes*, and other popular dishes. In recent years, however, it has been used also for desserts, like ice cream and cakes. Another classic staple of Mexican cuisine is *calabacitas*, known as Mexican squash; it is usually available in the late spring and summer and has been part of the Mexican diet for thousands of years. Similar to zucchini but of a lighter green-grayish color and sweeter flavor, it is used in many different dishes, including soups, stews, salads, or as a side dish. One of the most popular dishes with this vegetable is called *calabacitas con queso*. To prepare the dish, the squash is cut in small pieces and sautéed in oil with onions, garlic, and tomatoes then seasoned with salt, pepper, and oregano; it is served with crumbled *queso fresco* and *crema* on top. A variety of this squash comes in a round shape, the size of a small orange. Both types of squash also could be prepared stuffed with cheese and served in a tomato sauce.

Popular in Mexican cooking, chard is known in Mexico as *acelgas*; it is one of the most popular green leafy vegetables in Mexican cuisine. Originally from the Old World, it came to Mexico from Spain, although as its Arabic name indicates, it was probably brought to Spain by the Moors. Chard is traditionally served as a side dish, steamed or sautéed with onions, garlic, and tomatoes. It is also common in soups, stews, and salads or even in vegetarian tacos. Like *acelgas*, *espinaca* (spinach) was brought to Mexico by the Spaniards, who in turn got it from the Moors. It is not known precisely when it was brought to Mexico, but it is a very popular vegetable in the country today and is consumed regularly in many dishes, *quesadillas*, salads, and even as a main dish in the popular *tortitas de espinaca* (spinach patties stuffed with cheese and served in a tomato sauce). Before the arrival of the Europeans, Mesoamerican cultures had many wild greens known today as *quelites*, which is the generic name for all these edible wild greens like chicories, dandelions, and prickly lettuce, some of which people still collect from fields or even empty lots where they grow naturally.

Perhaps two of the best known, which are still widely used in Mexican cooking, are *verdolagas* (purslane) and *huauzontle* (*Chenopodium album*). *Huauzontle* is related to quinoa and amaranth and has remained an important food in Mexican cuisine. Originally considered a humble food for Lent, today it is seen as a delicacy. Greatly appreciated by the Aztecs, the plant has a long, thin, fibrous stem with many bunches of very small green flowers. These flowers are the edible part of the plant. Traditionally the buds are stripped from the branches, cooked in boiling water and salt, and formed into little patties stuffed with cheese then covered in an egg batter and fried; they are served in a tomato or spice sauce. *Verdolagas* are a succulent plant that grows in all parts of Mexico, but is particularly popular in the center and the north of the country. It is a tasty, fresh, crunchy plant that could be added to salads and soups or sautéed with oil, onion, and garlic for a side dish or vegetarian tacos. In Mexico it is cooked in a classic dish, *verdolagas con puerco* (pork with purslane), prepared with pork cooked in a green sauce and lots of *verdolagas*. It is considered one of the quintessential dishes of Mexican popular cuisine.

Another Mesoamerican vegetable, *chayote* (*Sechium edule*), is, like avocado, a fruit eaten as a vegetable and was originally from Mesoamerica and used by the Maya, Aztecs, Olmec, and other pre-Columbian peoples. Its shape resembles a large pear; it is green, juicy, and has a mild, sweet taste; the most common variety in Mexico is a prickly fruit covered in thorns, which can be removed with the skin when cooked; another type, with a smooth green skin and no thorns, is the more common outside of Mexico. Often used in salads, soups, stews, or even tacos, *chayote* can be boiled, grilled, steamed, or sautéed in oil with salt and pepper. *Chilacayote,* or chilacayote squash, comes in different sizes, from as small as an apple to as big as a small watermelon. Of a bright-green color and elongated shape, it is sprinkled with white spots on the smooth skin. It is very common in Mexican cooking, where traditionally it is eaten as a side dish or added in small chunks to stews; soups; and the traditional dish called *pipián*, a sauce made with chili peppers, spices, and toasted pumpkin seeds often served with either pork or chicken, or vegetarian if it is served with the *chilacayotes* only. The texture of its flesh is spongy and smooth, and the taste is mild, often absorbing the flavors of the other ingredients in the dish. It is common in Mexico to candy or crystalize *chilacayote* and serve it as a sweet snack or as a dessert.

Chili peppers, or *chiles*, are those quintessential vegetables that most people associate with Mexican cuisine. From salsas and guacamole to stews, soups, or even snacks, chili peppers are indispensable in Mexican cooking. There are many different types of chili peppers with a variety of flavors, from sweet to intense, to earthly, to extremely spicy, and all have been used to add particular flavors to Mexican dishes, either fresh or dy. Some of the most common fresh chili peppers in Mexican cooking are *jalapeños, poblanos, serranos, chilacas, manzano, pequín, cascabel, de árbol, chiltepin,* Anaheim, and *habanero*. Like chili peppers, *ejotes* (green beans) are another vegetable that has been in the national diet for thousands of years. Of Mesoamerican origin, *ejotes* are the early pods of the beans harvested and consumed when they are still young; fresh green beans have to be of a bright-green or yellow color, and they should snap when broken. They are used in soups, stews, and salads. *Elote* is the young ear of corn that is used as a vegetable in different stews, soups, salads, and even desserts. It can be eaten whole, grilled or boiled, and then covered in butter, mayonnaise, shredded cheese, salt, pepper, and chili pepper powder or lime juice. Another way of eating *elote* is by cutting the kernels and cooking them with salt and other herbs; this is a popular snack called *esquites*.

Jícama is a juicy tuber used in salads or sliced as a snack with lime juice, salt, and powdered chili pepper. It is also a traditional snack for children who gather around street vendors outside their school after classes. With a texture similar to a potato but sweeter and juicier, it is consumed all over Mexico and has become more present in the United States. *Nopales* are a variety of edible cactus known in the United Statas as prickly pear cactus. The cactus leaves are flat, large pads the size of a palm that are harvested and cooked young. In Mexico they are used in soups, stews, or salads; they can also be eaten pickled or grilled. A common way of eating them is grilled with cheese. However, the most traditional way of eating *nopales* is in a salad, known as *ensalada de nopalitos*, made with cooked cactus cut in strips and mixed with chopped onions, tomatoes, *jalapeño* peppers, and cilantro and dressed with lime juice, olive oil, and salt and pepper, as well as crumbled fresh cheese on top. Onions are not originally from Mesoamerica, yet they are an important ingredient in Mexican cuisine, particularly white and red onions; they are used in stews, soups, *moles*, salads, and, of course, salsas, together with tomatoes, chili peppers, and cilantro. It is also commonly used chopped as a garnish in tacos, enchiladas, *sopes*, and other dishes.

Potatoes are not originally from Mesoamerica either, but have been part of the Mexican diet since colonial times. Once the Spanish colonized Mexico and South America, the food they encountered in both regions began to travel. Tomatoes, chocolate, and corn were brought to South America, and potatoes were brought to Mexico. Tomatillo, also known in many parts of Mexico as *tomate verde*, is a green fruit covered with a brown husk. It is used in Mexican cuisine to prepare salsas and *moles*. It has a tangy, zesty taste, somehow citric, that resembles green apples and herbs. Of very malleable flavor, it blends well with onions, cilantro, and chili peppers, and it is an ideal complement to chicken and particularly pork. It is an excellent source of minerals and vitamins, especially vitamin A and C, and in some parts of Mexico it is used also for medicinal purposes. The tomato, one of the most popular foods worldwide today, is originally from Mexico and is indispensable in Mexican cuisine. It is a main ingredient in stews and sauces, as well as traditional Mexican *salsas*, such as *pico de gallo* or guacamole. Tomatoes are also added to soups and salads and used as a garnish for *sopes*, *tostadas*, or tacos. When it was taken to Europe by the Spaniards, it was first believed to be poisonous before becoming widely popular in Mediterranean regions.

Fruits

Cantaloupe, known in Mexico as *melón*, is one of the most popular fruits in the country. It is a traditional in salads; drinks; and as a snack with lime juice, salt, and powdered chili pepper. Together with watermelon and papaya, it is one of the traditional fruits served in the morning for breakfast or for a light lunch. The seeds of the melons are also used to prepare *agua fresca* (fruit-flavored water) by blending the seeds with sugar, water, and ice. Papaya, originally from the tropical parts of the American continent, is an elongated and oblong fruit of between 4 and 12 inches, with sweet, juicy flesh of a greenish-yellow color or dark orange; it contains innumerable black, small seeds wrapped in a jelly-like substance and a transparent membrane. It was cultivated and consumed by pre-Columbian Americans, but it was the Spaniards who took the fruit to other parts of the world. Today, Mexico is one of the main producers and exporters of papaya, where the fruit is still eaten fresh, in shakes with milk and sugar, in salads, or in mousses and other desserts. Watermelon, known in Spanish as *sandía*, is another popular fruit in Mexico. It is typical for breakfast or a light lunch, as well as in fruit salads or as a snack sliced with lime, salt, and chili pepper powder. It is also used to flavor water by adding chunks of watermelon and sugar to a large pitcher or blending the fruit with water and sugar.

Pineapple, known in Mexico as *piña*, is a very sweet, juicy fruit of yellow flesh and a rough skin. The fruit is originally from the tropical parts of America and was cultivated by Mesoamericans, particularly the Maya. When the Spaniards arrived in America, pineapple was one of the first and most exotic fruits they encountered, and they immediately took it to Europe, where it was offered to King Ferdinand of Spain, who declared it the best thing he had ever eaten. In Mexico, pineapples are used in drinks (*agua fresca* and *atole*) and in breads, cakes, fruit salads, ices, preserves, or crystalized; it is often eaten fresh either raw or grilled as dessert or with lime juice, salt, and chili pepper powder as a snack. Like pineapple, *capulín* is a traditional fruit originally from Mexico. It is a round, small fruit of aromatic, juicy, and sweet flesh with a smooth, dark skin of an intense dark color—almost black—and with a relatively large pit. Its flavor is similar to cherries, and it is used in *atoles*, *tamales*, preserves, or breads. It has been cultivated and consumed in Mexico for centuries. Also originally from America, *mamey* is an elongated fruit of medium size and rough, hard skin, with sweet, buttery flesh and a black, large, smooth pit. The flesh of the *mamey* is eaten fresh or mixed with milk, ice, and sugar to make *licuados* (fruit and milk drinks). It can be used to make different desserts, as well, like ice cream, breads, cakes, or mousses. Pre-Columbian Mexicans used the pit, peeled, roasted, or cooked, to flavor sauces and *moles* and to prepare drinks.

Figs were introduced to Mexico by the Spaniards early on and have remained very popular. Not only are they consumed fresh, dry, in

> When the Europeans arrived in America, the most exotic fruit they noticed was the pineapple. Fascinated by the way it looked and its sweet taste, they immediately took it to Europe. When it was offered to the Spanish monarch, Ferdinand, the first king in the Old World to taste it, he declared in awe that he had tried other exotic foods, but the flavor of the pineapple "excels all other fruits."

compotes, crystalized, in salads, breads, and other desserts, but they are part of the folklore of Mexico. According to a legend, a barren fig tree announced the first Mexican saint, St. Felipe de Jesús. In his youth, Felipe was an ill-behaved, disobedient young man, and when his mother declared to the family that he was destined be a saint, his nanny laughed, saying that it would be easier for the fig tree to produce fruit than for Felipe to become a saint. So, when Felipe was killed as a missionary in Japan, the fig tree gave a big, beautiful fig. *Membrillo* (quince) is a popular fruit in Mexico; it is of medium size, with yellow, smooth skin and aromatic flesh. It is mostly used in compotes, jams, pastes, desserts, and breads. Known to the Babylonians, Greeks, Romans, and Arabs, *membrillo* was brought to Mexico by the Spaniards, who inherited it from the Romans. Originally from Asia, mango traveled to Africa and to the Americas during the Portuguese colonization of Brazil. However, it came to Mexico most likely from Asia. Muslim missionaries brought mangoes to the Philippines in the fifteenth century, and from the Philippines passed to Mexico when the Philippines were under control of New Spain. Mangoes adapted well to the tropical areas of Mexico and became very popular fresh or in drinks and desserts.

Lima, or sweet lime (*Citrus limettioides*), is a round citrus fruit of green color, with a strong, pleasant aroma; slightly sweet, yellowish flesh; and thick skin with a protuberance on top. It is usually smaller than an orange but larger than a lemon. When it matures, it acquires a yellow color, although some traces of green remain on the skin. It is widely available in late fall and winter, and it is consumed fresh. It is very popular in many parts of Mexico for Christmas, since it is used to fill the traditional piñatas, along with chunks of sugarcane, *jícamas*, *tejocotes*, mandarins, oranges, and sometimes candy. Limes (*Citrus aurantifolia*) are one of the most popular fruits in Mexico and are used in many dishes or in breads, desserts, ices, and drinks. They are widely used in cooking as well and as a dressing, combined with olive oil or just salt and pepper or chili pepper powder. Tacos and soups are often presented with wedges of lime to squeeze on them. The generic name given to the fruit in most of Mexico is *limón* (lemon), since yellow lemons are less common in the country and are known as *limón real* (royal lemon), to distinguish them from limes.

Oranges are one of the most popular fruits in Mexico; they came to the country from Spain soon after the conquest and adapted marvelously well to the soil and climate; today they are one of the main crops cultivated in the nation. Oranges are omnipresent in Mexican markets, tables, and gardens, and they are consumed fresh or in desserts, jams, breads, cakes, salads, crystalized, or juiced. A very popular fruit in Mexico, *granadas* (pomegranates) are eaten fresh, in drinks like *granadina* or *atole*, and in cocktails like margaritas. They are used in salads as well as in some dishes like the traditional *chiles en nogada*. The pomegranate came to Mexico with the Spaniards and very soon propagated through the entire region. It is common to see pomegranate trees in family gardens and patios in most parts of the country, as well as in markets and farmers markets. Strawberries have existed in the wild in many regions of the world, and ancient humans have used them sporadically as food, but it was not until later that strawberries were cultivated and commercially produced; it was in France in the late 1700s that different types of strawberries were crossed to produce the contemporary strawberry. Strawberries, known as *fresas* in Mexico, have been cultivated in the country since the early 1800s at least, and they appear in Modernist poetry as symbols of beauty and passion. They are produced in large quantities in Mexico, making this nation the third largest producer worldwide. They are eaten fresh or baked in breads and cakes, as well as in drinks like *atole*, *aguas fracas*, and, of course, *licuados* with milk, vanilla, sugar, and ice.

Tuna (prickly pear) is a quintessential Mexican fruit, so emblematic, indeed, that it is even in the national coat of arms. Cultivated and eaten by Mesoamericans hundreds of years before the arrival of the Europeans, it is the fruit of the nopal cactus, and it is greatly appreciated in many regions of Mexico. The fruit itself is cylindric, small, and with sweet, juicy flesh, with innumerable small, dark seeds wrapped in soft flesh and an outer layer of skin covered with thin thorns. There are many varieties of *tunas*: white, green, yellow, or purple with a flavor that goes from very sweet to a little sour. They are eaten fresh, in drinks, or in preserves. *Tejocote* (*Crataegus pubescens*) is a fruit originally from central Mexico, cultivated and consumed since Aztec times. Its name comes from the Nahuatl word *texocolt*, which means hard berry. It is a small fruit, resembling a miniature apple with thin, smooth, yellow skin covered with brown freckles; its flesh is of yellow or orange color, juicy but firm, and of a sour taste. It is eaten raw or used in compotes or jams or caramelized and skewered on a wooden stick. It is also used in the preparation of drinks like *atole* or punch, as well as liquors in some parts of the country. *Zapote*, or sapote in English, is a generic name used to refer to several fruits of the Sapotaceae family. These fruits have sweet, soft flesh; their shape is most often round and not too big. The most common are the white sapote (*Casimiroa edulis*) and black sapote (*Diospyros digyna*). These fruits are eaten fresh or in sweets, drinks, and other desserts.

Beans

Bean is the generic name given to more than 400 varieties of seeds of the Leguminosae family commonly known in Mexico as *frijoles* (*Phaseolus vulgaris*). The plant was first domesticated in Mesoamerica thousands of years ago and has remained a staple of the diet of the peoples of the continent ever since. Today, beans are widely used in the world and cultivated in nearly every continent. In Mexico, they are used in stews and soups, and they are a traditional accompaniment for most dishes. They can be prepared in many ways using oil, condiments, herbs, vegetables, bacon, or other meats. The most popular beans in Mexico are pinto beans, *bayo* beans, *flor de mayo* beans, and black beans, but many more varieties exist and are used in regional cuisines. Garbanzo beans are not originally from Mesoamerica, but ever since they were introduced to Mexico, they have remained a favorite food because of their flavor, versatility, and low price. Mexico is among the main producers of garbanzo beans, and they are very popular in salads, stews, soups, and even desserts. A traditional food for Lent, garbanzos can be used as side dishes or even as a main dish in a tomato broth. They are also toasted; seasoned with salt, pepper, or chili pepper powder; and eaten as snack. Fava beans, or *habas*, are another edible seed of the Fabaceae family originally from the Middle East. *Habas* were introduced to Mexico after the Spanish colonization and became a regular food; they are a traditional dish for Lent and usually are prepared in soups, salads, and stews. *Lentejas* (lentils), like fava and garbanzo beans, originated in the Middle East and arrived in Mexico with the Spanish conquistadores and soon after were adopted by the entire population. They are traditional in soups or in stews.

Herbs and Spices

Like fresh chili peppers, *chiles secos* (dry chili peppers) are essential in Mexican cooking and have been for thousands of years. They are used mostly in sauces and traditional Mexican *moles*. Most of them are actually dried or smoked versions of fresh chili peppers. The most common are *chile ancho*, which is the dried version of the *poblano* pepper and has a mild, somehow sweet flavor. *Chile pasilla* is the dried *chilaca* pepper, and it is a long, dark, wrinkled chili pepper with a mild flavor, similar to that of *chile ancho*, although hotter. *Chile mulato* is also a dry poblano pepper that was picked when it was ripe; its flavor is sweet and fruity, but also a little smoky. It is hotter than *chile ancho* and *pasilla*. *Chile guajillo* is a long, small, flat pepper that has a sharp and tangy flavor; it is very popular in Mexican cooking and of moderate heat. *Chile chipotle* is the dry, smoked version of the jalapeño pepper; it is flavorful, smoky, and spicy, yet with a hint of sweetness. *Chile morita* is similar to *chipotle*, but not as smoky. *Chile de árbol* is a dry, small chili with smooth, red skin, used in salsas and other dishes. *Chile cascabel* is a small, round chili pepper of a dark reddish color and mild, fruity taste, not too spicy.

Achiote, also known as annatto, is the ground seed of the annatto tree (*Bixa orellana*). In Mexico it is traditionally made into a paste by mixing the annatto seeds with garlic and other spices, like oregano and cumin, and it is widely used as a condiment in stews and soups and as a rub for meats and vegetables. *Epazote* is the quintessential aromatic herb of Mexico. It is a long, green herb used by Mesoamericans for thousands of years. It is known for its distinctive aroma, which could be considered strong and disagreeable by some people. This was not unnoticed by the Aztecs, who called it *epazotl*, a word derived from *epatl* (skunk) and *tzol* (dirt). Despite its strong aroma, *epazote* is widely used in Mexican cuisine and adds a peculiar earthly flavor to many dishes; it is most commonly used fresh, but also can be used dry. Cilantro is another herb that is strongly associated with Mexican cooking; brought to Mexico by the Europeans, it soon became indispensable in Mexican cuisine, used in soups, *moles*, salsas, stews, and as a garnish for many traditional dishes. It has a strong flavor and aroma, and its seeds can also be used as a condiment. *Perejil* (parsley), along with cilantro and epazote, is one of the most important aromatic herbs used in Mexican cuisine and was also brought to Mexico by the Europeans; it is used like cilantro to flavor different dishes and in salads, as well as salsas and *moles*.

Vanilla, a native plant of Mesoamerica, is a climbing orchid from the semitropical regions of Mexico. With large yellow flowers, the flavor and aroma are extracted from the pod, a long green bean that can measure six to eight inches. This pod is treated and dried, acquiring a dark or black color, and its seeds are used in pastries and drinks. Industrially produced vanilla extracts are also common. In Mexican cuisine, vanilla is used in breads, cakes, desserts, and sweets; it is also used in shakes, liquors, and other drinks, like chocolate and *atole*. Like chocolate and tomatoes, vanilla is one of those important contributions of Mexico to world cuisine. *Canela*, or cinnamon, is not originally from Mexico; however, it is one of the most important ingredients in Mexican cuisine; consumed in many ways, including drinking it as a tea or in coffee, *atole*, and chocolate, it is an irreplaceable ingredient in most *moles*, sauces, stews, and desserts. Native to Sri Lanka, cinnamon came to America with the Spaniards, who inherited it from the Romans and the Moors. It adapted very well to the climate of New Spain and became cultivated aggressively; today Mexico is one of the bigger producers of cinnamon in the world.

Cumin, called *comino* in Mexico, is a traditional spice used abundantly in Mexican cooking, although in small quantities, since it could overpower other flavors. Originally from the Mediterranean region, it was known and used by the ancient Egyptians and Syrians. It came to Mexico from Spain, and like many other plants, it adapted to the climate of the Americas so well that it became an important spice in the cuisine of Mexico. It is used in many dishes from *moles*, soups, and stews, to marinades and rubs for meats or vegetables. Oregano is another popular aromatic herb all around the world. There are many varieties of this herb, which is native to Europe and the Middle East; the one used in Mexico, however, grows wild in semiarid and tempered areas of the country; it is called Mexican oregano (*Lippia berlandieri*) and is used in soups, stews, broths, and other dishes. It is one of the most popular herbs in Mexican cuisine. Rosemary, thyme, bay leaves, marjoram, and sage, as well as clove and allspice, are all herbs and condiments used in Mexican cooking for stews, sauces, and infusions.

Grains

Amaranto, or amaranth, is a plant native to Mesoamerica with long, edible leaves, sometimes called *alegría* (happiness). The part of the plant that is most appreciated is its seeds, agglutinated in an ear on the top of the plant, which can hold thousands of seeds. The dry seeds were used by the Aztecs for food—they were as important as corn and beans—but also for ceremonial purposes. A candy called *alegría*, made with amaranth and honey, dating back to Mesoamerican times, has always been popular in central Mexico. In recent years, amaranth has started to be appreciated in other regions of Mexico and the world. Chia is a seed that was widely used in Mesoamerica as well. The Aztecs ground it and mixed it with corn in *tamales* and other dishes as well as *atole*. In colonial Mexico, chia was mostly added to lemonade and other refreshing drinks. Today, just like

Influential Ingredients

amaranth, chia has seen a renewed interest for its nutritious properties and enjoys a growing popularity. No other grain is so profoundly connected to Mexican history, culture, and, of course, cuisine than corn (*maíz* in Spanish). Domesticated in Mesoamerica, corn is the crop that not only made it possible for early Americans to survive but provided the conditions for the great ancient civilizations to emerge, grow, and flourish in our continent. The Olmecs, Toltecs, Maya, and Aztecs all considered corn a gift from the gods and developed a cuisine that had this sacred crop at the center.

Early Mesoamericans domesticated this grass and developed a singular technique to cook it; the process is called *nixtalización*, which consists of soaking and cooking the grains in an alkaline substance, most commonly lime and water, but also ashes, to make it edible. Once cooked, corn was made into a dough that was used to prepare tortillas, *tamales*, and other dishes, as well as drinks like the traditional *atole*. *Arroz* (rice) is not a grain that originated in Mesoamerica, but it came to New Spain from the Philippines when that nation was under Spanish control. The *nao de la China*, or the ship from China, covered the route between Manila and Acapulco, bringing goods from Asia. Rice became important during colonial times, but never took a central role in the cuisine of New Spain. Today in Mexico, rice is consumed regularly as a side dish and as an ingredient in soups, traditional desserts like *arroz con leche* (rice pudding), and drinks like *horchata*. Contrary to what one may think, rice and beans are rarely served together in Mexican cooking and do not accompany every single main dish. Rice is often served as a second course by itself, cooked with a tomato puree and vegetables in a dish called *arroz a la mexicana*.

Nuts and Seeds

Almonds have been common in Mexican cuisine since colonial times, but they are not originally from America. It is believed they originated in the Middle East and from there they went to Europe. The Spaniards brought almonds to Mexico early during the colonial period, and since then almonds have been utilized in sauces, *moles*, drinks, and as snacks. They are also used in desserts and breads and to infuse tequila, which is then called *almendrado*, as well as *rompope* (Mexican eggnog) and other drinks. *Cacahuate* (peanut) is a plant native to America that produces a pod with two to three edible seeds—the peanuts themselves; it has been used in Mesoamerica for thousands of years, and the Aztecs introduced peanuts to the Spaniards, who introduced them to Europe. Peanuts are commonly used in Mexican cooking to thicken sauces, *moles*, and stews and as snacks with salt and chili pepper powder and sometimes lime juice. They are also consumed in candies and *palanquetas*, sweet bars traditionally made with honey and dried fruits. Pumpkins are originally from Mesoamerica and have been considered part of the traditional Mexican diet. The fruit is widely consumed in the country, especially in the fall; it is traditionally candied or cooked with sugar and spices, but it is also used in stews, soups, and side dishes. However, the seeds are greatly appreciated by themselves; they can be used for *moles*, stews, salsas, and as snacks, toasted with salt. Pumpkin seeds are the main ingredient in the traditional dish *pepián* or *pipián* (from *pepita*, seed), a thick, spicy sauce served with pork or chicken considered a classic of Mexican cuisine.

Sesame seeds are originally from Africa and were brought to Mexico most likely by the Spaniards—other sources mention African slaves. Although both are possible, it is logical to assume that it was the conquistadores who brought sesame seeds to New Spain because they were already an ingredient used in Spain and the name given to the seed in Spanish, *ajonjolí*, is of clear Arab origin. In Mexico, the seeds are used in moles and sauces, particularly in *mole poblano*, which uses the seeds in the sauce, and as decoration, sprinkled on top of the sauce and meat when the dish is served. The seeds are used as well in the preparation of breads, pastries, and candies. *Nueces* literally means nuts and in Mexico refers mostly to two types of nuts: *nuez de castilla* (walnut) and *nuez pecana* or *nuez cáscara de papel* (pecan). Originally from Mexico and the United States, pecan nuts are the most popular *nueces* in Mexico, used in many dishes and desserts. Walnuts, brought to America by the Spanish conquistadores, are also consumed and produced in Mexico. Known by the Babylonians and other ancient cultures, walnuts are considered the oldest food on record. Both pecans and walnuts are used in Mexico in *moles* and sauces, as well as bread, desserts, and drinks like *atole* and even *pulque*. Walnuts are one of the main ingredients in the traditional dish *chiles en nogada*, which is a poblano pepper stuffed with meats, spices, fruits, and nuts, covered with a white sauce of walnuts, cream, and cheese and topped with pomegranate seeds.

Meats and Fish

One of the most popular meats in Mexico, pork, was unknown in pre-Columbian America. Brought to the continent by Columbus and to Mexico in particular by Cortés, pork very soon became an important staple of the Mexican diet. Considering the importance of pork for the Spaniards, it is not surprising that pigs were the first animals they brought to America.

Influential Ingredients

Pork soon became a favorite of the Native Americans and was a popular food during colonial times. Like pork, beef was brought to Mexico from Spain and very soon became an important source of food. In Mexican cooking, almost all the parts of the cow are used—mostly in stews, soups, and, of course, *tacos*—but also as steaks. Chicken, just like pork and cattle, was introduced to America by the Europeans. Once New Spain was established, the colonizers brought many of their crops and domestic animals and chickens were among them. The acceptance of this bird by the indigenous peoples of Mexico was almost immediate, probably because they already had a domesticated bird: the turkey. *Guajolote* (turkey), a bird native to America, is one of the very few domestic animals Mesoamericans kept for food. The Spaniards often called them "chickens," and very soon after the conquest of Mexico they took them to Europe where they became very popular. In Mexico turkeys are called *guajolotes* (from the Nahuatl *hueyxolotl*) when referring to the live birds or when used in traditional meals or *moles*; however, when the turkey is roasted and stuffed, it is usually called *pavo*. *Pavo* is traditional for Christmas, while *guajolote* is traditionally used for other celebrations when served with *mole*.

Fish, and seafood in general, have always been important ingredients in Mexican cuisine, particularly in coastal regions, although they do not seem as popular as other traditional ingredients in Mexican cooking today. But this is misleading if one considers that Mexico has over 6,000 miles of coastline and that more than half of the states have access to the sea—that is in addition to the numerous rivers and lakes in the country. Fish and seafood were consumed regularly in pre-Columbian times, even in the highlands of Mexico. And during colonial times, many wrote about the abundance of food, particularly of fish, in New Spain as a sign of its being predestined to become an independent and powerful nation. Some of the fish abundant in Mexico are *robalo* (sea bass), *mero* (red grouper), *pargo* (Southern red snapper), *bagre* (catfish), *lisa* (flathead gray mullet), *trucha* (trout), *cazón* (dogfish), *pez espada* (swordfish), *pámpano* (pompano), *sargo*, and *huachinango* (red snapper). Most of these fish are still traditional in Mexico, but perhaps the two most emblematic in Mexican cuisine are *huachinango* (red snapper) and the *blanco de Pátzcuaro*, a small fish with white skin and flesh that make it look almost translucent. It can only be found in Lake Patzcuaro, thus the name, and is considered a delicacy, although today it is facing extinction. Another traditional fish is *charal*. *Charales* refers to many varieties of small, thin fish that live in lakes and lagoons in many parts of central Mexico. They are usually eaten dry in soups and stews or in little cakes covered in an egg batter and fried and then served in a tomato sauce.

Dairy Products

Like all dairy products, butter was brought to Mexico from Spain. It is used mostly in baking and to a lesser degree in cooking. However, it has remained a popular item for breakfast or dinner spread over bread with preserves, honey, or even sugar and cinnamon sprinkled on top. *Crema* is the Mexican version of sour cream, more similar to *crème fraîche* than American sour cream; Mexican *crema* is thinner and a bit sweeter than both the French and American versions. *Jocoque* is a dairy product traditional in western, central, and northern Mexico made by letting raw milk ferment lightly overnight until it becomes acid and acquires a sour taste; once it has fermented, a little *jocoque* from an old batch is added to the new and it is fermented completely. Depending on the region, the consistency could be similar to thick sour cream, Greek yogurt, or even a very soft cheese. In the state of Michoacán it is used to prepare a dish called *enjococadas*, which is similar to enchiladas, but the sauce used to cover the tortillas is made with *jocoque*.

Mexican cuisine uses many different types of cheese. Some of the most traditional are *queso añejo*, which is the opposite of *queso fresco* (fresh cheese). *Queso añejo* is the aged (*añejo* means aged) version of the same cheese. Its flavor is similar, although intensified. *Queso añejo* is frequently used in the same way *queso fresco* is used if a more pronounced flavor is preferred. The term could also be used in a generic way to refer to other aged cheeses. *Queso fresco* is a young, crumbly cheese, often salty, although of mild taste. It is very popular in Mexico, and its creamy consistency and bright, fresh taste is the perfect complement for heavy and spicy dishes. In Mexico, this is the cheese that is used to top most dishes, from enchiladas, *sopes*, and eggs to salads. It is also used to stuff *chiles rellenos* or *calabacitas*. It is similar to feta, but of milder taste.

Queso asadero is a cream-colored cheese from northern Mexico of mild to sharp taste with a nutty flavor that is usually melted or grilled (*asadero* means grilling in Spanish). It is typically used in *queso fundido*—grilled cheese sandwiches—and sometimes even in *quesadillas* or dishes au gratin. Like the term *añejo*, the term *asadero* sometimes is used as a generic term for grilling cheeses and is often confused with *queso Chihuahua* or even *queso Oaxaca* because of their flexibility and melting properties. *Queso Chihuahua*, like many other cheeses, is named after the region where it originated—in this case, the state of Chihuahua in northern Mexico. Unlike many Mexican cheeses, *queso Chihuahua* is aged with a dark cream color, stronger flavor, and pleasant aroma; it usually comes in a wheel that can be of different sizes, up to 22 pounds. It is a malleable cheese and can be grilled or melted and used in *queso fundido*. This cheese is also known as wheel cheese or as *queso menonita*, since it was the Mennonites from northern Mexico who first made it. *Queso Oaxaca*, as its name indicates, originated in the state of Oaxaca in southern Mexico. It is a stringy, elastic, white cheese of mild taste. Unlike many Mexican cheeses, it is not salty and usually is sold in balls formed wrapping the curds together like a twine. Made of cow milk, it is also known as *quesillo*, particularly in Oaxaca. Easy to separate in strings and perfect for melting, it is commonly used in *quesadillas* (it is actually sometimes known as *queso quesadilla*) or to cook au gratin.

Queso Cotija is yet another cheese named after the place where it was first made. Cotija is a town in the state of Michoacán, where this cheese has been produced since colonial times. *Queso Cotija* is an aged, salty, sharp, dry cheese made with cow milk and aged for at least three months, but up to one year. It is similar to parmesan. This cheese does not melt, but it is easy to crumble or to grate and is often covered with a chili paste that gives it a spicy flavor. *Queso manchego* is a Mexican cheese that takes its name from a traditional Spanish cheese made with sheep milk that has a sharp, strong taste and hard rind that is traditionally aged up to two years. The Mexican *machego* is made with cow milk and has a mild flavor. It is usually not aged, and it melts very easily, making it highly versatile. Recently, when Mexico and the European Union had to renegotiate a trade agreement, the duplication of the name *manchego* became an issue, since Spain argued that *queso manchego* was produced in the La Mancha region and therefore was a denomination of origin. Mexico, however, argued that its version had a long tradition in the country and was fundamental in Mexican cooking. In the end, Mexico was allowed to call its cheese *manchego*, as long as it would say in the label that it was a Mexican product. *Queso panela* is a rubbery, soft cheese that cannot be melted or crumbled. It is white and has a mild taste, and like *fresco* and *añejo*, it is a little salty. It is used to stuff vegetables; cut into small cubes, it is added on salads and other dishes. It is also served alone as an appetizer or a snack. Another name for this cheese is *queso canasta*, in reference to the traditional baskets in which it is sometimes molded. *Requesón* is a popular dairy product in Mexico and Spain. The Mexican version is made with the whey that results from making cheese, and the consistency is similar to ricotta cheese. It is used, like *jocoque*, to add flavor to some meals. It is spread on bread with honey or preserves or on *tostadas* with salsa; it is also used to stuff the little fried corn cakes called *gorditas* and *tlacoyos*; in some regions it is also used in breads or desserts. Traditionally in Mexico, *requesón* is made from cow milk.

Guacamole Taquero (Green Sauce with Avocado)

Yield: Serves 8 to 10

6 large tomatillos
2 chile serrano or jalapeño chili peppers
½ small white onion
4 sprigs cilantro
Salt to taste

Equipment: medium pot, blender, mixing spoon.

1. In a medium pot place the tomatillos, chili peppers, and onion; cover with water. Bring to a boil and cook for 8 minutes.
2. Transfer all ingredients to a blender with ½ cup of the water from the tomatillos. Blend for a couple of minutes.
3. Add cilantro and avocado and blend for another few minutes. Season with salt to taste.

To serve, transfer salsa to a bowl and use it to accompany grilled meats, tacos, and other foods.

Ensalada de Jicama (Jicama Salad)

Yield: Serves 4 to 6

1 large *jícama*
2 medium carrots
1 large cucumber
½ red onion
¼ cup chopped cilantro
1 large lime
Salt to taste
Ground chili pepper

Equipment: mixing bowl or salad bowl, measuring cup

1. Wash all vegetables. Peel and julienne the *jícama*, carrots, and cucumber.
2. Slice the red onion.
3. Mix all the cut vegetables in a large bowl.
4. Squeeze the lime over the vegetables, add salt, mix well, and sprinkle with the chili pepper.

Serve the salad as an appetizer in small bowls or as a side dish for fish or grilled meats.

Nopalitos Navegantes (Cactus Soup)

Yield: Serves 6 or 4

4 *pasilla* chili peppers
5 large tomatoes
2 cloves garlic
½ medium white onion
3 tablespoons vegetable oil
5 large *nopales*, cooked and cut in thin trips or diced
1 sprig of *epazote* or a teaspoon of dry *epazote*
6 eggs, optional
Salt to taste

Equipment: small pot, medium pot or medium stewpan, blender, strainer, mixing spoons

1. In the small pot bring 2 cups of water to a boil; add the chili peppers and turn the heat off. Let them rest for 10 minutes. Seed the peppers.
2. Place the tomatoes, onion, garlic, and seeded peppers in a blender; blend, adding some of the water from the peppers as needed to form a smooth mix.
3. Heat the vegetable oil in the medium pot or stewpan; strain the tomato and *pasilla* mixture into the pot and cook for about 10 minutes.
4. Add 4 cups of water and when it starts to boil add *nopales* and *epazote*. Simmer for a few minutes and season with salt. If using eggs, break each egg, one at a time, directly into the soup and allow the eggs to cook.

Serve the soup without the eggs in individual bowls as a first course; if adding eggs, you may use it as a main dish. Serve the soup and 2 eggs in a large bowl with warm corn tortillas.

Chiles Rellenos (Stuffed Poblano Peppers)

Yield: Serves 6

6 poblano peppers (make sure they are the same size)
1 pound *queso fresco*
1 cup flour
4 eggs separated
6 tablespoons vegetable oil
4 medium tomatoes
½ small white onion
1 clove of garlic
Salt and pepper to taste

Equipment: comal or griddle, mixing bowls, electric mixer, frying pan, spatula, medium skillet with lid, mixing spoons, blender, measuring cups

1. Roast peppers in a *comal* or griddle, turning them constantly to roast evenly. Place them in a plastic bag or cover with a kitchen cloth. Let them rest for 15 minutes until the skin comes off easily. Rub the skin off with a cloth; with a sharp knife, cut the peppers lengthwise and seed them. Carefully wash and clean the peppers.
2. Stuff the peppers with the *queso fresco* and close them. If needed, use a toothpick to keep them securely closed.
3. Beat the egg whites with a pinch of salt until they form stiff peaks. Add the yolks one at a time and beat until just incorporated.
4. Place the flour in a large mixing bowl. Roll the peppers in the flour, coating them and shaking off the excess flour.
5. Heat the oil in the frying pan; dip the peppers in the egg batter and fry in hot oil until golden on both sides. Place the peppers on paper towels to absorb the excess oil.
6. Cut the tomatoes in quarters and place in a blender. Add the white onion cut into large chunks and the garlic. Add ½ cup of water and blend to form a smooth mix.
7. Heat the oil in the skillet, and when hot strain the tomato mixture and simmer for 10 minutes; season with salt and pepper. Transfer the drained stuffed peppers to the tomato sauce and cover; simmer for a few minutes to warm the peppers.

To serve place a chile relleno *on a plate and cover with enough of the tomato sauce; accompany with warm corn tortillas.*

Crema de Calabacitas (Cream of Squash)

Yield: Serves 4 to 6

5 large Mexican squash (zucchini can be used instead)
1 medium white onion
2 garlic cloves
3 tablespoons butter
1 cup milk
1 cup heavy cream
Salt and pepper to taste
Sour cream
Crackers, optional

Equipment: medium pot, medium sauté pan, blender, measuring cups, measuring spoons, mixing spoon

1. In a medium pot, bring squash and ½ onion to a boil and cook over low heat for a few minutes.
2. Once the squash is soft, transfer to a blender with the onion and 1 cup of the water used to cook the squash.
3. Mince the garlic and chop the remaining onion. In a medium sauté pan melt the butter and add the onions; sauté for a few minutes until translucent. Add the garlic and sauté just until fragrant. Add the contents of the blender and simmer over low heat for 10 minutes.
4. Add milk and simmer for about 5 minutes.
5. Add the heavy cream slowly and whisk to incorporate; lower the heat.
6. Simmer for a few minutes and remove from the heat. Add salt to taste.

Serve the cream in individual bowls and add a large spoonful of sour cream to the middle of each bowl; sprinkle with fresh ground pepper. Drop a few small crackers on top, if using, or place them on the side.

Sopa de Lentejas (Lentil Soup)

Yield: Serves 8 to 10

1 pound lentils
2 tablespoons olive oil
2 garlic cloves minced
½ medium white onion finely chopped
1 large tomato chopped
1 cup cubed carrots
1 cup cubed celery
6 cups water
1 bay leaf
Salt and pepper to taste

Equipment: Strainer, medium soup pot, mixing spoon

1. Wash and drain the lentils, making sure you remove any debris. Set aside.
2. Heat oil in the soup pot. Add onions and sauté for 3 minutes. Add the garlic and sauté until fragrant (about 2 more minutes). Add the tomatoes, carrots, and celery and sauté until soft, about 5 minutes.
3. Stir in the drained lentils, water, and bay leaf. Bring to a boil. Reduce the heat to low and simmer for about 30 minutes or until the lentils have the desired consistency. Season with salt and pepper.

Serve the soup in individual bowls accompanied with half a bolillo bread or warm corn tortillas.

CHAPTER THREE

Appetizers and Side Dishes

The word *comida* in Mexico is so generic and so versatile. It literally means food, and yet it is so specific in the right context, since it is also used to refer to the main meal of the day, which happens usually in the early afternoon and is called *la comida*. Traditional Mexican *comida* or special occasion dinners include a starter, traditionally soup or salad; after that, rice or a dry pasta is served, followed by a main dish, often meat in a sauce, a stew, a chili pepper sauce, or simply grilled or fried. Vegetables, and occasionally fruits, are traditional side dishes, with tortillas, salsa, and beans almost always placed at the center of the table for people to help themselves. The main dish (called *plato fuerte* in Spanish), whether it includes meat or not, is often accompanied by several side dishes. To talk about appetizers and side dishes in Mexican cuisine requires a brief explanation. Like in most places, in Mexico, eating habits can change from region to region, depending on many factors, including age, class, education, and ethnicity; also, the etiquette of eating changes depending on various circumstances. According to chef and food historian, Ricardo Múñoz Zurita, modern times have changed the traditional way of eating in Mexico, and if "in the past the number and order of dishes [in a meal] was very strict and followed a precise protocol" (58), today *comidas*, or dinners, could "have three or four courses, and only in very special occasions they could last long hours" (58). If traditional meals in Mexico used to be an elaborate ritual lasting a long time and including several dishes, modern times have made that an impossible everyday occurrence.

Some traditions, remain, however, and most meals in Mexico today include at least three courses. This section of the book discusses some traditional appetizers and side dishes in Mexican cuisine; the boundaries between these two categories, however, are not very clear and a dish could be either an appetizer or a side dish, or even a main course, depending mostly on the quantities. When they are served before the meal in very small quantities or while drinking a cocktail, a glass of wine, or a beer, they usually are called *aperitivos* (appetizers), and they are intended to stimulate the appetite; when they are served at the beginning of the meal, they are called the *primer plato* (first course); if followed by another course, the dish that follows is called *segundo plato* (second course). Today, most meals include only one course before the main dish, and this could be one of those traditionally considered first or second course, just in a smaller portion, which could also be eaten as snacks (and then be called *botanas*) at different times of the day or when sipping drinks at a bar. To look at several dishes, and to have a more representative view of the dishes popular in the entire country, this text will focus on five principal regions: central Mexico, southern Mexico, northern Mexico, the Yucatán Peninsula, and the coastal areas—with the understanding that many of the appetizers and side dishes "typical" of one area could be popular in other areas as well, with some variations.

Central Mexico

The term "central Mexico" refers to the following areas: Mexico City; the states of Mexico, Puebla, Tlaxcala, Queretaro, Morelos, Hidalgo, Guanajuato, Aguascalientes, Zacatecas, and San Luis Potosí; and parts of Jalisco, Michoacán, and Guerrero. Some of the traditional dishes most people would serve as appetizers are *quesadillas*. When offered as an appetizer *quesadillas* are usually smaller and fried, similar to a samosa; the fillings tend to be the traditional ones: chicken, cheese, potato, and pork. Also traditional as appetizers, the *quesadilla de comal* are freshly made tortillas, cooked on a *comal* and filled with the same standard ingredients, but also mushrooms with cheese, zucchini blossoms, and *cuitlacoche*. *Sopes*, *tlacoyos*, and *chalupas* are all possible appetizers; these foods are little corn cakes topped with beans, cheese, lettuce, onion, and sometimes a meat. They will be discussed in more detail in Chapter Eight, when discussing street foods. Another appetizer that is sometimes considered a traditional street food is *taquitos dorados* or *flautas* (flutes). These are rolled tortillas, filled with shredded chicken, and deep fried until golden and crunchy. They are served topped with crumbled fresh cheese, cream, shredded lettuce, and salsa.

A little more complex, and usually reserved for special occasions, are two appetizers very popular in Mexico City: *quesadillas de cuitlacoche* or crêpes with *cuitlacoche*. Considered a delicacy, this fungus has always been appreciated in Mexico. Other appetizers, in contrast, are much simpler and consist of cooked or pickled vegetables. *Hongos al ajillo*, mushrooms in garlic sauce, is one example. Another example are *chiles*

Appetizers and Side Dishes

curados, pickled jalapeño or serrano peppers with other vegetables, mainly cauliflower, carrots, green beans, and mushrooms; often before a meal, particularly when having a cocktail or a beer before eating, little bowls of pickled peppers and other vegetables are served to stimulate the appetite. Fruit peeled and sliced, particularly *jícama*, pineapple, or cantaloupe, is also a traditional appetizer served with lime juice, salt, and chili pepper powder.

Queso fundido (melted cheese) or *queso con chorizo* (melted cheese with chorizo) are traditional appetizers as well; the melted cheeses are served in little clay pots with small corn tortillas for people to make tacos with them. Less common are cheese plates, which in Mexico are generally served as appetizers with slices of bread rather than at the end of the meal. Pates are sometimes served as appetizers as well as cold cuts, pickled pig's feet, or pickled pig's skin called *cueritos*. *Chicharrón*, crunchy fried pork rind, is also popular as an appetizer, often served with tortillas to make tacos or simply with a salsa to use them as chips. Salads are popular as a first course; the most traditional is made with shredded lettuce, tomatoes, and onions dressed with salt and lime juice, sometimes also olive oil; another traditional salad is made with peeled and sliced cucumbers and onions in lime juice, salt, and chili pepper powder. Radishes are popular as well, alone with sea salt or sliced and dressed with lime juice and salt. More elaborate salads, like Caesar salad, Cobb salad, Greek salad, tomato and avocado salad, or caprese salad, are also common.

Perhaps the most traditional is the *ensalada de nopalitos* (cactus salad), which is sometimes served also as a side dish. It is made with *nopales* (cactus pads) cooked and cut in strips or squares with chopped tomatoes, onions, jalapeño or serrano chili peppers, and cilantro. This salad, when offered as an appetizer, is often served with warm corn tortillas to make tacos; as a side dish, it is served accompanying grilled meats or placed on the table in a large serving bowl so people can help themselves. Other salads with cooked vegetables, such as *chayote* salad, artichoke salad, green bean salad, asparagus salad, zucchini blossom salad, or spinach salad, are common; often they are served as a first course or as side dishes; if served as a first course, they are served on a plate in a generous amount at the beginning of the meal; if served as side dishes, they are often served in the same plate as the main dish, particularly if this is a meat or vegetable served without any sauce, such as grilled meats or vegetable patties (*tortitas*). Regardless of what or how many side dishes are served in a meal, beans, warm tortillas, and a salsa are always on the table.

Soups, like salads, are often served as a first course. If soup and salad are served in a meal, the soup is served first, followed by the salad. Soup is sometimes in Mexico called a dry soup, which is either rice Mexican style or spaghetti in tomato or cream sauce. These dry soups are served alone and rarely in the same plate with the main dish. Spaghetti is usually cooked in a tomato sauce or fried with butter and cream and then served with crumbled fresh cheese on top. The Mexican-style rice, also called *arroz rojo*, is washed, strained, and sautéed in oil and then cooked in a tomato sauce with peas, cubed potatoes, carrots, and jalapeño peppers. This is by far the most popular way of preparing rice. Other variations, however, include *arroz verde*, which is rice cooked with herbs like cilantro, parsley, and poblano peppers; *arroz blanco*, which is cooked like *arroz rojo*, but without the tomato sauce; or *arroz amarillo*, which is cooked with turmeric or even achiote. In all these cases, the rice is cooked with cubed vegetables, peas, and whole serrano or jalapeño peppers.

Other soups traditionally served as first courses are lentil, fava beans, and *nopales* soup, simple soups cooked with onions, garlic, spices, and sometimes chili peppers. *Sopa de fideos* is a popular pasta soup made with very thin spaghetti cooked in a tomato sauce; it is one of the most traditional soups in home cooking. Equally traditional as first courses are chicken soup and other soups related to it, like *sopa de tortilla* or *caldo tlalpeño*. *Sopa de tortilla* is a chicken soup with vegetables and strips of fried corn tortillas added for crunchiness and consistency; this soup is served with chopped onions, cream, and cheese on top. *Caldo tlalpeño* is similar, except that the broth of the soup is made with chipotle peppers and it is served with chopped onions, avocado, cheese, and cream. *Consomé de pollo* or *caldo de pollo* is also very popular; it is a very light chicken soup, with few vegetables, often some chickpeas, and little or no chicken meat; it is closer to a chicken broth, and it is served with chopped onions, chili peppers, and wedges of lime, often as an appetizer. It is traditionally made with many different parts of the chicken, especially the bones, giblets or gizzards, and even feet, so the chicken flavor is very concentrated.

Other extremely popular soups are the called *cremas*. These soups are made with the main vegetable pureed and cooked with chopped onions, garlic, herbs, and cream or milk. Some of the most traditional are *crema de elote* (corn cream), *crema de champiñones* (mushroom cream), *crema de espinaca* (spinach cream), *crema de chile poblano* (poblano pepper cream), *crema de flor de calabaza* (zucchini blossom cream), *crema de papa* (potato cream), and *crema de zanahoria* (carrot cream). Perhaps the most emblematic of them all is the *crema de calabacitas* (squash cream). For this soup, the squash (or zucchini) is cut in large chunks, cooked in water with salt and onion and then blended until very smooth. Meanwhile, in a large pan, some oil or butter is heated and a small onion is finely chopped and

Appetizers and Side Dishes

sautéed; when the onion is translucent, the blended squash is added and cooked for a few minutes. A little water is added, as well as a cup of cream; all the ingredients are simmered for a few minutes over a very low heat. Finally, it is seasoned with salt and pepper and served with a spoonful of sour cream on top.

Side dishes are usually vegetables cooked in oil or with cream and served together with the main dish. The vegetables could be any vegetable imaginable, including leafy green vegetables like chard, spinach, *verdolagas* (purslane), or *quintoniles* (amaranth greens). Some of the most traditional vegetable side dishes are *hongos con epazote*, mushrooms cooked in oil and chopped onion and garlic flavored with *epazote*; *chayotes* sautéed in oil and oregano or in a cream sauce; and *calabacitas con queso*, a classic of Mexican cuisine. *Calabacitas con queso* is squash cut into small cubes and sautéed in a little vegetable or olive oil with chopped onions and garlic, as well as poblano pepper strips, sweet corn kernels, and a sprig of parsley; the dish is flavored with oregano, salt, and pepper and cooked until the flavors are combined. Once all the vegetables are done, the dish is served with a spoonful of sour cream on top and plenty of crumbled fresh cheese.

Southern Mexico

It is hard to determine what is southern Mexico and what is, for example, the Yucatán Peninsula or the Gulf Coast. However, the following states—Oaxaca, Tabasco, Chiapas, parts of Guerrero, and Veracruz—have many traditions in common, a close history, and clear common ethnic components, as well as a similar climate, that justifies presenting them here together. Many of the appetizers mentioned previously are traditional in this region as well, with some variations. *Sopes*, *quesadillas*, *tlacoyos*, *gorditas*, and *taquitos dorados* are all familiar and served as appetizers. Nonetheless, there are some variations; one of the most traditional appetizers in the region, for example, is the famous *gorditas de frijol*, *gorditas* filled with a bean paste, popular in Veracruz. Similar to *tlacoyos*, the *tlayudas* are another popular appetizer typical of Oaxaca; the *tlayudas* are large thin tortillas fried until crisp and spread with refried beans; topped with shredded cabbage, onions, and chicken or steak mostly, but also chorizo, or pork, as well as cheese, cream, and a hot salsa. When served as appetizers, two or three *tlayudas* are placed on the table and they are shared by several people. Similar to the fried *quesadillas*, the *empanadas oaxaqueñas* are small corn tortillas filled with ground beef and onion, folded, and fried in oil until golden.

Traditional appetizers are the popular *tamales*; the *tamales* from the southern region are wrapped and cooked not in a corn husk but in banana leaves and are sometimes known as *tamales oaxaqueños*. One of the most traditional of these *tamales* is *tamalitos de chipilín*. These *tamales* are prepared with the traditional corn masa, lard, and salt, but also with leaves of *chipilín* (longbeak rattlebox) and fresh cheese or shredded chicken for the filling. These *tamales* are popular particularly in the states of Tabasco and Chiapas; also popular in Tabasco is the *tamalitos de pejelagarto*, the emblematic fish from the state; these *tamalitos* are filled with the fish cooked with achiote, epazote, and other herbs. Other *tamales* popular in this region are *tamalito de chaya con chicharrón*, which are made with a filling of pressed pork mixed with chopped *chaya* (tree spinach); *chaya* is a local plant that has been eaten in southern Mexico since the Maya. Traditional in the state of Veracruz are the famous *tamales veracruzanos*, with a filling of *hoja santa* (acuyo) and pork marinated in a *chipotle* sauce. *Pituales* are another kind of *tamal* popular in Chiapas made with mashed beans mixed with the corn dough.

Tortillas are almost always served with most foods in Mexico, and in Tabasco, Chiapas, and parts of Veracruz, the tortillas can also be mixed with other ingredients for flavor and variety. Some of the most common are *tortillas de frijol*, which are made with the masa or corn dough mixed with refried beans; once all the ingredients are incorporated, the dough is made into regular tortillas cooked on a *comal*; *tortillas de chicharrón* is another popular version made with fried pork rind or pressed pork mixed with the dough; *tortillas de yuca* are made just like regular tortillas, but in this case yuca is mixed with the dough; another popular variety is the *tortillas de plátano verde*; these tortillas are made with a mixture of corn dough and green plantains cooked and mashed. Like tortillas, plantains are a staple of southern Mexican cuisine and are especially popular in appetizers and side dishes. Some of the most popular appetizers and side dishes

---

Mexicans love *tamales*, and to assure success in their preparation, people have developed a series of rituals considered absolutely indispensable. For example, before preparing *tamales*, you have to make the sign of the cross over the dough; any sad person must leave the kitchen where *tamales* are being prepared, as must any pregnant woman; only one person can mix the dough, and they must be in a good mood. Fail to do this, and *tamales* will "throw a tantrum." If that happens, you must beat the pot with a stick or dance around the pot.

Appetizers and Side Dishes

made with plantains are *plátanos machacados*, which are slices of green plantain cooked and pressed, sometimes two or three together, until they form a tortilla-like circle, which is then fried and served warm with salt; *machuco de plátano* is mashed plantains fried in lard with onions and salt.

Other more elaborate dishes are *molotes de plátano*, very traditional in the state of Oaxaca. *Molote* in Mexico means a bundle, so this appetizer is little fried patties or rolls made with cooked and mashed plantains, sugar, salt, and bread crumbs, usually fried in lard, but vegetable oil is used as well; to prepare the dish, the rolls of cooked and mashed plantains are filled with black beans, pork, or beef and then fried and served as appetizers with Mexican cream or sour cream on the side, as well as shredded *queso añejo* or any salty cheese that contrasts with the slightly sweet rolls or patties. The same appetizer in Tabasco is called *platanito relleno*. Like in other parts of Mexico, melted cheeses mixed with peppers or other vegetables are popular as appetizers, usually served with warm corn tortillas to make tacos. Cooked vegetables in a chili pepper sauce are often placed on a table in small clay pots with warm tortillas to make tacos as appetizers. And like in other parts of the country, pickled chili peppers and other vegetables are common appetizers, especially when sipping a cocktail or a beer. Besides pickled vegetables, sliced fruits like *jícama*, pineapple, and papaya with lime juice, salt, and powdered chili pepper are popular appetizers.

Soups are a popular first course in this part of the country as well; some of the traditional soups common in southern Mexico are unique to the region. *Caldo de gato* is one of those dishes; it is a soup with pork and chicken cooked in a broth with spices; chili peppers; garbanzo beans; and vegetables like potatoes, green beans, carrots, and squash. It can be a hearty soup that could be served as a meal, with tortillas and lime wedges, but it typically is offered as a first course, served in smaller quantities. *Sopa de ajo* (garlic soup), popular in the state of Oaxaca, is a soup with a large amount of garlic cooked in a broth with herbs, spices, and chili peppers served with slices of bread and melted cheese on top. Another popular soup in the state of Veracruz is the famous *chilpachole*, a soup made traditionally with fish but that could also be prepared with other meats—crab meat and shrimp are particularly popular for this dish. The basic *chilpachole* soup is made with *pasilla* or *ancho* chili peppers, onion, garlic, *epazote*, and fish broth, as well as the meat of choice. *Caldo de pescado* is a simple fish soup made with tomatoes, chili peppers, herbs, and chunks of fish simmered until tender; sometimes vegetables like carrots and *chayote* are added to make a heartier soup. Another version, *caldo verde de pescado*, is made the same way, but with tomatillos instead of tomatoes. Both *caldos* are served as a first course in clay bowls topped with chopped onion and lime wedges. In Oaxaca and Veracruz, black beans are the most popular beans, usually cooked with *epazote*. These beans can be served as a side dish, but also can be added to soups, as in the case of the traditional black bean soup, which is made with beans, chorizo, onions, and garlic.

Rice—green, red, or white—is popular as a first course in the south, the way it is in other parts of Mexico, but in this region it is also combined with other ingredients, like the popular rice with seafood; likewise, pasta, either dry or in soups, is fairly common in traditional home cooking. Rice, like beans, can also be a side dish. Other side dishes popular in southern Mexican cuisine are *chayotes con oregano*, which is *chayotes* cooked in water and then sautéed in oil and flavored with oregano, salt, and pepper. *Chayotes rellenos* (stuffed *chayotes*) are another side dish that can be served also as a main dish. For this dish, the *chayotes* are cooked and cut in half lengthwise; the seed is removed and most of the flesh is spooned out and mixed with meat, spices, herbs, and bread crumbs to create the filling. The filling is then placed in the hollow *chayotes* and covered with butter or oil and sprinkled with cheese. The *chayotes* are then baked until the cheese melts and the *chayotes* are golden. If served as an appetizer, they are cut in smaller pieces and served; if offered as a main dish, two halves are placed on a plate and accompanied with a salad. Pickled vegetables and chili peppers are common side dishes, as well as salads, like the traditional lettuce, tomato, and onion salad or the cucumber salad. Mashed plantains are a common side dish; they can be cooked, boiled, fried, and pureed, but a simple way of serving them is fried topped with Mexican cream.

Mushrooms, wild or cultivated, are a traditional side dish as well. They can be cooked with epazote, garlic, and onions or can be pickled. A traditional dish from Veracruz, for example, is *setas con vinagre*, wild mushrooms in vinegar. This side dish can also be made with regular mushrooms or even Bella mushrooms. Squash, green beans, or spinach, as well as other *quelites*, are common side dishes, usually cooked in a tomato or chili pepper sauce or sautéed in oil. Particularly popular are yuca and potatoes. *Papas con rajas* (potatoes and poblano peppers) is a traditional side dish, as well as *papas con chorizo*. In both cases the potatoes are cooked in water, peeled, cut, fried in oil or lard, and mixed with *chorizo* or the poblano peppers cut into strips and covered with heavy cream. *Papas en escabeche* are pickled potatoes, and they are a traditional side dish; the same can be said of *papas enchiladas*, which are potatoes cooked whole or cut in half and then marinated in a chili pepper paste; they can either be baked or sautéed in oil.

Appetizers and Side Dishes

As noted earlier, rice is common as a first course or as a side dish, and so are beans in multiple forms—*de la olla*, or straight from the pot, with chorizo or pork, with sauces, or refried. Beans, just like rice, are never served in the same plate as the main dish; they are instead placed on the table in a serving bowl so people can take what they want and add them to their plate or make a taco with them. Also, rice and beans are almost never served together, except in the case of a traditional dish popular in Veracruz and Oaxaca called *moros y cristianos* (Moors and Christians), known in the United States as rice and beans. For this dish, the beans and rice are cooked separately, while in a large skillet onions, garlic, tomatoes, and other spices are sautéed in hot oil; then the beans and rice are added to the pan with the tomatoes, onion, and garlic.

Northern Mexico

The states included here—Baja California, Baja California Sur, Durango, Sonora, Chihuahua, Coahuila, Nuevo León, and parts of Tamaulipas and Sinaloa—are all in the north of the country, but they are very different from each other, particularly since some of them, like the Californias, Sinaloa, Sonora, and Tamaulipas, have large coastal areas and the rest do not. Nonetheless, there are some similarities in their cuisines, derived particularly from the meat and dairy products popular in that part of Mexico. Like in other regions, corn is an essential part of the cuisine; however, wheat is also an important grain. So corn tortillas alternate with flour tortillas in the northern diet. Here as well, *quesadillas* are a favorite appetizer, but the favorite filling is cheese; shredded beef is also popular, as well as chorizo sometimes mixed with potatoes or even eggs. These *quesadillas* tend to be smaller and cooked in a *comal* with little oil. They are served with a salsa and crumbled *queso fresco*. *Tamales* are also common in the north; however, the *tamales norteños*, or Monterrey-style *tamales*, as they are also called, tend to be smaller than *tamales* from southern Mexico and are prepared with less dough and abundant filling, mostly consisting of pork marinated in spices and chili peppers.

Another traditional appetizer is *taquitos*, which are rolled tortillas filled with shredded beef in this case and fried; they are served with shredded lettuce, chopped onions, salsa, *queso fresco*, and cream. *Taquitos de tuétano* (also called *tacos de médula*) is another popular appetizer in the north; it is made with bone marrow cooked for a long time until soft and buttery and spooned in small corn tortillas with salt and salsa to make tacos. Traditionally the cooked bones with the marrow are placed in a bowl and people spoon the marrow out into their own tortillas. It is a simple and delicious way of accompanying an ice-cold beer before a meal. An equally simple and delicious appetizer is grilled meats, including chorizos, cut in small bites and served in a large plate with toothpicks for people to grab what they want. Dry beef is also popular as an appetizer, particularly in Nuevo León, Coahuila, and Chihuahua. Usually the dry meat is lightly toasted on a *comal* or a griddle and served on a large plate with wedges of lime and a vinegar-based salsa. More unusual, but still popular, pieces of goat meat are often served as an appetizer, particularly when served with small flour tortillas and salsa to make tacos.

Cheese is a very important ingredient in northern Mexican cuisine and rightly so since the region is one of the most important cheese producers in the country. So often an appetizer consists of chunks of cheese served with cold beer before a meal. Other times, the cheese is prepared as *queso fundido* or melted cheese, served in little clay pots with small flour tortillas. The cheese could sometimes be mixed with other ingredients like *chorizo* or vegetables, such as potatoes or, more commonly, rajas (strips of chili peppers) sautéed in oil. A traditional way of preparing this dish is by toasting, seeding, cleaning, and cutting into strips two or three Anaheim chili peppers, sautéing them in oil with onion and tomatoes, and simmering with cream or milk before adding lots of *asadero* or *menonita* cheese, which is simmered until it melts and mixes with the peppers. Another version of the dish popular in the state of Chihuahua is *queso fundido con cerveza*, which follows the same process previously described, but the chili peppers are simmered with a good, strong beer before adding the cheese. All these cheese appetizers are served in clay pots with plenty of tortillas, preferably flour tortillas, and a salsa.

Most of the main dishes in this part of Mexico are meat based; from pork and beef to goat or lamb, meat reigns supreme in the region. Fish is also important, particularly in the large areas with access to the sea. So, first courses and side dishes tend to be simple, intended to accompany the meats, rather than compete with them. First courses, like in other parts of Mexico, tend to be salads, soups, or rice. One popular salad in the state of Sonora is lettuce, tomatoes, onions, and pickled Anaheim chili peppers. Cucumber or *jícama* is also used in salads, as well as fruits like oranges and other citric fruits. Lentils, fava beans, garbanzo beans, and split pea are popular for soups, as well as pasta. Like in the rest of Mexico, beans are popular and mostly served as a side dish, but also could be served as soups, particularly when prepared in dishes like *frijoles borrachos* (drunken beans)—beans cooked with onions, garlic, tomatoes, chili peppers, cilantro, and dark bear. This dish can be served as a soup for a first course or to accompany grilled meats, like the traditional *cabrito* (roasted baby

Appetizers and Side Dishes

goat) from Nuevo León. Another bean side dish is *frijoles maneados* (beans Sonora style)—beans cooked with chorizo, chili peppers, and lots of melted cheese on top. *Frijoles charros*, another variation of *borrachos*, is now considered a classic of Mexican cuisine. For this dish, the beans are cooked with onions, tomatoes, bacon, chorizo, and *chicharrón*, all mixed and slowly cooked until tender.

The Yucatán Peninsula

The Yucatán Peninsula encompasses three states: Yucatán, Quintana Roo, and Campeche; these states share cultural traits that make their cuisine similar. From the ancestral Maya influence to the contemporary tourism boom and a cosmopolitan presence, these states have developed a rich cuisine. However, the traditional dishes are remarkably similar to the ones from neighboring states like Tabasco or Veracruz. Like in those regions, many appetizers are corn based. Similar foods to *quesadillas*, *tlacoyos*, or *gorditas*—those corn patties filled with beans or meat and topped with shredded lettuce, onions, cream and cheese—are also popular in the Yucatán region, except that there they are called *panuchos*, and when prepared by dipping them in pumpkin seed sauce are called *papadzules*. *Taquitos* are prepared in Yucatán as well, but the rolled tortillas are often stuffed with fish, fried, and served with shredded cabbage. Like in the southern region, plantains are an important staple of the Yucatán diet. Dishes like plantain patties or rolls stuffed with cheese are popular as well in Yucatán, where they are called *platanito relleno*. Like in other regions, salsas are common here too, and one of the most popular is *salsa de chile habanero* or *salpicón de habanero*. It is simply habanero peppers, and sometimes serrano peppers, sliced and mixed with chopped onions cooked with lime, bitter orange, and grapefruit juice. The chili peppers are left in the juices for several hours and then are seasoned with salt.

Xnipec is another salsa prepared with tomatoes, cilantro, red onion, and habanero chili peppers dressed with bitter orange juice and salt; this salsa could easily be a salad, except that it is very spicy. Red onion marinated in vinegar for hours and then seasoned with salt is called *cebolla curtida*, and it is widely used as a condiment on tacos or grilled meats; sometimes it contains sliced habanero peppers as well. Salads are popular; besides the traditional lettuce, tomato, and onion, another popular salad is *ensalada de jícama*, which is actually made with diced *jícama*, chopped red onions, peeled and sliced oranges, and chopped cilantro seasoned with salt and chili pepper powder. Radishes (*rábanos* in Spanish) are also very popular in salads, the most traditional of which is prepared with sliced radishes, red onion, jalapeño or serrano peppers, and cilantro, served with a dressing of oil, bitter orange and lime juice, and salt; it is topped with pieces of fried pork rinds. Mushrooms, wild as well as cultivated, are used pickled, in salads, or cooked in oil with spices or a tomato sauce and served with corn tortillas. A popular dish is prepared with a type of wild mushroom called *chiquinte* and is prepared by cooking the mushrooms in a thick tomato sauce with corn dough and spices, topped with fresh cheese.

Soups, like in most of Mexico, are popular in the Yucatán region as a first course. Besides the traditional lentil and fava bean soups, chicken, fish, and beef are popular. But perhaps the most famous soup from the region, a soup that is invariably included in the lists of traditional Yucatán cuisine, is *sopa de lima* (lime soup). This soup is made with chicken cooked in a light broth with peppers, red onion, habanero peppers, and sliced limes; flavored with cilantro and lime juice; and served with little strips of corn tortillas fried in oil until crunchy. Cream-based soups are popular as well, like the traditional *crema de elote* (sweet corn cream), which is frequently intensified with cilantro, leeks, and celery; after all the vegetables are pureed, they are sautéed in butter and cooked with cream and milk. More traditional of the region is the refreshing *crema de aguacate* (avocado cream), a cold soup made with vegetables, spices, avocados, light cream, and lime juice. For the soup, the vegetables are sautéed in butter and then blended with the cream and mixed with the avocado and lime juice to create a creamy, velvety soup, which is served chilled with chopped onions and avocado slices.

Like in other regional cuisines, grilled, sautéed, or boiled vegetables, such as *chayotes*, green beans, carrots, squash, or potatoes, are often served as side dishes. But a very traditional side dish is beans. In the north and the center of the country, beans are almost always present on the table; like in the south of Mexico, black beans are preferred. Cooked with lard and *epazote* or avocado leaves for flavor, black beans are served as a side dish or are used in more elaborate dishes like *frijoles negros en chilmole*. *Chilmole* is a dark sauce made with spices and vegetables grilled or toasted, or even charred to add color and flavor to the sauce; it can be used in different dishes with pork, chicken, or turkey, but also beans. Another way of preparing beans similar to *frijoles charros* is *frijoles con puerco*; for this dish, the beans are cooked and then simmered with tomatoes, chili peppers, spices, onion, garlic, bitter orange juice, habanero peppers, and chunks of pork meat, including the bones and skin for flavor. This dish is so satisfying that it could be served as a main dish; however, most of the time it is served as a side dish along with white rice.

Appetizers and Side Dishes

The Coastal Areas

At least half of the Mexican states have direct access to the sea, which gives their cuisines a distinctive flavor. Many of the appetizers and side dishes discussed previously are popular in these states, as are dishes with fish and seafood. One of the most traditional appetizers in these regions is *ceviche; ceviche* is a popular dish made with raw fish cooked in lime juice and combined with tomatoes, chili peppers, onions, herbs, and spices. It is usually served with tortilla chips or on top of a tostada as an appetizer. The most traditional recipe includes white fish cut into bite-size pieces and marinated in lime juice for 24 hours or more, after which it is mixed with chopped onions and cilantro, minced jalapeño or serrano peppers, chopped tomatoes, chopped avocado, vegetable oil, salt, and a hot salsa. It is served in small glasses with tortilla chips as an appetizer, before a meal and while enjoying a cold beer. Although the traditional *ceviche* is made with fish, shrimp, crab, octopus, or clams are also used; sometimes they are combined in what is called *ceviche mixto*.

Also popular as an appetizer is *coctel de camarón*, which is prepared with shrimp cooked and mixed with chopped onions and cilantro in tomato juice with catsup, oil, lime juice, and a splash of hot sauce, like Tabasco, Cholula, or Valentina. They are served in individual glasses topped with cubed avocado and salty crackers. Shrimp fried in olive oil and lots of garlic are often served as appetizers as well, either by themselves or on a tostada. If prepared in a chili sauce or a spicy tomato sauce, they can be served with corn tortillas or tortilla chips. *Tostadas* are a favorite, and easy, way of serving appetizers; usually the hard corn tortillas are topped with any ingredient and dressed with salsa and maybe cheese. The traditional seafood *tostadas* are *tostadas de pescado* (fish), *de ceviche, de pulpo* (octopus), or *jaiba* (crab). Another popular appetizer in coastal areas is *tamalitos de marsicos*, which are little *tamales* filled with fish or seafood and made with coconut milk instead of chicken broth. They are smaller than the traditional *tamales oaxaqueños* and wrapped in banana leaves. The *tamalitos* are usually placed on the table in a serving plate for people to eat one or two with drinks before a meal.

Caldo de pescado is a light fish soup prepared with chunks of fish cooked with water, onion, garlic, and other aromatic herbs; chopped vegetables like carrots and potatoes are often added to the soup, as well as pureed tomatoes and chili peppers. It can be served as a main dish, but most of the time it is served as a first course. The *sopa de mariscos* is prepared just like the *sopa de pescado*, but with seafood or shellfish instead of just the fish. Similarly, the *caldo siete mares* (seven seas) is a soup prepared with seven types of seafood: shrimp, clams, scallops, fish, sea snails, octopus, and crab legs cooked in a broth with tomatoes, herbs, chili peppers, vegetables, and spices. There are several variations of this soup, but the seven types of seafood are always the same, and in some markets people can buy the seafood already mixed together and prepacked in plastic bags. These soups are usually served in small clay cups with chopped onions and lime wedges as a first course, although some of them are heavy enough to be served as a main dish.

As in most regions discussed here, side dishes in coastal areas are often grilled or cooked vegetables, prepared in sauces or chili sauces, as well as fried or sautéed with spices. Tubers like potatoes, yuca, or sweet potatoes are particularly popular; so is green plantains cooked and mashed or mixed with other ingredients. Legumes like lentils and fava beans, and chiefly black beans, are also popular first courses, as well as the traditional red, green, and white rice. Since many main dishes are fish and seafood, salads tend to be very traditional as side dishes, from the simplest one made with lettuce, tomato, and onions to more complex ones including different vegetables and fruits, or even seafood, like the traditional shrimp and mango salad popular in several southern states made with chunks of mango, onions, tomatoes, chili peppers, cilantro, and shrimp dressed with lime juice, olive oil, salt, and pepper. Similarly, a popular salad from Tabasco is made with papaya, avocado, tomatoes, onions, greens, peppers, and cilantro, with a dressing of lime juice, olive oil, paprika, salt, pepper, garlic, and a little bit of sugar. In the state of Yucatán, the most popular salad is a citrus salad made with oranges, grapefruits, limes, red onions, and avocados dressed with bitter orange juice, olive oil, salt, and pepper.

Sopes (Little Corn Cakes)

Yield: Serves 4 to 5

1½ cups masa harina
1¼ cup warm water
6 tablespoons lard or vegetable oil
1 cup cooked beans, pinto or black
2 cups lettuce, finely shredded
1 cup shredded *queso fresco*
½ medium white onion, finely chopped
1 cup Mexican cream or sour cream
1 cup shredded chicken, optional
1 cup cooked and crumbled chorizo, optional

Equipment: *comal* or griddle, mixing bowls, frying pan, measuring cups

1. In a large bowl mix the masa harina and water until it forms a soft dough. Add more water if needed. The dough should be soft and malleable. Cover with a wet kitchen towel.
2. In a frying pan heat 2 tablespoons of lard or vegetable oil and add the beans; mash the beans and fry until they form a spreadable paste.
3. Divide the masa dough into 8 or 10 pieces of the same size. Roll the pieces into balls. Place the balls, one at a time, between two sheets of plastic and form thick circles of about ½ inch using a tortilla press or a rolling pin. Wet the dough if it cracks. Pinch the edges of the circle of dough all around to form the *sopes*.
4. Heat the *comal* or griddle and ½ tablespoon of lard or oil. Place 2 or 3 *sopes* on the *comal* or griddle and cook with the oil for a couple of minutes; flip the *sope* and cook for another minute. Transfer to a plate and cover to keep warm while you finish all the *sopes*.
5. Spread the bean paste over each *sope*; add chicken or chorizo, if using; and top with shredded lettuce, chopped onions, crumbled cheese, and cream.

To serve, place a couple of sopes on a plate and add salsa de molcajete *if you want.*

Caldo de Habas (Fava Bean Soup)

Yield: Serves 6

1 tablespoon vegetable oil
1 medium white onion finely chopped
2 cloves garlic, minced
3 medium globe tomatoes or 4 large Roma tomatoes, cubed
1 pound fava beans, cooked
4 cups water
2 cups *nopales*, diced and cooked
Salt and pepper to taste
4 sprigs cilantro

Equipment: large pot, mixing spoons, blender, measuring cups

1. Heat the oil in the large pot, then add the onion and sauté until it becomes transparent, stirring frequently. Add the garlic and sauté until fragrant, about 2 more minutes.
2. Add the tomatoes and bring to a simmer. Cook until they form a chunky sauce, about 8 minutes.
3. Add the fava beans and 4 cups of water to the pot, reserving 1 cup of cooked fava beans.
4. Blend the reserved cup of fava beans with enough water to create a smooth paste.
5. Stir in the fava bean paste, cooked *nopales*, and cilantro into the pot and mix well with all ingredients; season with salt and pepper.
6. Simmer for about 10 minutes to allow the flavors to blend.

Serve hot in individual bowls and accompanied with a slice of toasted bread or warm corn tortillas.

Calabacitas Rellenas (Stuffed Squash)

Yield: Serves 6

6 Mexican squash
4 cups water
½ small white onion
2 cloves garlic
4 large Roma tomatoes, roughly chopped
1 teaspoon dry oregano
3 tablespoons olive oil
6 thick slices *queso fresco*, the size of the squash
Salt and pepper to taste

Equipment: large pot, deep sauté pan, mixing spoons, blender, strainer

1. Place the squash in a large pot and cover with water. Bring water to a boil and cook the squash until done, but still firm.
2. Remove the squash from the hot water and let cool. Reserve 2 cups of the water.
3. Meanwhile, put the onion, garlic, tomatoes, oregano, and a cup of the water from the squash in a blender. Blend until smooth.
4. In a sauté pan heat the olive oil and strain the tomato mix. Bring to a simmer, lower the heat, and cook for 10 minutes. Season with salt and pepper. If needed, add more of the reserved water to keep the sauce silky and not too thick.
5. While the sauce is cooking, scoop the flesh out of the squash very carefully so as not to pierce the skin and stuff them with the *queso fresco* (if you cannot find *queso fresco*, you may use feta cheese instead).
6. Place the stuffed squash in the sauce and heat, bathing them with the sauce a few times.

Serve one squash and plenty of sauce on a plate with warm corn tortillas or accompanied with white rice.

Papas con Rajas (Potatoes and Poblano Peppers)

Yield: Serves 6

2 pounds potatoes
3 poblano peppers
3 tablespoons vegetable oil
1 small white onion
1 cup Mexican cream
Salt and pepper to taste

Equipment: medium pot, large sauté pan, mixing spoon

1. Place potatoes in a large pot, cover with water, and bring to a boil; cook the potatoes until almost done. Let them cool.
2. Meanwhile, roast the poblano peppers over an open flame. Place in a plastic bag and steam for a few minutes; peel the skin off with your hands or a kitchen towel. Seed the peppers and cut them into long, thin strips.
3. Once the potatoes are cool enough to handle, peel them by pulling the skin (it should come off easily; this is the traditional way of peeling potatoes in Mexico, but you can also peel and cut the potatoes before cooking them). Quarter the potatoes or cut them into 1½-inch cubes.
4. Chop the onion; in a large sauté pan heat the oil over medium heat and add the onions; sauté the onions for a few minutes, until translucent.
5. Add the potatoes and cook them for 5 minutes; then add the pepper strips and cook for a few more minutes.
6. Add the cream and season with salt and pepper. Simmer for a few minutes to allow the flavors to mix.

Serve papas con rajas *as a side dish by placing them in a plate at the center of the table and allow people to serve themselves.*

Appetizers and Side Dishes

Chayotes con Queso (*Chayotes* with Cheese)

Yield: Serves 5 to 6

3 medium *chayotes*
½ medium white onion, finely chopped
3 tablespoons olive oil
1 tablespoon butter
1 tablespoon oregano
Salt and pepper to taste
½ pound *queso fresco*, cubed

Equipment: medium pot, sauté pan, mixing spoons

1. Peel and cut the *chayotes* into cubes; place the *chayotes* in a pot and simmer for 10 minutes or until the *chayotes* are done, but still firm. Remove from heat and drain.
2. In a sauté pan, heat 2 tablespoons of olive oil and the butter; add onions and sauté until translucent.
3. Add the drained *chayotes* and oregano; season with salt and pepper, sautéing for a few minutes. Remove from the heat and let cool slightly.

To serve, combine chayotes *and* queso fresco *in a serving bowl, mix well, drizzle with remaining olive oil, and place on the table.*

Frijoles Charros (Mexican Cowboy Beans)

Yield: Serves 6 to 8

1 pound of *pinto*, *bayo*, or other similar beans
1 tablespoon lard
6 strips bacon
½ pound chorizo, or *longaniza* if available
½ medium white onion
½ medium white onion, chopped
2 garlic cloves, minced
3 large tomatoes, chopped
4 dry *chile de árbol* peppers, whole
½ pound pressed pork or fried pork rind
Salt to taste
3 sprigs cilantro

Equipment: large pot (preferably a Mexican clay boiling pot), sauté pan, mixing spoons

1. Place beans and ½ onion in the large pot; cover with abundant water and bring to a boil. Simmer on low until done, about 2 hours. In traditional Mexican cooking, beans are never soaked; however, you may do that if you want, or you can also cook them in a pressure cooker—just make sure you stop cooking them when the beans are almost done.
2. When beans are soft but not yet done (about 1 to 1½ hours), place the lard in a sauté pan and cook the bacon cut in small pieces in the lard; when the bacon is almost done, add the chorizo or *longaniza* cut in small pieces. Cook for a few minutes until golden brown. Add the chopped onion and cook until translucent; add the garlic and cook for a few seconds until fragrant; add the chili peppers and brown, stirring constantly; add the tomatoes and let them simmer with the rest of the ingredients for a few minutes; finally add the pork rind or pressed pork and cook for another few minutes. Season with salt.
3. Transfer the contents of the sauté pan to the pot with the beans, making sure there is enough water to make a thick soup, and simmer for 15 minutes or until the beans have the preferred consistency. Adjust the salt and remove from heat.

To serve, place enough beans and pieces of the meats in a small bowl or a cup and serve as a side dish for grilled meats.

CHAPTER FOUR

Main Dishes

Three important meals are served during an ordinary day in Mexico. Like in most countries, the first one is served in the morning, the second meal around two in the afternoon, and the last one in the late evening or early hours of the night. The importance of the middle meal is such that it is simply called the *hora de la comida* (hour of the meal) or just *la comida*. The other two meals are *desayuno* (breakfast) and *cena* (supper). A couple of small meals offered in between are sometimes traditional, with *merienda*—light refreshments, usually coffee, tea, chocolate, or even lemonade and a pastry—often served in between *comida* and *cena*. *La comida* was for generations the main meal of the day, a meal for which the family would gather around the table. However, as cities got bigger and more congested and as modern life became more demanding, going home in the middle of the day became less a real possibility, and *comida* became less practical. It is still the main meal of the day and a family affair whenever possible, but mostly on weekends and holidays. The rest of the week, most people eat at a restaurant, cafeteria, or one of the popular *cocinas económicas* that abound in Mexico City and many other cities around the country. In most cities in Mexico one can find numerous cafés, chain restaurants, family-style restaurants, or even stands in a market where people can sit down and have a large meal during *la comida*.

If *la comida* is the main meal of the day, that does not mean that breakfast and dinner are not important. On the contrary, breakfast could be an abundant meal, and for many Mexicans it is quite important; it usually happens early morning for most people getting ready to go to work or for children before going to school. If breakfast is eaten late, it is called *almuerzo*. Dinner is also important, although traditionally it is lighter and often nothing more than leftovers from *la comida*, and sometimes even just a hot beverage—coffee and milk, tea, chocolate, or *atole*—and bread. However, on special occasions or when going out with friends for dinner, it can be an elaborate event, similar to *la comida*. But as happened with *la comida*, eating habits in Mexico have changed, and *la cena* is becoming more important. Breakfast has also been going through a process of transformation, in part because of the proliferation of American products; so for increasing numbers of Mexican families, breakfast has become lighter with a granola bar or a bowl of processed cereal. Despite these changes, the typical dishes for the daily meals have remained rather unchanged. Some dishes have transcended their regional origins and have become standard dishes of Mexican home cooking all over the country, adapted to regional taste and ingredients; others have remained dishes consumed on special occasions. Following are some of the most traditional main dishes for the meals of the day.

Breakfast

Breakfast, or *desayuno*, is the first meal of the day. Depending on how much time people allow for breakfast, it could be as simple as bread, usually *pan dulce*, and coffee or something more elaborate, including eggs, beans, and some meat. The most traditional breakfast includes eggs sunny-side up (*huevos estrellados*), scrambled (*huevos revueltos*), or in a special sauce, often served with beans and tortillas; sometimes chocolate or *atole* can be served instead of coffee. The most popular egg dishes are *huevos a la mexicanan* (eggs Mexican style), *huevos con chorizo* (eggs with chorizo), *huevos con nopalitos* (eggs with cactus), *huevos rancheros* (eggs country style), *huevos a la albañil* (eggs construction worker style), *huevos ahogados* (drowned eggs), *huevos a la diabla* (eggs in devil sauce), and *huevos divorciados* (divorced eggs).

Despite the colorful names, they all are simple breakfast dishes, some as unassuming as a couple of scrambled eggs with other products, such as scrambled eggs with *chorizo* or scrambled eggs with cactus leaves that have been previously cut in small pieces and cooked, and, of course, the classic *huevos a la mexicana*, scrambled eggs with chopped onions, tomatoes, and jalapeño peppers. Other more elaborate ways of preparing eggs are *huevos rancheros*, which consists of two eggs sunny-side up placed on two tortillas slightly fried in oil or lard and covered with a spicy tomato sauce and topped with crumbled cheese (most commonly *queso fresco*) and sometimes cream.

Another popular dish with eggs in a sauce is *huevos a la albañil*. *Albañiles*, or brick layers, are the traditional construction workers in México; this dish is named in their honor and is very popular in Mexico City. The dish consists of scrambled eggs cooked and covered with a juicy sauce that could be red (tomato based) or more traditionally green (tomatillo based);

Main Dishes

it is served with refried beans and warm corn tortillas and sometimes it is topped with crumbled *queso fresco*. Likewise, *huevos ahogados*, or drowned eggs, are cooked in an abundant sauce made with tomatoes, garlic, onions, oregano, salt, and pepper. The sauce is prepared by blending all the ingredients and frying them in oil, letting the sauce simmer for a few minutes before cracking in the eggs and cooking them in the sauce until the egg white is firm and translucent and the yolk somewhat firm. Usually this sauce is not spicy. Unlike *huevos ahogados*, *huevos a la diabla* are also eggs in a red sauce; however, this sauce is very spicy. The humorous association of the heat of the chili peppers with fire and the red of the sauce with the devil give this dish its name.

Huevos ahogados and *huevos a la diabla* are similar to *huevos rancheros*, except that the sauce for *a la diabla* is traditionally made with *chile pasilla* and tomatoes and is therefore really spicy; the other difference is that *huevos rancheros* are placed on a tortilla with a slice of ham in between before bathing them with the sauce. Another egg dish with a picturesque name is *huevos divorciados*, which consists of two eggs "divorced" because of the irreconcilable differences between the green and the red sauce. This dish is simply two fried eggs, sunny-side up, placed on a plate and covered with a green tomatillo-based sauce and a red tomato-based sauce. Like all these egg dishes, the *huevos divorciados* are often served with refried beans and crumbled *queso fresco* on top. Some recipes call for fried tortillas placed under the eggs, like *huevos rancheros*, and then topped with the sauces. But the most traditional dish does not use fried tortillas. As mentioned before, some dishes are particular to a region, even though they may be prepared in other parts of Mexico as well. Some of the most recognizable ones are *huevos motuleños* (eggs Motule style), *huevos a la veracruzana* (eggs Veracruz style), *huevos a la oaxaqueña* (eggs Oaxaca style), and *machaca con huevo*, a traditional dish from the northern state of Nuevo León.

The *huevos motuleños* are the Yucatán answer to *huevos rancheros*. They are originally from the town of Motul de Carrillo Puerto (hence their name; *motuleño* is the demonym of Motul). This dish is assembled with two eggs sunny-side up placed on two fried tortillas that have been spread with refried black beans; then the eggs are covered in a sauce of tomatoes and habanero peppers and topped with diced ham, cooked peas, and crumbled *queso fresco* or grated *queso añejo*. It is served with slices of fried plantain. *Huevos a la veracruzana* and *huevos a la oaxaqueña* are regional dishes from Veracruz and Oaxaca, respectively. The eggs Veracruz style are scrambled eggs in a tortilla and smothered in pureed black beans, topped with chorizo and cheese. Eggs Oaxaca style consists of eggs scrambled and cooked in a big circle, without breaking them, as an omelet (in Mexico this way of cooking eggs is called *en torta*). Once the eggs are cooked, they are covered in an abundant sauce made with tomatoes, a traditional chili pepper from the state of Oaxaca called *chile de agua*, onion, garlic, and *epazote*. Some recipes suggest adding *nopalitos* (cooked cactus), and others suggest serving the dish with crumbled *queso añejo*. Another traditional egg dish, this one from the north of the country, is *machaca con huevo*. *Machaca* is beef that has been seasoned, shredded, and dried (similar to beef jerky). The dish is made by combining scrambled eggs, tomatoes, onions, and jalapeño peppers with the *machaca*.

Eggs are the most popular item for breakfast in Mexico. However, other popular foods Mexicans eat for breakfast, particularly if one does not have a lot of time and wants to grab something on the go, are *tamales* and *atole*; these traditional foods are common in central and southern Mexico, but in Mexico City they are an institution, particularly in the form of a dish that most Mexicans love to hate called *guajolota*, a *tamal* inside a *bolillo* or *telera*, often accompanied by a steaming cup of *atole*. In other parts of the country, the breakfast on the go is most commonly a piece of sweet bread and either *café con leche* or chocolate. Other street foods that people may eat for breakfast, often while commuting to work, are *gorditas*, *sopes,* or even *quesadillas*—variations of cakes made of corn dough filled or topped with pork, chicken, cheese, cream, or beans. Another popular breakfast dish is *chilaquiles*, usually prepared for breakfast on weekends or holidays since it is more elaborate. The traditional *chilaquiles* are prepared with tortilla chips fried and soaked in a spicy sauce, either red or green, and simmered until the tortilla chips are soft; it is served topped with Mexican cream, crumbled *queso fresco*, onion rings, and sometimes chicken, steak, or fried eggs.

Comida

La comida was, and continues to be, the most important meal of the day for most Mexican families. Modern life has changed this tradition, at least in most urban centers; nonetheless, many people still get together for *la comida* even if it is not the entire family. Given the cultural diversity of Mexico, the size of the country, and the diversity of climates and ecosystems, it is understandable that the main dishes prepared for *la comida* are many and could vary greatly from region to region. Generally speaking, the average *comida* consists of three courses: a soup, a main dish, and a dessert; sometimes it is four if a soup is followed by a salad or a "dry" soup—most commonly Mexican rice or thin noodles in tomato sauce

Main Dishes

called *fideos*. The main dish could be a generous portion of meat, poultry, fish, or a vegetable prepared in either a sauce or a *chile* (a chili pepper sauce that is often spicy). The dishes presented here are everyday dishes known all over Mexico. They are an invitation to enter the world of traditional home cooking, rather than an exhaustive record of the cuisine. The list of main dishes is divided into the conventional categories of meat, poultry, seafood, and vegetables, providing information about the dishes and their origin.

Meats

Farm animals were unknown in the Americas before the arrival of the Europeans. Meat came in the form of game and was complemented with fish and shellfish from the lakes and rivers of the interior and the coasts. After the arrival of the Europeans, however, chicken, beef, lamb, goat, and particularly pork were introduced and mixed with the native ingredients. Today, pork and chicken are the most popular meats, followed by beef, lamb, and goat, a delicacy in northern Mexico.

Pork

Pork dishes are numerous, and variations of the same dish are common in different regions. Perhaps one of the most common, a combination of flavors that is distinctly Mexican, is pork in green sauce. The green sauce is prepared with tomatillos, onions, green chilis (often serrano or jalapeño peppers), and garlic. Sometimes cilantro or epazote is added to the sauce, but the classic sauce is the simplest with three or four ingredients; the acidity of the tomatillos and the heat of the chili peppers complement the fatty meat excellently, and it is one of the classical combinations of Mexican cuisine. Sometimes, cubed potatoes, Mexican squash, *chilacayotes*, or *chayotes* are added to the dish. A famous variation of this dish is *puerco en chile verde con verdolagas*. The dish is basically the same, except that it is cooked with *verdolagas* (purslane) instead of any other vegetable. The flavors and texture of the *verdolagas* are so characteristic that the dish is considered a different one than the one including other vegetables. More elaborate than the *chile verde*, *mole verde* is another traditional way of preparing pork. It is a dish of tomatillo, green chilies, spices, and green aromatic herbs; in some instances, it includes pumpkin seeds or sesame seeds to thicken the sauce.

Another popular dish with pork is *puerco en adobo*; adobo is a sauce made with tomatoes, different types of chili peppers, onions, spices, and vinegar. Some recipes use citrus juices, like lemon, lime, or bitter oranges instead of vinegar; chef Patricia Quintana also recommends grapefruit. Generally speaking, the adobo is used to marinate the meat (usually pork tenderloin) for a few hours before roasting it in the oven, but also can be used as a sauce, particularly with chunks of stewing pork half-cooked in water that will finish cooking in the thick *adobo*. In all cases it is served garnished with pickled onions. The flavor and the color of the *adobo* change depending on the ingredients used and can be from a light red color to almost black with a tangy or sweet taste. In some parts of the country, particularly in the southern states, *adobo* is also called *recaudo* or *recado* in the Yucatán Peninsula. Adobo can be used as well as a glaze for pork ribs in a process that resembles BBQ country ribs. Adobo also can be used with chicken, beef, lamb, and rabbit, but pork is the most traditional meat used.

Other traditional dishes with pork are *chiles*. *Chile* is the generic name given to stews prepared with chili peppers, tomatoes or tomatillos, onion, garlic, and spices. One of the most traditional of these dishes is called *chile colorado* (because of the rich red color of the sauce from the chili peppers of the same name); it is traditional in northern Mexico but present in other regions as well. Pork is also cooked in a tomato sauce (*caldillo de jitomate*) seasoned with onion, garlic, oregano, salt, and pepper, with cubed carrots, potatoes, and peas. Given the simplicity of this dish, it is likely to appear in the everyday menus more frequently than *chiles* or *moles*. Two dishes that are a little more elaborate but still considered simple enough to be prepared for an ordinary meal are *lomo adobado*, which is a pork loin marinated in adobo and roasted in the oven, and *lomo relleno* (stuffed pork loin), which is a loin of pork butterflied; filled with a mix of chorizo or ground beef, potatoes or other vegetables, onion, spices, salt and pepper; and rolled to its original shape. It is served with potatoes or rice on the side. Also popular for *la comida* are pork chops, which are prepared in a green sauce with vegetables; on hot days, they are grilled or cooked in a frying pan and served with a salad.

Beef

Beef, like pork, was brought to Mexico by the Spaniards during the colonial period; in fact, some historians think that it was Cortés himself who brought some cattle to Mexico from Cuba. By 1560, a relative of Cortés had a ranch with *toros de lidia*, the bulls used for bullfighting. All through the 1600s and 1700s cattle ranches were established in New Spain, taking advantage of the rich grasslands of central and southern Mexico; later, after Mexico became independent and started a process of modernization, cattle ranches were widely promoted in the northern part of the country in semiarid regions from the actual states of Nuevo León to Chihuahua and Sonora. Cattle, however, was mostly used to produce milk and dairy products. Cheeses, cream, and butter were fairly common items in the diet of colonial Mexico; the flesh of these animals was less common, considering the value of the animals as producers of milk. Nonetheless, beef is also part of the traditional Mexican diet, particularly thin cuts of meat, called *bisteces,* as well as a typical cut called *arrachera,* similar to skirt steak. Other traditional cuts of meat in Mexico are *diezmillo, chamberete, costilla, agujas, filete* or *solomillo, falda,* and *aguayón.* A common way of consuming beef in Mexico is in stews and *chiles.* Grilled steak and American-style cuts of meat, including ground beef, are less common.

One of the most popular dishes with beef is *carne de res en chile pasilla.* This traditional way of preparing beef consists of chunks of beef, preferably with some bone, boiled until they are tender and then added to a sauce made with onions, tomatoes, spices, and *pasilla* chili peppers. Sometimes halved small potatoes or quartered large potatoes are added to the dish, as well as peas and diced carrots. It is served with tortillas and pinto beans on the side. Similarly, *carne de res en chile ancho* is a dish made with chunks of beef cooked and served with a sauce made with *ancho* peppers instead of *pasilla.* Other variations of these simple dishes are made with *chipotle, morita,* or *mulato* peppers or a simple tomato, onion, and garlic sauce. A very traditional dish with beef is *mole de olla,* literally *mole* sauce in a pot, and it is actually a soup rather than a sauce, thus the pot reference. The traditional *mole de olla* is prepared with guajillo chili peppers, garlic, onion, and *epazote* or cilantro. Usually, the meat is cooked in water with spices and a mix of *guajillo* peppers, garlic, and onion previously blended, plus a sprig of epazote or cilantro; it is served with wedges of lime and chopped onion for garnish.

Albóndigas en chipotle (meatballs in a chipotle sauce) is a traditional dish made with ground beef. The most common way of preparing *albóndigas* is by making balls of ground beef mixed with bread crumbs or cooked rice, salt, pepper, and sometimes chopped onions and parsley; cooked in water until done; and served in a sauce made with tomatoes, onion, and *chipotle* peppers. *Picadillo* is a simple dish with ground beef cooked with onions, garlic, diced tomatoes, carrots, peas, and squash. Some variations include raisins, parsley, almonds, capers, and even plantains or pineapple. Sometimes *picadillo* is also used to fill *chiles rellenos* or in a dish called *ropa vieja,* which traditionally is made with leftover meat. The traditional *ropa vieja* is prepared with the leftover meat (or picadillo) and sometimes vegetables cut in small pieces and fried in oil and served as a salad with lettuce, tomatoes, and onion. There are many variations of this dish, but in general it is a way of using remaining food from the day before.

Another popular way of eating beef is *bistec*. *Bistec* (derived from the English beefsteak) is a generic name for a very thin piece of beef, often sirloin, flank, or brisket, that is sometimes pounded with a mallet to tenderize it. The favorite way of cooking *bistec* is *encebollado*, which consists of cooking the meat in a little bit of oil and abundant amounts of onion. Equally popular and easy to make is *bistec a la mexicana*, which is cooked with chopped tomatoes, onions, and jalapeño or serrano peppers. *Bistec* can also be prepared in a green or red sauce or a *chile*. Sometimes *bistec* is prepared dry, as in *bistec enchilado*. In this case, the meat is marinated or rubbed with chili powder and spices and then cooked on a griddle or a pan. Often, the *bistec* is also seasoned with salt, pepper, and some spices and broiled on a grill, along with scallions or spring onions and sometimes *nopales*. When grilling the meat, depending on the region, it could be seasoned with garlic, olive oil, drops of vinegar, lime juice, or even beer. Similar to *bistec* is a cut called *arrachera*, a thin skirt steak sometimes marinated with added spices, a favorite in the northern part of Mexico, but popular all over the country. *Arrachera* is almost always cooked on a grill and served with tortillas and salsa or occasionally with a side dish of refried beans or *frijoles charros* and guacamole. Another popular beef dish is *milanesa de res*, a *bistec* pounded thin, breaded, and fried in oil on both sides until brown. It is served with a simple salad on the side.

Poultry

Like pork and beef, chicken was brought to Mexico by the Spaniards. However, Mesoamericans had already domesticated turkeys and probably kept ducks and other wild birds in their backyards. But turkey is the most quintessential American bird. Turkey remains popular in Mexico, mainly for holidays like Christmas, New Year's Eve, weddings, birthdays, and other family celebrations; in fact, in Mexican slang, turkey or *mole* are synonymous with a feast. So, chicken, not turkey, is the poultry used for everyday meals. Many chicken dishes consist of a stew with tomatoes, onions, garlic, spices, and chili peppers. *Pollo en chile verde* is perhaps one of the simplest and most common dishes; it is made with an entire chicken cut into individual pieces and boiled in water with salt and onions and served in a sauce prepared with tomatillos, onions, serrano or jalapeño peppers, and sometimes garlic and cilantro. Depending on the region or

Main Dishes

preference, some vegetables could be added, like diced potatoes, squash, or even *chilacayote* or *nopales*. Sometimes peanuts are added to the mix before blending it to thicken the sauce, in which case it is called *encacahuatado* (from *cacahuates*, peanuts). *Encacahuatado* can also be an elaborate dish for special occasions when prepared with dry chilis, like *ancho* or *guajillo*, and spices like cinnamon, clove, garlic, allspice, toasted peanuts, and toasted sesame seeds. Because it is a little more time consuming, this dish is preferred for special occasions or Sunday family meals.

Like *encacahuatado*, *mole pepián* or *pipián*, or simply *pipián*, is a sauce traditionally served with chicken that is usually reserved for special occasions, like birthdays or anniversaries. The main ingredient in this dish is roasted pumpkin seeds, which are called *pepitas*. *Pipián* is made with onions, garlic, spices, toasted pumpkin seeds, sesame seeds, dry chili peppers, and sometimes a vegetable like chilacayote or potatoes. The traditional meat served with *pipián* is chicken, but sometimes turkey or pork can be used instead. Even though it is an elaborate dish, today is common to see it in everyday menus since it is easy to find a prepared paste made with all the ingredients already toasted, cooked, ground, measured, and mixed in most markets. All that is needed to prepare a *pipián* nowadays, then, is mixing the paste with water or chicken broth and heating it. It is usually served with white rice or warm corn tortillas.

Other stews made with chicken are chicken in a sauce made with tomatoes, onion, garlic, salt, and pepper. A popular dish called *enchipotlado* is also made with a tomato sauce, except that it includes *chipotle*; sometimes also heavy cream. *Pollo a la mexicana* is prepared with chunks of chicken fried in oil and then covered in chopped onions, tomatoes, and jalapeño or serrano peppers. It is served with corn tortillas and beans on the side. The simplicity of this dish makes it a favorite meal for a busy weekday *comida*. Another dish relatively easy to prepare is *tinga de pollo*. *Tinga* consists of a sauce prepared with chipotle peppers, garlic, onions, and tomatoes, as well as shredded chicken. Sometimes, depending on the region, sausage or *chorizo* and cubed potatoes are added. The *tinga* is served as a main dish with tortillas. It can be used as well to prepare the traditional *tostadas de tinga*, which are prepared with toasted corn tortillas (or *tostadas*) topped with a generous portion of *tinga*, garnished with shredded lettuce, crumbled fresh cheese, and Mexican crema. *Tinga* is also used in tacos *de tinga*. Both *tostadas* and tacos make a light, informal meal and sometimes are served at casual or family gatherings.

Pollo con champiñones is a dish that can be served during a weekday, but is most likely prepared on Sundays. This dish is a one-pot meal that is delicious and a little more elegant. It consists of a chicken cut into serving sizes and cooked in a white wine sauce with plenty of onions, oregano, thyme, mushrooms, and a bay leaf. The chicken is first browned in olive oil, then the onions are added and cooked until they are translucent. At this point a couple of cups of white wine are added, as well as sliced mushrooms, thyme, and the bay leaf; the meat and vegetables are seasoned with salt, pepper, and oregano and simmered until the chicken is done. It is usually served with white rice and a salad on the side. Chicken can also be grilled, fried, or roasted and accompanied with a salad or a vegetable side dish. An example of this is *pollo empanizado* (chicken Schnitzel), which is very popular in Mexico and a favorite for hot summer days; it is served with a salad of lettuce, tomatoes, cucumbers, onions, and radishes dressed with lime juice, olive oil, and salt and pepper. A simplified version of this dish is *pechugas asadas*, literally grilled chicken breast, in which the chicken breast is pounded and seasoned with salt and pepper and then is cooked on a griddle or a pan and served just like chicken Schnitzel.

Another traditional dish is *pollo al oregano*. A version of this dish popular in Oaxaca, according to Bricia López, is made by cooking the chicken in water until all the water has evaporated and then adding a mix of spices and oregano. But for the most part, *pollo al oregano* is simply any way of preparing chicken in which oregano is the predominant spice. Casseroles are rare in Mexican cooking; however, there are some exceptions, like a popular dish in Mexico City called *budín azteca* or *pastel azteca*. This dish is a tortilla and chicken casserole perfect for cold days. Similar to some American versions of enchiladas, the *budín* is prepared with either a red or a green sauce and layers of tortillas with shredded chicken in between; the traditional sauce is red, but a green tomatillo sauce is also used. The *budín* is topped with shredded Oaxaca or Chihuahua cheese and baked until the cheese melts. It is served with sour cream or Mexican cream on top.

> Josefina Velázquez de León, a self-taught cook, singlehandedly dragged Mexican food out of the stuffy colonial kitchens and the rustic huts of the countryside and placed it on modern tables. In the 1930s and 1940s, Josefina started to self-publish her books with recipes she collected all over Mexico and sold them by mail; she also opened a culinary school intended for housewives to teach them how to cook with modern techniques and utensils. As food historian Jeffrey Pichler writes, "she adapted village recipes to the needs of urban cooks." More than anybody else, she is responsible for Mexican home cooking.

Main Dishes

Fish and Seafood

Most Mexican restaurants abroad offer a variety of dishes with pork, chicken, beef, and lots of vegetables, rice, and beans, but hardly any fish or seafood, apart from shrimp fajitas and perhaps shrimp *a la diabla* or *al mojo de ajo*; occasionally fish tacos appear on the menu, but even these dishes seem a little out of place and are not guaranteed in most Mexican restaurants. The same is true of most restaurants in Mexico, except for seafood restaurants. This lack of seafood and fish in most mainstream menus is puzzling considering that Mexico has over 5,000 miles of subtropical coastline with white sandy beaches and crystalline green or blue waters that make it a top tourist destination. The country is literally surrounded by water with the Atlantic on the east, the Pacific on the west, and the Caribbean Sea in the southern tip, in addition to rivers and lakes of considerable size like Lake Chapala and Lake Pátzcuaro in central Mexico. Nonetheless, almost nobody associates Mexican food with fish and seafood. The reason, of course, is not because it doesn't exist, but because the Mexican food that became popular is the food from the big colonial cities of central Mexico, as well as the mining towns, cities, and cattle haciendas of the northern region.

Coastal cuisines were less influential until recently. Today, among the most popular restaurants in big cities are the so-called *ostionerías* (oyster bars) and *marisquerías* (seafood restaurants). These restaurants specialize in fish and seafood and are traditional even in places that have no coastline. Fish and seafood, then, are traditional foods in coastal regions, but are appearing more in other parts of the country as well. One of the most popular dishes is *caldo de pescado*, a soup prepared with different kinds of seafood, fish, vegetables, and herbs like oregano, bay leaf, or parsley in a broth of tomato, onion, and often chili peppers. Another favorite way of eating fish is simply fried. *Mojarras fritas* are a popular dish for Lent, but can be present all year round. It is a simple and light dish served with a simple salad, making it a favorite dish for spring and summer months. Frying is the most popular way of preparing fish in Mexico, and the difference between *mojarras fritas* and *filete de pescado frito* (fish fillet) is strictly the size. Usually smaller fish are fried whole, while larger fish are cut and the pieces fried in oil. *Huachinango*, however, is the fish that is best known in Mexican cuisine, particularly *huachinango a la veracruzana*. This is a complex dish in which a red snapper is cooked whole and served in a delicious sauce that combines olives, capers, tomatoes, garlic, onion, bay leaf, and oregano. The traditional recipe calls for the sauce and the fish to be cooked together; however, other recipes make the sauce first and then bake the fish covered in the sauce.

Coastal cuisine includes ingredients like oysters, clams, scallops, crab, langoustines, octopus, lobster, even shark and turtle, which is a protected species now and therefore its consumption is illegal. Some fish are exclusive to a specific area, like the *blanco de Patzcauro*, a small, delicate fish with white meat and silver skin that can only be found in the waters of Lake Patzcuaro in the state of Michoacán; or the emblematic *pejelagarto* from the rivers of the state of Tabasco, which looks like a cross between a fish and an alligator and is considered a living fossil. These fish are rare outside of their region of origin, but many other fish are common all over the country, as well as shrimp and octopus. Shrimp are usually cooked in olive oil and lots of garlic, called *al mojo de ajo* or *al ajillo,* or in *coctel de camarón* (shrimp cocktail), a dish prepared with shrimp cooked in lime juice and mixed with olive oil, tomato sauce, chopped onion, and cilantro garnished with avocado slices and served with lime wedges, salty crackers, and hot sauce on the side. Another version of this dish but with more ingredients like oysters, octopus, crab meat, and even small chunks of fish is called *vuelve a la vida* (literally come back to life); this dish is popular in many parts of the country, particularly because it is considered an effective remedy for hangovers but also because it is delicious and nutritious.

Octopus is also popular in many parts of the country, usually cooked in a sauce made with tomatoes, onions, garlic, oregano, bay leaf, and thyme. When the octopus's ink is added to the sauce, this dish is called *pulpo en su tinta*. It is usually served with white rice and other vegetables as a main dish, but can be served in small portions as an appetizer. *Ceviche* is another popular way of eating octopus; to prepare it this way, the octopus is first cooked in boiling water and salt and then cut in small pieces and mixed with lime juice, chopped onions, cilantro, tomatoes, and olive oil. Although it is called *ceviche*, it technically is not, since *ceviche* refers to the process of cooking fish with lime juice. Octopus is also grilled, usually over an open fire or a grill, marinated with lime juice and olive oil.

Vegetables

Vegetables in a traditional Mexican meal are usually a side dish; maybe even an appetizer. However, vegetarian dishes are not at all unusual as main dishes for a *comida*. Traditionally, there are some dishes that are intended to be main dishes for a meatless meal, which could happen a couple of times a week in most families. The basis of the Mesoamerican diet was mostly beans and corn, a combination still present in Mexico, but other ingredients were equally important, among them squash. And one of the most traditional vegetarian dishes is *calabacitas con queso*. The basis for the dish is Mexican squash cubed and sautéed with onions, diced tomatoes, and oregano. The *calabacitas* are served hot or warm with crumbled fresh cheese on top and Mexican cream. Another traditional vegetarian dish is *tortas de huauzontle*. Huauzontle (*Chenopodium nuttalliae*) is popular in central Mexico but fairly common in other regions as well. For the *tortitas* (patties), usually the florets are separated from the branches and cooked in boiling water and salt. Then they are drained and squeezed to get rid of the excess water and compressed in small balls with a slice of cheese in the center. *Tortas* or *tortitas* is a generic name given to a dish consisting of patties made with a variety of ingredients, often with a piece of cheese in the middle.

Potatoes, carrots, squash, spinach, green beans, broccoli, corn, cauliflower, cactus, even flowers like zucchini blossoms or *flores del colorín* (*Erythrina coralloides*) are the most common ingredients for the *tortitas*. Leafy greens are also common in *tortitas*, but often eaten in tacos with salsa. The most popular of them are *quintoniles* (*Amaranthus hybridus*), *acelgas* (chard), and *espinacas* (spinach). The way of cooking all these vegetables is the same, and because of its simplicity, it is a favorite of many families for a quick lunch that is nutritious and delicious. The easiest way to make them is by sautéing them with chopped onions in some oil and served with a *salsa de molcajete* and warm corn tortillas to make tacos. Sometimes, the *acelgas* or spinach can be cooked and prepared in *tortas*, in a similar way to *huauzontles*. *Chiles rellenos* is another popular dish. The traditional stuffing for *chiles rellenos* is cheese, but it can be anything from ground beef to fish, shrimp, chicken, or other vegetables. They can be served naked, on a bed of greens and covered with cream, or can be *capeados* (covered in egg batter and fried), served in a tomato sauce. The traditional way of preparing and serving the dish, however, is stuffed with fresh or *añejo* cheese, *capeado*, and in a tomato sauce. This is one of the most traditional meatless meals that is intended as a main dish. Squash can be prepared in a similar way in *calabacitas rellenas*, with round *calabacita criolla* (Mexican squash) cooked, the flesh spooned out, and filled with cheese.

Cena

This chapter began by mentioning that the most important meal of the day in Mexico is *la comida* and that *cena*, the last meal of the day, is less important. However, modern life has made it more difficult to follow this schedule, since most people cannot go home to enjoy a large meal in the middle of the day. Today it is not unusual for Mexican families to adopt a more American-like eating schedule. The traditional *cena* used to be light, mostly bread, cheese, milk, or leftovers from *la comida*. Dinner was usually a one-dish affair combined with milk or coffee and milk and sweet bread. *La comida* remains today, at least in theory, the main meal of the day; however, more and more people are eating a lighter *comida* on the street, at a restaurant, or a café and a heavier *cena* at home. In those cases, details about *la comida* also apply to *la cena*—larger portions, three or four courses, a main dish and side dishes, etc. Children and young adults for the most part still eat a traditional *cena* with milk, *atole*, chocolate and milk, or *café con leche* and sweet bread or bread with butter sprinkled with sugar and cinnamon. There are not special dishes per se for dinner, except that it always includes sweet bread and a hot drink. Most people have *la cena* traditionally between 7:00 and 8:00 p.m.

Main Dishes

Huevos Divorciados (Eggs in Two Sauces)

Yield: Serves 4

Red sauce
2 medium tomatoes
1 jalapeño or cuaresmeño chili pepper
½ small onion or ¼ medium onion
1 garlic clove
1 tablespoon vegetable oil
Green sauce
6 large tomatillos
2 garlic cloves
1 *jalapeño* or cuaresmeño chili pepper
½ small white onion or ¼ medium white onion
2 sprigs cilantro
1 tablespoon vegetable oil
8 large eggs
Salt to taste
Crumbled fresh cheese

Equipment: Medium pot, 2 medium sauté pans, fraying pan, spatula, mixing spoons, measuring spoons

1. Place the tomatoes and chili pepper in a medium pot; add enough water to cover them; bring to a boil and cook for a few minutes.
2. Transfer the tomatoes and pepper to a blender and blend with the onion and garlic until smooth.
3. Heat oil in a sauté pan and add the tomato mixture; cook for about 5 minutes; season with salt. Reserve.
4. In the medium pot boil tomatillos, onion, garlic, and chili pepper with enough water to cover them. When the tomatillos swell and start to open, remove them from the heat.
5. Transfer the ingredients and cilantro to a blender and blend until smooth.
6. In a sauté pan heat the oil and add the tomatillo mixture and simmer until done, about 5 minutes. Season with salt. Reserve.
7. In a frying pan add enough oil to fry two eggs at the same time. Fry the eggs sunny-side up. Remove from heat when the yolk is hard on the sides and still soft in the center.

To serve, place eggs on a plate and cover one with red sauce and one with green sauce; top with crumbled cheese. Serve with warm corn tortillas.

Mole de Olla (Spicy Beef Soup)

Yield: Serves 6 to 8

1 pound bone-in beef short rib
1 pound cross-cut beef shank or oxtail
1 pound chuck steak
1 large onion
4 garlic cloves
2 sprigs *epazote*
6 *guajillo* chili peppers
Salt to taste
2 corn cobs, cut into 3 or 4 pieces each
2 medium carrots cut into large chunks
1 *chayote* cut into chunks the size of the carrots
2 medium potatoes, quartered
¼ pound green beans, whole
2 medium squash cut into chunks the size of the *chayotes*
2 limes, quartered

Equipment: Large pot, small pot, blender, mixing spoons

1. Place the meat in a large pot with ½ onion, 2 garlic cloves, *epazote*, and a pinch of salt; add 8 to 10 cups of water and bring to a boil; reduce heat and simmer for 1½ hours and remove the *epazote*, onion, and garlic. Check the meat regularly after 1 hour to avoid overcooking.
2. In a small pot bring 3 cups of water to a boil and add the seeded chili peppers; let them rehydrate in the hot water for 10 to 15 minutes.
3. Place the peppers in a blender with 1 cup of the soaking water, the remaining onion, and garlic; blend until smooth. Reserve.
4. After the meat has been cooking for 1 hour, or when it is almost done, strain the chili pepper puree into the pot with the meat. Add the corn and simmer for 10 minutes.
5. Add the carrots and *chayote* and simmer for 5 minutes.
6. Add the potatoes and simmer for another few minutes.
7. Add the green beans and simmer for a few minutes.
8. Add the squash and simmer for just about 2 minutes. The meat should be tender by now and all the flavors well incorporated. Season with salt to taste.

Serve the soup in individual clay bowls, making sure you include in each one pieces of all the vegetables and meats; place on the table the quartered limes and warm corn tortillas.

Pollo a La Crema de Chipotle (Chicken in Creamy Chipotle Sauce)

Yield: Serves 6 to 8

1 chicken cut into 8 pieces
1 medium white onion
2 garlic cloves
3 tablespoons vegetable oil
3 to 5 whole chipotle peppers in adobo
1 cup heavy cream
½ cup shredded Chihuahua cheese (or any cheese to melt)
1 cup milk
1 cup chicken stock
Salt to taste

Equipment: 1 large pot, 1 large sauté pan, blender, measuring cups, mixing spoons

1. Put the 8 pieces of chicken with ½ onion and salt in a large pot. Bring to a boil, lower the heat, and cook for 25 minutes or until chicken is almost done.
2. Meanwhile chop the remaining onion and mince the garlic; in the sauté pan sauté the garlic and onion in 1 tablespoon of oil until the onion is translucent.
3. Transfer the onion and garlic to a blender and add the chipotle (the amount you like), the cream, the cheese, and the milk; blend until very smooth.
4. In the sauté pan add the remaining oil and heat; when hot, add the chicken and brown very lightly; lower the heat and add ½ cup of chicken stock and then the contents of the blender. Simmer over very low heat for a few minutes; add small amounts of the remaining chicken stock to keep the sauce from getting too hot and to add flavor.

Serve one or two pieces of chicken per plate, depending on the size, and cover the meat with plenty of sauce; serve with warm corn tortillas.

Bistec en Chile Pasilla (Beefsteak in *Pasilla* Sauce)

Yield: Serves 6

3 pounds top sirloin, thinly sliced
6 *pasilla* chili peppers
3 medium tomatoes
Vegetable oil
4 small potatoes, peeled and cubed
1 clove of garlic
½ small white onion
Salt to taste

Equipment: Large skillet, blender, medium pot, mixing spoon

1. Seed *pasilla* peppers and place them in a medium pot with the tomatoes and enough water to cover them; bring the water to a boil and cook for 10 to 15 minutes.
2. Heat the oil in the skillet; season steaks with salt and add them to the skillet. Cook them for a few minutes.
3. Remove the tomatoes and peppers from pot and transfer to the blender. Blend with the onion and garlic.
4. Strain the tomato and pepper mixture in the skillet with the steaks and season with salt; add the potatoes and cover. Simmer for 10 minutes or until potatoes are done.

Serve the steaks on a large plate with plenty of sauce and a side of pinto beans; accompany with warm corn tortillas.

Tortitas de Papa (Potato Patties)

Yield: Serves 4

2 pounds potatoes, peeled
2 eggs
½ cup bread crumbs
1 cup grated Cotija or añejo cheese (parmesan can also be used)
3 tablespoons vegetable oil
Salt and pepper to taste
1 small head lettuce
2 large tomatoes
½ medium white onion
1 lime
2 tablespoons olive oil

Equipment: mixing bowls, large pot, frying pan, spatula, mixing spoons

1. Place the potatoes and ½ tablespoon of salt in a pot; cover with water and bring to a boil. Lower the heat and cook the potatoes until soft. Transfer the potatoes to a bowl and let them cool.
2. In a mixing bowl, mash the potatoes and add eggs, bread crumbs, and cheese. Mix all the ingredients well and season with salt and pepper.
3. Heat the vegetable oil in a frying pan; make 8 patties with the potato mix and fry them in oil for a few minutes until golden on both sides.
4. Transfer the patties to a plate with paper towels to drain the excess oil.
5. Meanwhile, shred the lettuce and slice the tomatoes and onions; place all vegetables in a bowl, and dress with the juice of 1 lime, olive oil, salt, and pepper.

To serve, place 2 potato patties on a plate accompanied with the lettuce and tomato salad.

CHAPTER FIVE

Desserts

Compared with the rich, diverse, and ancestral foods of Mexico, and considering how open Mexican cuisine has been through the centuries to other influences, particularly European and, recently, Asian and American foods, there is a surprising scarcity of desserts, particularly cakes, pastries, and other baked goods, in Mexican gastronomy. Mexico, the country that gave chocolate and vanilla to the world, has very little use for them in its cuisine, besides drinks and certain dishes where they are used as condiments. Sweet bread (including *churros*) is common in Mexico, but it is usually served at dinnertime and sometimes for breakfast, never as dessert; cookies are rare and often eaten as snacks. Cakes, for the most part, are reserved for birthdays and special occasions, like weddings and maybe even First Communions. Home baking is not really a tradition in Mexico. That does not mean Mexicans abstain from eating dessert or that they do not enjoy a sweet here and there, particularly after a hearty meal. But in general, people prefer simple treats, usually bought at a *dulcería* or candy shop. Often after a meal, a plate of small, traditional sweets or a bowl with candied fruit is placed at the center of the table, all of which tend to be extremely sweet.

Most *comidas* in Mexico traditionally end with *fruta de la estación* (seasonal fruit); desserts, properly speaking, are considered out of the ordinary and are served mainly at formal dinners and special occasions or when people eat out. And most of the traditional desserts in Mexico, in fact, tend to be cooked, steamed, or even poached, but rarely baked. Some of the traditional desserts in Mexico are really old and can be traced back to colonial times. Among the earliest ones mentioned by chroniclers and historians are compotes, *confites* (sweets), *mazapanes* (marzipan), and sugar icings; later, in one of the earliest collections of recipes, the cookbook from the San Jeronimo convent in Mexico City, the list is complemented with *ates* (fruit pastes with sugar), as well as desserts that are still traditional in Mexico, like *buñuelos* (light fritters with sugar or syrup) and *jericalla* (a crust similar to crème brûlée). These were some of the traditional desserts in Mexico for centuries, and even though pastry chefs and other bakers from Austria, France, and Italy moved to Mexico in the eighteenth and nineteenth centuries, cakes and baked goods remained treats for special occasions or for afternoon gatherings in the cafes of the big cities. Perhaps because of this, desserts, particularly baked desserts with creams and icings, when served after a dinner, acquired a reputation as fancy foods; even so, some simple desserts were popular, and more elaborate baked desserts are common today.

Being that fresh fruit is the most traditional way of ending a meal, it is not surprising that a big dessert category is simple sweets derived from fruits, specifically *frutas cristalizadas,* or candied fruits. It is common when ending a meal in Mexico to place a plate or a tray with slices of shining pineapple, papaya, pumpkin, apple, pears, oranges, figs, peaches, and all kinds of other fruits—regional, national, and international—cooked and covered in layers of syrup until it hardens and gives the fruit a glossy, crystal-like appearance. The traditional method consists of washing, cutting, and peeling the fruit, then cooking it in sugar for several hours. After the fruit is cooked, it is left to rest overnight and cooked in sugar again; once this is done, it is left to rest for another eight to ten days, depending on the type of fruit or the consistency desired, before bathing it in a final sugar syrup to glaze them. Although many fruits can be candied, the most traditional ones are pumpkin, pineapple, figs, papaya, oranges, pears, sweet potato, chilacayote, prickly pear, lemon, and limes stuffed with shredded coconut. However, recently, many candy makers have been experimenting with different fruits in an attempt to promote their products and to attract new customers; some of these are fruits that have entered the Mexican market recently, like kiwis, but others are more traditional, like *acitrón* (an endangered cactus native to central and northern Mexico) and *nopal,* as well as dry chili peppers and other vegetables like tomatoes and cucumbers.

Besides candied fruits, *frutas en almíbar* is another popular way of serving fruits as desserts in Mexico. *Frutas en almíbar* are sometimes called *frutas en conserva,* and even though the terms are generally used interchangeably, *en conserva* means preserved; in Mexico that means mostly fruits, but sometimes other vegetables are preserved in a similar way, mostly by cooking them in sugar and water and storing them in syrup (*almíbar*) or by making them into jellies, marmalades, or jams. So, *frutas en almíbar* are fruits cooked and served in a syrup made of sugar and water, although sometimes other spices like anise seeds, cinnamon, cloves, allspice, orange zest, or even fig leaves are added for flavor. Like in the

Desserts

case of *frutas cristalizadas*, the fruits used in *frutas en almíbar* are usually seasonal and regional, like peaches, pears, figs, or guavas. Besides these, other traditional *frutas en almíbar* used in Mexico are pumpkin, plums, cashews, *tejocotes*, *nanches*, pineapple, papaya, mango, oranges, lemons, apples, and quince. It is an easy and traditional dessert common in informal family dinners. A traditional way of serving them is with whipped cream or cheese.

In some regions, the *fruta en almíbar* is called *dulce de fruta*. For many people, they are the same thing; however, one difference is that *dulce* is a somewhat thicker syrup often made with water, sugar, and spices and the fruit is more incorporated with it, almost like a marmalade or even a paste; *dulces* are also often made with a combination of two or more fruits. Some of the most traditional—although, as always, the fruits used depend on the region and the season—are *dulce de papaya*, traditional in southern Mexico, particularly in states like Tabasco, Quintana Roo, or Yucatán. Other popular *dulces* in the southern region of Mexico are *dulce de piña*, *coco*, and *guanabana*, as well as those made with less conventional fruits like *dulce de grosella* (raspberry), *dulce de sandía* (watermelon), *dulce de icaco* (coco plum), *dulce de mango*, and *dulce de nanche*. Different fruits are used, depending on the region. So, among some of the most traditional *dulces* in central Mexico are *dulce de capulín*, *dulce de tuna* (prickly pear), *dulce de ciruela* (plum), *dulce de tejocote*, *dulce de membrillo* (quince), *dulce de manzana* (apple), *dulce de naranaja* (orange), and *dulce de limón real* (lemon).

A few *dulces*, however, are made with milk instead of water, like *dulce de mamey* or *dulce de camote* (sweet potato). For these *dulces*, the pulp of the *mamey* or the *camote* is mixed with milk, sugar, and cinnamon and cooked until it becomes very thick; then the mixture is poured over a hard surface and left to cool and harden; finally, it is cut into squares and served on a plate. Similar to these *dulces*, there is a traditional candy often served as dessert or as a snack at fairs, markets, and parks all over the country called *jamoncillo*; it is a fudge-like candy made with milk, cinnamon, and sugar, but depending on the region, it could also include other ingredients like nuts, almonds, pumpkin seeds, raisins, pine nuts, chopped candied fruits, or shredded coconut. To prepare this candy, the milk is simmered over a very low heat with sugar and cinnamon; it is cooked for a long time, stirred constantly with a wooden spoon until the milk thickens and the mixture comes away from the side of the pan. Once this is done, it is poured on a baking sheet or a hard surface to cool. As it cools, it also hardens; once it is firm enough, it is cut into squares or little bars. Sometimes it is put in the oven for a few minutes to create a hard crust, while keeping the center soft and creamy. Like most Mexican candies, *jamoncillos* can be made at home or bought at traditional candy stores or markets.

Like *jamoncillo*, a *cocada* is a traditional candy that is found in parks, markets, fairs, and even schools to be eaten as a snack but that can also be served at the end of a meal. It is similar to a coconut macaroon; however, most traditional *cocadas* are made with just sugar, coconut water, and shredded coconut. The coconut is boiled in water and sugar until it gets thick, and once it has acquired the desired consistency, it is cooled and shaped into small circles and left to dry. Alternatively, it can be put in the oven for a few minutes to create a crunchy crust while keeping the center soft. This candy is very popular all over Mexico, including in the center and mountainous regions, where there is no coastline; it could be soft or crunchy, and depending on the region, it can be combined with other fruits like pineapple, sweet potato, lime, raisins, dried fruits, or even nuts or seeds. In many southern regions, it is common to mix the basic ingredients with milk, eggs, cinnamon, and other spices. In other regions, the *cocadas* are flavored with liquors or spirits, like brandy or rum, and sometimes they are also colored with food coloring. The most traditional *cocada* is sold in markets and candy shops, but in some parts of the country it is common to make it at home. *Cocada* is traditionally the candy that people can buy in fairs, markets, and candy shops, while *dulce de coco* is the one made at home, often offered to guests with a cup of coffee or after a meal. There is a variation of the sweet called *duquesa* (duchess), which is prepared by making a large circle with coconut, eggs, and sugar cooked on a griddle, like a tortilla, and folded like a taco shell, then filled with caramel or with a coconut-flavored meringue.

Cocadas are considered artisanal sweets; that means they are prepared and sold mostly by small or family businesses, following traditional methods. Although the sweets have changed with time, they still remain closer to the original. The same can be said of *palanquetas* (nut or seed bars), *alegrías* (amaranth bars), and *camotes*. *Palanquetas* are seeds, nuts, or a mix of them, sometimes with dried fruits, all blended with a thick syrup made with sugar or *piloncillo*; the mixture is spread on a sheet and left to dry; when it hardens, it is cut into individual bars, squares, or circles. The most traditional *palanquetas* are made with peanuts, but pecans, walnuts, pine nuts, or pumpkin seeds are also popular; often they are decorated with nuts or raisins. *Alegrías* (happiness) are basically *palanquetas* but made with amaranth instead of nuts and a simple syrup, although honey is sometimes used. *Alegrías* are special because they seem to have originated in the time of the Aztecs. There is ample documentation of a tradition common in some festivals when "amaranth dough figures were made [. . .] and eaten in the households" (Clendinnen, *Aztecs*, 250). These figures often represented their gods, so when the Spaniards saw this tradition, they took it for a parody of the Christian rite of communion, banning their consumption.

Camote is a generic word for a tuber in Mexican Spanish; however, the word is most commonly used to refer to sweet potatoes. These vegetables are popular cooked in a *piloncillo* syrup with cinnamon, clove, and sometimes guavas. Alternatively, they can be grilled or baked with brown sugar and cinnamon. It is a traditional sweet in the fall and for celebrations like Day of the Dead. The sweet called *camote poblano*, or *camote de Santa Clara*, is perhaps the most famous snack made with sweet potatoes. It is prepared by cooking the flesh of the sweet potato with sugar or *piloncillo* and water until the syrup thickens and the potatoes are done; sometimes other fruits like pineapple or coconut are included to give the mixture a thicker consistency. Once all the ingredients are cooked, they are blended or mixed into a paste; once the paste cools down, a small amount of it is rolled and shaped in the form of a cigar and left to dry for a day or two. Finally, the cigar-shaped candies are covered in a glaze of sugar and water to acquire a thin, shiny layer. The *camotes* can be of different flavors and come in different colors representative of those flavors—pineapple, lime, coconut, strawberry, and orange being the most popular. These *camotes* are usually bought in candy stores, but more and more people are making them at home to serve them as desserts.

However, when it comes to homemade desserts, people usually think of *arroz con leche* (rice pudding) and *flan* more than they do of *dulce de coco* or *camote en dulce*. Perhaps one of the most iconic Mexican desserts, *flan* is actually a popular dessert in many Latin American countries, as well as Spain. The most traditional *flan* in Mexico is made with milk, eggs, sugar, and vanilla. The milk is mixed with sugar and vanilla and cooked for a few minutes and then cooled; after it is lukewarm, the eggs are added to the mixture and incorporated well. The batter then is poured into a mold or ramekins with caramelized sugar at the bottom, covered with aluminum foil, placed in a baking dish with enough water to come halfway up the mold or ramekins, and baked until it sets. When the *flan* is ready, it is unmolded and covered with extra caramel. The variety of *flan* is relatively large, and sometimes fruits, dried fruits, or nuts are added. Two very popular variations of *flan* in Mexico are *flan de naranja* (orange flan), which is made in the same way as the traditional *flan*, but some orange juice and orange zest are added to the mixture; and *flan napolitano*, which is made with condensed and evaporated milks, eggs, and sometimes almonds or cream cheese; it is steamed rather than baked, and its consistency is much smoother than that of traditional *flan*.

If making a *flan* is still a beloved tradition in many houses, the reality is that industrialization has for a long time "simplified" the process by introducing powdered *"flan"* to prepare in minutes. It consists of a vanilla-flavored powder that can be mixed with hot milk and put in the fridge until it sets. This *flan* is sometimes called *flan de caja* (boxed flan), *flan de paquete* (packaged flan), or *flan instantaneo* (instant flan). It is popular in Mexico, particularly for a quick treat or an informal dessert. Its appeal is guaranteed in a way because it resembles another popular dessert, *gelatina* (Jell-O). This is a dessert made with gelatin; water or juices; and often chunks of fruit, nuts, or raisins. It can be made with milk as well, or it can be flavored with wine or liqueurs, most commonly sherry. It is popular in Mexico for most occasions, including birthdays. This dessert has been prepared in Mexico for a long time, and even Josefina Velázquez de León, the pioneer of Mexican home cooking and Mexican cookbooks, includes several recipes, called *jaletinas*, in her book *La Cocina Económica* (Economical Kitchen), among them a *jaletina* de papaya with oranges, as well as *jaletinas* de lime, tamarind, and cantaloupe. Some modern chefs have embraced this traditional dessert and experimented with flavors like sapote, hibiscus and red wine, pineapple, and carrot, as well as *tres leches*. However, the most popular way of making *gelatinas* is to buy the prepared powder in the flavor of your choice and mix it with water or milk and then place it into the fridge to set. They are so popular that it is common to find them in bakeries or neighborhood stores as well.

Like *flan* and *gelatinas*, *arroz con leche* is ubiquitous in Mexico; popular in all regions of the country, it is served at practically all tables, from the humblest to the most aristocratic, because of its simplicity and flexibility. Traditionally, the dessert is made with milk, rice, sugar, raisins, and cinnamon. The preparation consists of cooking the rice in milk with sugar and a cinnamon stick, moving constantly to keep the rice from sticking to the bottom; once the rice is cooked and the milk has thickened, the vanilla and raisins are added. It is served cooled or chilled with powdered cinnamon on top. But like most desserts, it often changes depending on where and who is preparing it. It could be served warm, room temperature, or chilled; it can be very thick or soupy; or it can be served in small individual cups or in a large bowl for people to serve themselves at the table. Some common variations include cooking the rice in the same way as mentioned before but with some lemon or orange peel added to the cooking mixture and served with lemon or orange zest on top as decoration. This dessert is one of the most popular ones, and it is almost invariably one of the two or three options offered in most *cocinas*, restaurants, and cafés; it is also popular most weekdays at home when dessert is served.

A more traditional dessert, *capirotada* is derived from a popular dish in Spain of the same name that goes back to medieval times; however, the Spanish *capirotada* is savory and consists of layers of dry, old bread soaked in broth with different pieces of meat in between the bread. In Mexico, on the contrary, *capirotada* is always a sweet dessert, consisting of layers of fried old bread soaked in *piloncillo* syrup or milk with dried fruits, spices, nuts, or seeds baked with the bread; many versions of the dish include cheese as one of the ingredients. It is usually served warm or at room temperature topped with more of the dried fruits, commonly raisins, and bits of other candied fruits, peanuts, almonds, and cheese, if used. Depending on the region, some variations may occur, and different ingredients, including coconut, plantains, bananas, or even tomatoes, could also be used. The dish is especially popular for Lent, but some modern versions have incorporated different ingredients like liquor or other types of syrups and prefer to serve it with whipped cream or vanilla ice cream, making it a popular dessert for other times of the year as well.

Like *capirotada*, *jericalla* is a traditional dessert originated most likely in what is today the state of Jalisco, but popular in the entire Bajío region and other parts of Mexico; it resembles certain traditional European desserts like crème brûlée or *crema catalá*, from which it most likely is derived. According to some legends, the dessert was invented by a nun tending a hospice in the city of Guadalajara, who called it *jericalla* in honor of the city of her ancestors, Jérica, in Valencia, Spain. Like most legends about the conventual origins of many Mexican dishes, there is no proof of its veracity. Instead, the resemblance to the Catalonian dessert *crema catalá* and the clue given in the name (Valencia is part of the Catalonian-speaking communities in the Iberian Peninsula) strongly suggest it is a Mexican version of *crema catalá*. In both cases the main ingredients are milk, sugar, cinnamon, egg yolks, and vanilla; some versions include a little cornstarch or flour and lemon or orange peel. The most traditional *jericalla* is prepared by boiling the milk with the cinnamon and the vanilla, beating the yolks with sugar, and incorporating mixture slowly into the warm milk. Once the mixture is ready, it is poured into individual serving bowls or ramekins, which are placed in a deep dish with water coming to the middle of the containers; then they are baked until set and firm. Once done, they are placed under the broiler for a few minutes to brown the top of the custard. When cooled, they are refrigerated for a few hours and served chilled.

Another traditional dessert that vaguely resembles a European sweet is *gaznate*. Although at first sight it may look like cannoli—a tube of crunchy pastry with a sweet filling—the cylindrical shell of the Mexican dessert is made with flour, water, eggs, oil, and salt only, and the filling is traditionally a pink meringue. Like many other Mexican sweets mentioned here, the *gaznates* are usually sold in candy stores, markets, and, until recently, on the street and public parks by street vendors called *merengueros*, who used to carry a large basket or a wooden tray with folding feet to turn it into a portable table with *gaznates* and multicolored meringues arranged on it and covered with plastic or cellophane. It is a traditional sweet snack popular in Mexico City and the states around it, but it can also be served after a meal. As with other traditional sweets, modern variations, particularly if prepared at home to serve as dessert, experiment with different fillings, including *dulce de leche*, cheese, or fruit mousses like guava, as suggested by chef Paulina Abascal. Other cooks suggest whipped cream, flavored custards, caramels, or chocolate whipped cream. Many of these home versions also flavor the shell with spices or even liqueurs. Whereas in Mexico the dessert is called *gaznate* (gullet), a similar dessert popular in Spain, filled with cream, is called *canutillo* (small tube).

A traditional Mexican dessert that does not resemble another European dessert is *chongos*. *Chongos* are made with milk curdled and cooked in a syrup of brown sugar, water, and cinnamon. To make the *chongos*, milk, preferably *leche bronca* (or raw milk), is warmed and mixed with rennet or any other coagulant and left to curdle. When the curd has formed, it is cut into smaller pieces and simmered in water and cinnamon over low heat. After cooking for a long time and removing some of the excess whey, the sugar is added, forming a thick syrup in which the small pieces of curd continue to simmer at low heat until they curl a little, resembling little braids (in Mexican Spanish, *chongo* means "hair bun" or "curl"). Once the *chongos* are ready, they are left to cool and put in the fridge for a few hours or overnight. This dessert is traditionally served chilled in a cup or glass with abundant syrup. The dessert is most commonly known as *chongos zamoranos*, since they are considered the official dessert of the city of Zamora in the state of Michoacán, where they are the most popular and where according to tradition they were invented; however, there are versions of the same dish in other states, including one from the state of Durango—although it goes by the same name, it is actually made with slices of sweet bread soaked in syrup, butter, and eggs; baked; and topped with shredded cheese and cinnamon. It is more similar to *capirotada* than *chongos zamoranos*.

When it comes to traditional Mexican fare, few foods are more authentic than *tamales*, which have been passed on through generations, from pre-Hispanic times to our own, almost untouched. Most people outside of Mexico are familiar with the *tamales* filled with chicken or pork in either a

Desserts

red or green sauce. However, these little bundles of corn dough wrapped in a corn husk and steamed until cooked are so versatile that the fillings could be practically anything, from pork, chicken, even fish to vegetables, cheese, and, of course, fruits. *Tamales de dulce* are sweet *tamales* filled with either dried or fresh fruit. They are traditionally served for breakfast or in celebrations, particularly children's birthday parties. The most recognized *tamal dulce* is made with corn dough, usually colored pink, mixed with lard or oil, sugar, and raisins; sometimes it is flavored with spices like anise or cinnamon. It is traditional in central Mexico, but some variations can be found in other parts of the country as well. Among the most popular *tamales dulces* are *tamal de fresa* (strawberry), *tamal de piña* (pineapple), *tamal de zarzamora* (blackberry), and *tamal de capulín*.

A wave of new chefs have been experimenting with new flavors and techniques to complement traditional Mexican foods. The main change with *tamales* is that more and more often, they are being prepared and served as dessert. As mentioned earlier, traditionally *tamales* were used for breakfast or special occasions like birthday parties for kids or the feast of Candlemas. Occasionally people may buy them for *la merienda* from the numerous sellers offering them on street corners, outside subway stations, or from vendors in a *triciclo*, a traditional tricycle for adults adapted to carry merchandise from street to street in big cities. But the *tamales* that appear in restaurants as dessert are less traditional and more modern. They are usually smaller and come in a variety of flavors, mostly fruits, but also nuts, spices, or even sweet liquors. Chef Fany Gerson, author of *My Sweet Mexico*, offers recipes for the traditional raisin and pecan *tamales*, as well as strawberry, but also for an unusual lime *tamal*, or *tamal de limón*. Likewise, Diana Kennedy recounts a traditional chocolate *tamal*, popular in Aguascalientes, which includes cinnamon, vanilla, pecans, and cocoa powder that is flavored with Kahlúa liqueur.

As mentioned at the beginning of this chapter, Mexico does not have the tradition of baked desserts that is seen in the United States and northern Europe, since most desserts are Mediterranean in origin and depend on fire, spices, fruits, and sugar and rarely on butter and milk. However, there are some exceptions. Bread arrived early in Mexico during the colonial period, and by the eighteenth century pastries were already popular in New Spain, mostly from pastry shops and rarely prepared at home. These are some of the most popular baked desserts in Mexico, although most of them are relatively recent. The first one, a cake that claims to go back to colonial times, called *postre del virreinato* (viceregal dessert), is included in Patricia Quintana's *The Taste of Mexico*. It is probably not colonial—it cannot be found in any book or hardcopy reference, although there are a few references online, but they seem to follow Quintana's recipe. This cake is most likely inspired by the colonial preference for candied fruits, nuts, and spongy cakes soaked in liqueurs. It consists of a layer cake soaked in sherry, with a custard mixed with small pieces of dried fruits in between layers; frosted with cream; and topped with toasted pine nuts, almonds, candied figs, oranges, and limes. Another similar version of this dessert, called *suspiro de novia* (bride's sigh), is prepared by chef Ricardo Muñoz-Zurita.

The traditional sweet breads, the ones that most likely existed during colonial times in Mexico, were soft and spongy cakes made with egg whites, sugar, egg yolks, and flour soaked in syrup or liqueur, called *mamones* (suckers), *marquesotes*, or *bizcochos*. But even these cakes were most likely prepared in convent kitchens and sold to sustain the religious institutions; bakeries, which were highly regulated, sold bread of different qualities for the different social classes. These bakeries remained practically untouched until the late 1800s, when Spanish immigrants modernized what Robert Weis calls "the most archaic industry of urban Mexico" (72) at the time. Around that time also French cuisine became fashionable with the upper classes, and the French cafés and French and Austrian bakeries made and sold cakes and other pastries, zealously guarding their recipes. Cookbooks appeared in Mexico in the late 1800s, but most of them were intended for professional cooks and included mostly international (namely French) dishes. Mexican food, per se, was considered more or less regional and traditional. The changes brought by the revolution of 1910 transformed that, and since the new government wanted to create a national Mexican identity, it arduously worked to collect and revalorize everything Mexican, including food.

As result, cookbooks by trained chefs started to appear with a Mexican flair, but still French techniques. It was not until the 1930s and 1940s, when an untrained cook started to self-publish her own books and sell them by mail to her subscribers, that Mexican food started to become "national." As mentioned, her name was Josefina Velázquez de León. She not only published recipes she collected through her numerous travels to all the regions of the country, but she also opened a culinary school intended for housewives, not professionals. Her intention was to help these ladies learn how to cook to maximize their family finances and even earn some extra cash by baking at home, utilizing modern techniques and utensils. Ms. Velázquez de León popularized baked goods, adapting different recipes, including some old Mexican ones. She published books dedicated to baking (home baked goods, cake decorating, and modern cakes) and on how to use modern inventions like blenders, pressure cookers, and electric mixers, particularly in her revolutionary *Como cocinar en los aparatos modernos* (How to Cook with Modern Appliances).

Some of her recipes include pancakes (called hotcakes in Mexico); chocolate, cream, and strawberry cakes; *mamones*; muffins (*mofins*); donuts (*donas*); *churros*; *buñuelos*; corn sweet cakes; raisin bread; *roscas*; and all kinds of cookies, including *polvorones*, peanut butter, and black and white cookies. The increased access to gas ovens and other modern appliances in urban areas also made it possible for families to use Josefina's cookbooks *Pasteles modernos* (Modern Cakes) and *Repostería casera* (Home Baking). Even though, as mentioned before, there was no tradition of baked goods in Mexico, in the twentieth century women started to bake cookies and cakes more than before, and one type of cake that became a staple was *roscas* (a type of Bundt cakes) and *panqués* (pound cakes), all thanks to Josefina Velázquez de León. Still, these foods were, and up to a point still are, reserved for special occasions. *Rosca* (which literally means round) is the type of cake that is most likely to be baked at home; the flavors vary depending on the region, the occasion, or the family, but the most common are vanilla, chocolate, or marble. Other flavors are also popular, like *rosca de naranja* (orange), *rosca de nuez* (pecan or walnut), *rosca de limón* (lemon), and *rosca de piña* (similar to pineapple upside-down cake). Recently, people have been experimenting with traditional Mexican flavors in *roscas* like *camote* (sweet potato), *calabaza* (pumpkin), or even *chayote*.

One dessert that most Americans identify immediately as Mexican is *pastel de tres leches*. Although not as traditional as most people may think, this soupy cake has gained popularity recently. The use of condensed and evaporated milks reveals the rather "modern" origins of the dessert. Even though condensed and evaporated milks have been available since the late 1800s, their popularity in Mexico came much later. *Tres leches* is a rather simple cake made with butter, sugar, flour, eggs, and vanilla; once the cake is baked, it is cooled and covered in an abundant sauce made with whole milk, evaporated milk, and condensed milk (hence the name: *tres leches* means three milks in Spanish). The result is a very moist and sweet cake that is either covered with meringue or whipped cream, sometimes adorned with strawberries, or ganache. There are many variations, understandably, since it is not only popular in Mexico but in many Latin American countries as well. In fact, Nicaragua, Venezuela, Puerto Rico, Guatemala, and Cuba all claim that the dessert was invented there.

The most likely scenario, however, is the one described by MM Pack, who writes that the cake as it is known today is fairly recent and most likely the invention of Nestlé, the Swiss producer of canned milk, who had manufacturing plants in Mexico since the 1930s. In order to take full advantage of the new market in Mexico and Latin America, Nestlé printed recipes on the labels of their cans of milk, instructing people on how to use their products. One of the recipes was for *pastel de tres leches*. The cake wanted to offer a "modern" version of some traditional breads popular in Mexico, like *sopa borracha* (layers of fried bread with cream, milk sauce, rum, raisins, cinnamon, and vanilla in between), and other cakes and breads soaked in rum or sherry, like *mamones* or *capirotada*, mentioned before. Bread covered or soaked in a liquid is not an uncommon food in Mexico, but is mostly for children or sick people. This is an even more important tradition in Spain, a tradition that dates back to medieval times and was brought to Mexico during the colonization of America. In fact, *sopa* (soup) in Spanish originally meant bread soaked in milk or other liquid. Today this meaning of the word coexists with the more traditional definition of a liquid food with ingredients such as vegetables or meats.

Another dessert that is less common than the *tres leches* cake but also made with evaporated and condensed milks—raising the possibility that it may have also originated as a promotional recipe by the Nestlé or another similar company—is one called *carlota*. However, it is also suspiciously similar to a French dessert called Charlotte, so it is possible the Mexican *carlota* is an adapted version of this dessert. The *carlota* is rather simple and requires, besides evaporated and condensed milks, *galletas marias* (Marie biscuits) and lime or lemon juice. This is why the dessert is sometimes called *carlota de limón*. Despite being a simple dessert, it is popular for late spring and summer, since it is a refreshing dessert, usually served out of the fridge or even the freezer. The most traditional method of preparing it consists of placing a layer of *galletas marias* at the bottom and the sides of a spring-form or cheesecake pan, then pouring a mixture of the milks and the lemon or lime juice over the cookies, followed by a layer of *galletas marias* and milk mixture, alternating until everything is used. The dessert is then placed in the fridge or freezer to set. It is served chilled and decorated with lemon or lime zest and whipped cream. Other versions include fruits like strawberries or mixed cocoa with the milk and help it set by adding gelatin.

Like the *carlota*, the *pavlova* is most likely an adaptation of a dessert created in another country that nonetheless is very popular in Mexico. Named after the Russian dancer Anna Pavlova, the dessert probably came to Mexico via France. Even though Pavlova herself performed in the country twice, in 1919 and 1925, and was widely admired for including in her repertoire a series of folk dances from Mexico, the dessert most likely was not invented there; however, the dancer's popularity contributed to its

Desserts

acceptance in the country. The dessert is light and delicious, and its simplicity is the perfect way to end a heavy and spicy dinner. The traditional *pavlova* consists of layers of meringue flavored with lemon juice and whipped cream forming a "cake," topped with fruit, most commonly strawberries or other berries in season. Gabriela Cámara, a chef based in Mexico City and San Francisco, recommends a simpler version of the dessert she serves at her celebrated restaurant Contramar by making a large meringue disc covered with cream, berries, and pumpkin seeds.

These last two desserts are not immediately identified with Mexico, but they are present enough in restaurants, cookbooks, and family tables to justify including them in this review of Mexican desserts.

There are other traditional baked desserts that are popular; however, it is a lot less clear when they became popular in Mexico. These pastries are likely to be served for breakfast or *merienda*, but could also be served as desserts. The first one is called *garibaldi,* and it consists of a sweet cake, similar to a cupcake, covered with honey and sugar sprinkles. It was invented, according to tradition, by an Italo-Mexican family of bakers, the founders of El Globo, one of the oldest and most traditional bakeries in the country. *Niño envuelto* (literally, wrapped child) is a thin, rectangular cake; rolled and filled with marmalade, jelly, or cream and fruits; and sprinkled with powdered sugar; the most popular filling is strawberry or guava jelly. However, there are many other options, including strawberries and cream, caramel, chocolate, even Nutella. *Milhojas* (a thousand leaves) is a cake made with layers of puff pastry and cream; like the previous pastries, it can be made at home or most likely bought in slices at a *panadería* for breakfast. *Isla flotante* (floating island), like other desserts mentioned previously, is an adaptation of the French dessert of the same name, *ile flottante*. But while the French island is a meringue floating in *crème anglaise*, the Mexican version traditionally is a pound cake in a sauce of milk and cinnamon baked together. Both versions are popular in Mexico and are offered at many restaurants.

More traditional than the previous desserts, *gorditas de nata* is a sweet little cake that used to be sold by women sitting outside churches on Sundays or holidays; it is halfway between a cookie and a thick, small pancake. They are traditional in many parts of the country, but particularly in central Mexico and Mexico City. They are made with flour, sugar, eggs, cinnamon, milk, lard, and cream (*natas*). To make them, the cream and sugar are mixed well; the eggs are added one by one, mixing well after each egg to incorporate them into the dough; the milk, lard, and cinnamon are also added with baking powder to make a firm dough. The dough then is formed into round cookies and cooked on a griddle or *comal* until it is brown on both sides and cooked all the way through. The dough also can be slightly stretched on a hard surface, if making them at home, and cut into small discs with a cookie cutter and cooked on a griddle. Other similar sweets are popular in different regions of the country with the generic name of *suspiros* (sighs), which are prepared in a similar way to *gorditas de nata*, except that some of them are grilled, some are baked, and some are made into little balls and fried, like donuts. Of these, one of the most popular is called *suspiro de monja* (nun's sigh).

Finally, let's dedicate a few words to a popular dessert that is almost always present in most restaurants among the several options to end a meal: frozen treats—or as they are more commonly known in Mexico, *helados* and *nieves*. Neither one of these desserts is originally Mexican; however, they have been present on the tables of the nation for so long and have developed some local flavors that they are by now considered quintessentially Mexican. *Helado* (frozen in Spanish) is simply *ice cream*, and it is popular in Mexico not only in special places called *heladerías* but also at home or in restaurants for dessert. The most popular flavors are the ones standard all over the world—strawberry, chocolate, vanilla, and pistachio—with some local flavors like *mamey*, *cajeta* (caramel), or *elote* (sweet corn). In recent years, however, chefs and adventurous foodies have experimented with different native ingredients, some expected and some truly unusual, like avocado, cheese, rose petals, and even *mole* sauce. At least one company, Helado Obscuro, has experimented with different liquors and spirits to create alcoholic ice cream. The term *helado* can be used to refer to any kind of iced treat. However, technically it refers to ice cream, while *nieves* refers more properly to ices made without dairy.

Nieve literally means snow, and the full name of this dessert is *nieves de sabores* (flavored snows). It is made with water, sugar, juices or other ingredients for flavor, and sometimes little bits of fruit. Some of the most

---

Ice was widely used in colonial Mexico, mostly to prepare ices, ice creams, or to add to drinks to enjoy during the hottest months. It was brought to Mexico City and other cities from the nearby snow-covered volcanos and high mountains surrounding the cities, where ice could be harvested all year round, and it was also popular in the Port of Varacruz, where it was brought from the Pico de Orizaba volcano, covered in hay or ashes to keep it cold. It was a very expensive luxury; nonetheless, according to German traveler Alexander von Humboldt, people "in the coast could enjoy everyday refreshment of ices and iced water."

Desserts

popular are *nieve de limón* (lime), *nieve de coco* (coconut), *nieve de guanabana*, *nieve de grosella* (raspberry), *nieve de piña* (pineapple), and *nieve de melón* (cantaloupe). Like in the case of *helado*, some unusual flavors have recently appeared in different parts of Mexico with flavors like *jalapeño* pepper and *nopal* (cactus), including some alcoholic *nieves* as well, like hibiscus and *mezcal* or lime and tequila and *pulque*. A poor cousin of these *helados* and *nieves* is *raspados*; *raspados* are cups of shaved ice covered in syrups of different "flavors" and some amazing colors, like electric blue and intense yellow, red, and green. The traditional flavors are raspberry, lime, pineapple, tamarind, and *rompope* (eggnog). They are popular in the entire country, particularly for the hottest months of the year, and are considered a street food since they are sold by men pushing a wooden cart with the block of ice covered with a cloth and the multicolored bottles with the syrups hanging on the side.

Jericalla (Mexican Crème Brulé)

Yield: Serves 8

3 cups milk
1 stick cinnamon, Mexican preferred
1 large orange peel
1 teaspoon vanilla extract
6 egg yolks
1 cup sugar
2 tablespoons cornstarch

Equipment: 8 ramekins (3 oz capacity), baking dish large enough to hold ramekins, medium pot, whisk, mixing bowls, measuring spoons

1. In a medium pot bring the milk, orange peel, and cinnamon to a boil; add ¾ cup sugar and vanilla. Whisk until sugar dissolves. Remove the cinnamon stick and orange peel and let cool.
2. Beat the egg yolks with 1 tablespoons of the cooled milk mixture and the remaining ¼ cup sugar. Add to the milk mixture and incorporate well.
3. Pour into the ramekins. Place the ramekins in the baking dish and fill with water to cover the ramekins halfway up. Baked in a preheated oven at 315 degrees for 30 minutes. Place under the broiler for a couple of minutes to create a crust. It should look burnt in some spots; that is normal.
4. Cool in the refrigerator for a few hours or overnight.

Serve a ramekin per person; if you want to, you can top them with strawberries.

Garibaldis (Mexican Cupcakes with Apricot Preserve)

Yield: Serves 12

1½ cups all-purpose flour
1 teaspoon cornstarch
1½ teaspoons baking powder
¼ teaspoon salt
1½ sticks butter
1 cup sugar
2 large eggs
½ cup heavy cream
¼ cup vegetable oil
13 oz jar of apricot preserves
White sugar sprinkles
¼ cup of brandy or orange liquor, optional

Equipment: 12-cup muffin pan, mixing bowl, measuring cups, measuring spoons, sifter, electric mixer, 12 paper baking cups

1. Preheat oven to 350 degrees Fahrenheit. Grease and flour the 12-cup muffin pan.
2. In a bowl sift the flour, cornstarch, baking powder, and salt. Set aside.
3. With an electric mixer, beat the butter until it begins to change color; add the sugar and beat well.
4. While beating on medium low, add the eggs, one at a time, the heavy cream, and the oil.
5. Add the flour mixture while beating on low; mix well, but just until all ingredients are incorporated.
6. Divide the batter in the muffin pan and bake for 18 minutes or until the cakes are done and a toothpick inserted in the center comes out clean. Let them cool.
7. Meanwhile, place the apricot preserves in a small pot and heat over medium heat until it softens. Add the liquor, if using, to make the preserve more workable, or add a little bit of water.
8. Dip the cupcakes, upside down, in the softened apricot preserve and cover with abundant white sprinkles to cover the entire cake; place in a paper baking cup.

Serve the garibaldis with hot coffee for dessert or with a glass of milk for supper.

Flan de Naranja (Orange-Flavored Flan)

Yield: Serves 8

3 cups milk
Peel of 1 medium orange
1 tablespoon vanilla extract
1½ cups sugar
½ cup water
4 eggs
3 egg yolks
1 teaspoon orange extract
8 thin slices candied orange

Equipment: medium pot, small pot with lid, one round cake pan, large baking dish, measuring cups, measuring spoons, mixing spoon

1. In a medium pot bring milk, orange peel, ½ cup sugar, and vanilla to boil under medium heat. Remove from heat just when it is about to boil and cool and remove the orange peel.
2. In a small pot, mix ½ cup sugar and water over high heat and whisk until the sugar dissolves and thickens, making a dark caramel. Pour the caramel over the cake pan, making sure it covers the bottom of the pan. Set aside.
3. Whisk eggs, egg yolks, and remaining ½ cup sugar until integrated.
4. When milk is cool, incorporate it into the egg mixture, slowly whisking to avoid scrambling the eggs in case the milk is still warm. Add the orange extract and whisk to incorporate.
5. Pour into the cake pan and place the cake pan in the large baking dish; add water to cover halfway up the side of the cake pan.
6. Bake in a preheated oven at 350 degrees for 50 minutes. Remove from the oven and let cool. Refrigerate for several hours or overnight.

To serve, unmold flan on a plate, cut into individual portions, and decorate with thin slices of candied orange.

Desserts

Arroz con Leche (Rice Pudding)

Yield: Serves 10

2 cups long grain rice
3 cups water
1 cinnamon stick
Peel of 1 orange
1½ cups sugar
8 cups milk
½ cup raisins
1 teaspoon vanilla extract
Ground cinnamon to taste

Equipment: large pot, measuring cups, mixing spoon

1. In a pot, bring rice, water, cinnamon stick, and orange peel to a boil. Add sugar and stir to dissolve; lower the heat and cook over medium to low heat until done, about 15 minutes.
2. Gradually add the milk, lower the heat, and continue to stir occasionally to prevent the rice from sticking to the bottom of the pot, but do not overmix. Simmer until the rice is cooked and almost all the liquid evaporates.
3. Add raisins and vanilla extract; remove from the heat and remove the cinnamon and orange peel. Let cool.

To serve, place the rice pudding in a serving bowl and sprinkle with the ground cinnamon. Serve at room temperature or chill for a cool dessert.

Rosca de Camote (Sweet Potato Bundt Cake)

Yield: Serves 10 to 12

1 cup lard or vegetable shortening
1½ cups brown sugar
3 medium sweet potatoes, peeled, cooked, and mashed
1 teaspoon vanilla extract
3 eggs
3 cups flour
2 teaspoons baking powder
1 teaspoon ground cinnamon
1 teaspoon baking soda
Pinch of salt
1 cup *piloncillo*, chopped
1 cup cream
4 tablespoons milk
¼ cup cornstarch
1 cinnamon stick
¼ cup dark rum

Equipment: Bundt cake mold, mixing bowls, mixer, measuring cups, measuring spoons, mixing spoon, medium pot

1. In a mixer, cream butter and sugar. Add vanilla and beat for a minute. Add sweet potatoes and mix well. Add eggs.
2. Mix flour, baking powder, baking soda, ground cinnamon, and salt. Add to mixer and combine well with the other ingredients.
3. Pour in the greased and floured cake mold and bake in a preheated oven at 350 degrees for 90 minutes or until done. Take the cake out of the oven and let cool.
4. While the cake is cooling, mix the cream and *piloncillo* over low heat, whisking constantly to dissolve the *piloncillo*. Add the cinnamon stick and cornstarch previously dissolved in the milk and simmer for a few minutes.
5. Add rum and simmer for a few more minutes. Remove the cinnamon stick and let cool; serve at room temperature.

To serve, slice the cake and pour rum sauce over it.

CHAPTER SIX

Beverages

"Water is life" is a mantra frequently heard in school, the news, everyday conversations, and science documentaries. It is true that one can survive longer without any food than without water. Water is where life originated, according to paleontologists, and what astronomers are looking for in other planets as a telltale sign of life. Here on Earth, water is fundamental for our existence and that of animals and plants, but it is also a major source of illnesses, and it could be the cause of death of people and domestic animals alike, as the *Washington Post* reported in August 2019, when several dogs died in North Carolina and Georgia, poisoned by toxic algae that "need sunlight and stagnant, nutrient-rich water, which is most common in lakes, ponds and canals but can also be present along the coast of bays, gulfs and oceans" (Mettler). Water is also a universal solvent that absorbs toxic chemicals and other contaminants. The giver and taker of life, water is a symbolic element that connects us with the supernatural, not only in the numerous creation myths that refer to water but also in rituals, like cleansing, purification, and baptism.

It is not surprising that the supplying of clean water has always been a main concern for most societies through history, from the Romans and Greeks; to the Maya and Aztecs; to modern London, Paris, New York, or Mexico City. And if water is fundamental for life, drinking other liquids could also be beneficial and a pleasure; in fact, great food goes together with delicious drinks. Just like a cuisine goes beyond just satisfying one's hunger, drinking different beverages is more than just satisfying one's thirst. It is fascinating to discover the different drinks that humans have created over the centuries and how they have influenced civilization. Most historians agree, for example, that the origin of alcoholic drinks was probably when the first humans came across fermented fruits and liked the way it made them feel when they ate them and drank the juices; later, after they learned how to ferment alcoholic drinks, they also noticed they were safer to drink than water, since the fermentation, and later distillation, purified them.

Alcohol was important for humans because it was safer to drink but also because of its mind-altering properties. So, it might seem to us that alcohol is an invention of civilization; however, it is actually a prevalent element in the universe, according to Patrick McGovern, and it may have had an important role in the presence of life on Earth, since "if alcohol permeates our galaxy and universe, it should come as no surprise that sugar fermentation (or glycolysis) is thought to be the earliest form of energy production used by life on Earth" (2). There is evidence of prehistoric societies using alcohol, and the ancient civilizations of the Near East as well as Egypt have left ample testimony of its consumption, often in social or ritualistic ways. Since ancient times, wine and beer have been an important part of the diet of Europe, Asia, and North Africa. Even in Mesoamerica, McGovern thinks, the need for alcoholic beverages was the force behind what he calls the impossible task of domesticating corn, an impossibility that "was likely overcome by an overpowering desire of humans to alter their consciousness by alcohol" (205).

The same can be said of cacao, since according to McGovern, it was first appreciated for the sweet, fermented juices produced in the ripened fruit laid out in the sun of tropical Mesoamerica, a practice observed in the indigenous people from Guatemala by the time of the arrival of the Spaniards, who noticed that they would pile the fruit in their canoes, where they would let the pulp ferment to produce a mildly alcoholic beverage. As McGovern writes, "Before the early Americans learned how to make the chocolate beans into chocolate bars, sauces (*moles*), and beverages, they were captivated by the wine that came from the cacao fruit" (212). Other alcoholic and nonalcoholic beverages were already traditional of Mesoamerica by the arrival of the Europeans. Some were made by fermenting plants such as cacao, corn, or agave plants and others by mixing them with fruits and sugars like honey or agave sap. After the colonization of America, other beverages were created by mixing local and European ingredients and techniques. This chapter will review some of the most traditional beverages that for centuries have accompanied (and contributed to) the creation of the traditional cuisine of Mexico. Some of them are ancient, like *pulque* or *atole*; others date to colonial times, like tequila and *mezcal*; and other have been incorporated into the Mexican diet more recently, like beer. All of them are by now, however, considered an integral part of Mexican gastronomy.

The most popular nonalcoholic beverages in Mexico can be divided into two categories: hot drinks and cold drinks. Hot drinks are usually consumed in the morning for breakfast or in the evening for dinner. Sometimes, depending on the region or the time of the year, they could also be consumed in *la merienda*; rarely with *la comida*. The most common hot beverage is *café de olla*. In most Mexican houses, coffee means *café de olla*, which is prepared with boiling water, coffee, and cinnamon. Usually the water is boiled with a cinnamon stick, and when it starts to boil, ground coffee is added, simmered for a few minutes, and removed from the stove. The coffee then is strained and served with sugar. This is a conventional drink for breakfast and dinner; it is not very strong and it is served to all the members of the family, including children, albeit often with milk. Even if coffee is the most popular hot beverage, it does not mean it is the most traditional. Coffee came to Mexico late. It is not a native plant, and it was not cultivated there until the late 1700s. Coffee plants were originally cultivated in Arabia and brought to Europe around the 1600s. As legend goes, the plant was zealously kept in the royal gardens of the king of France, but made it by contraband to Martinique around 1720, where it prospered, and from there it spread through the Caribbean.

Coffee came to Mexico from Cuba and the Dominican Republic in the late 1700s. But it was not until the country became independent from Spain that the cultivation of coffee started to be systematic, mainly in plantations established by German and Italian immigrants in the mountains of the southern region of the country. Coffee prospered and was well established by the late 1800s, but it was not a national industry until the early twentieth century when the post-revolutionary government started to promote aggressively the cultivation and industrialization of the crop. This made coffee accessible and affordable; the fact that its preparation did not require a lot of time and effort—in addition to the stimulant effects of caffeine—made it a favorite drink for the people, particularly the working masses. Before that, it had been a luxury item. Considering the efforts of the Mexican government to develop a national coffee industry and the aura of intellectuality attached to drinking coffee, inherited from the nineteenth-century bohemians and their love for French culture, the first thing that surprises one is how limited coffee culture is in Mexico compared to France, Italy, Spain, and even South America and how difficult in general it is to find great coffee in most cities. This, perhaps, explains the surprising popularity of Starbucks, which by 2017 had already established stores in every single state of the country, making Mexico the seventh nation in the world in terms of Starbuck stores; the coffee giant made good, gourmet coffee available practically everywhere. As the digital English-language newspaper *Mexico News Daily* puts it, "Sitting down to a latte or frappuccino is more common in Mexico these days than enjoying a traditional *café de olla*" ("Starbucks Celebrates").

Besides *café de olla*, Mexicans love *café con leche*, which is traditionally strong coffee mixed with hot milk in equal quantities. The traditional *café con leche* is served in most cafés and restaurants in the country, but the one most people consider the quintessential *café con leche* is the one served in La Parroquia, a traditional café and restaurant in the Port of Veracruz. It is a favorite drink for dinner, and it is almost always served with sweet bread, churros, or a slice of cake; lighter versions with *café de olla* are common as well. Despite being one of the largest producers of coffee in the world, Mexicans rarely drink coffee through the day, and cafés like the ones popular in France, Italy, Portugal, or Spain are rare, even though they did have a presence in the nineteenth century, particularly during the frenchified years when Porfirio Díaz was in power, when cafes were popular with the aristocracy and intelligentsia. This activity, seen as elitist, was never popular with the masses; more popular cafés (basically small restaurants and American diners) like Sanborns and later Vips became standard during the twentieth century, but still the coffee they served was weak.

Unlike coffee, chocolate was always popular. Chocolate is perhaps one of the most valued contributions of Mexico to the world; it was already appreciated by the Aztecs and the Maya; as Inga Clendinnen explains, "The beverage most coveted by the Mexica lords was not the intoxicating pulque but chocolatl: the ground beans of the cacao tree beaten to a sweet foamy froth with honey and maize gruel, then gently warmed" (*Aztecs*, 195). This beverage was sometimes mixed with other spices and chili peppers. The Spanish conquistadores saw its value, first as stimulant since it contains caffeine and theobromine but also because it had an aura of mystery about it, since it was reserved for the nobility and warriors, considered a gift from the gods. Chocolate, thus, was taken to Europe and mixed with milk and sugar, where it became a huge sensation among the aristocracy of the old continent. Soon after its arrival in Europe, according to historian Jorge F. Rivas Pérez, chocolate "was celebrated in texts and works of art [. . .] and great fortunes were amassed from its cultivation and trade" (93–4). It was also the drink favored by the aristocracy of the colonies, particularly New Spain, where it was appreciated "because it was native to Mexico and cacao was widely cultivated in the region" (93).

Even though chocolate was drunk in Mexico during the colonial period by all social classes, it was favored by the aristocracy and was a drink associated with bishops, abbots, nuns, the viceroy, and the most distinguished families of the colonial aristocracy. As the production increased and prices dropped, it became even more popular with the people, although for the most part it was a beverage enjoyed on special occasions. The other popular hot drink during colonial times was *atole*, a drink that was made traditionally with water, *masa* (corn dough), or corn flour diluted in the water and mixed with *piloncillo*, honey, or sugar and spices like cinnamon, vanilla, or chocolate; sometimes it was flavored with pureed fruits, like pineapple, strawberry, or guava. *Atole* is popular even today, particularly for young children who drink it for breakfast sometimes instead of coffee. It is also a traditional drink served at birthday parties and other celebrations with sweet bread, *tamales*, or cake.

The drink goes back to pre-Columbian times, when it was made with water and honey, and according to some historians, it was often the only thing *macehuales* (working people) ate all day to keep up their strength. That is why it was also considered medicinal and a good source of nutrition for sick and elderly people, as well as children. Even though corn is the cereal used for the drink since the time of the Aztecs, other grains were used in later days, namely amaranth, rice, and wheat. There is an almost endless selection of flavors, since it can be mixed with any fruit or spice; it usually assumes the name of the flavoring ingredient, for example, *atole de nuez* (walnut *atole*), *atole de fresa* (strawberry *atole*), *atole de canela* (cinnamon *atole*), etc. Less common today, but popular in ancient times are the savory variations that use salt and chili peppers instead of sugar; there is even a type of *atole* called *atole agrio* (sour *atole*) made with fermented corn dough.

A variation of the drink, also very popular, is called *champurrado*. *Champurrado* is an *atole* prepared for special occasions mostly; it is made with water or milk or both, corn dough, sugar or *piloncillo*, cinnamon, vanilla, and chocolate. Although some ingredients may vary, it always includes the ones mentioned here or a combination of them, with corn dough and chocolate being the most important ones. It was considered a special *atole* in ancient times, since both the corn and the cacao beans had to be ground in a *metate* (a utensil made of volcanic stone tilted and supported by three feet, used to grind grains and spices). Today, *champurrado* is still popular for special occasions, and its preparation is easier, mostly because the chocolate used is sold already prepared, ready to dissolve in water or milk; however, *champurrado* remains a favorite drink for popular festivities.

Another common hot beverage, although less popular than coffee or *atole*, is tea, which refers to herbal infusions that are used in traditional medicine, as well as for small gatherings or as afternoon refreshments. Traditional medicine in Mexico relies greatly on infusions, and it is common to hear people recommending *un té* for specific ailments; some of the most common teas, which could also be drunk as refreshments, are *té de manzanilla* (chamomile), *té de borraja* (borage), *té de yerbabuena* (mint), *té de tila* (linden), or *té de azahar* (orange blossom). Common as well are *té de canela* (cinnamon) and *té de limón* (lemon grass), which are widely used for their supposedly digestive properties. Tea, strictly speaking, is not very popular in Mexico, although recently there has been a boom of tea and tea-related products, and experts anticipate that tea consumption in the country will continue to grow (Ramírez).

Cold drinks, on the other hand, are usually served with *la comida*, at taco stands and other street food venues, or at big family gatherings and other celebrations. The most traditional cold drinks in Mexico are called *aguas frescas* (literally fresh waters). *Aguas frescas* are drinks prepared with fresh fruit, water, sugar, and ice. They can be made with literally any fruit available, but the most traditional are *agua de piña* (pineapple), *de sandía* (watermelon), *de melón* (cantaloupe), *de fresa* (strawberry), *de papaya*, *de limón* (lime), and *de guayaba* (guava). To prepare them, the fruit is either blended to form a pulp or chopped in small pieces, or juiced in the case of lime and lemons; the pulp or chunks of fruit are then added to the water, along with sugar to taste. Big chunks of ice are added to keep the drinks cold. It is still common to see in markets, street food stands, and in traditional *cocinas* and *fondas*, the *vitroleros* (glass jars in the shape of a small barrel) with the *aguas frescas* of different bright colors aligned on the counter. Other *aguas frescas* are made with infusions, like *agua de jamaica* (hibiscus iced tea) or *de tamarindo* (tamarind); in both cases, the tamarind and hibiscus flowers are boiled in water and, when cooked, added to water with sugar.

A variation of the *aguas frescas* is the ones sold at juice stands or the traditional *juguerías* of most markets. This type of *aguas* is made by blending the sugar, water, and fruit and straining it in a tall glass to be served. Unlike the traditional *aguas frescas*, which are made in advance, the *aguas* from *juguerías* are prepared individually when ordered. Also, they tend to be more elaborate and creative. Besides the mentioned fruits, one could order specialties like *agua de alfalfa*, which is prepared by blending alfalfa, lime, sugar, pineapple, and *pingüicas* (point leaf manzanita). In addition to *aguas*, the *juguerías* sell fresh-squeezed juices, all made, as well, when ordered. The most popular are orange, grapefruit, carrot, beet, and celery juices, or combinations of them, like the famous *vampiro* (vampire), which is beet and orange juices mixed together, with a splash of lime. These establishments are popular, particularly in Mexico City and in the central states of the country. Recently, they have started to cater to a vegan and vegetarian clientele and have become more common in other regions of the country.

Licuados are another type of cold beverage popular in Mexico; they are also sold at *juguerías*. *Licuado* is a drink made with milk, sugar, fruit, and sometimes vanilla and cinnamon. It is prepared by adding all the ingredients to a blender and blending them until smooth (*licuado* literally means blended); sometimes ice is added, but most frequently it is made with very cold milk. The most common fruit for *licuados* is banana, but also papaya, guava, *mamey*, strawberry, and mango are used; however, banana and strawberry are the most traditional. *Licuado de plátano* is a classic; it is prepared with cold milk, bananas, sugar, and vanilla extract all blended until very smooth and then served in a tall glass sprinkled with powdered cinnamon on top. It is not infrequent to add a couple of eggs or just the yolk of the eggs to the *licuado*, especially when used to replace breakfast or to complement lunch. It is considered very nutritious and often consumed as a meal when in a hurry. Other variations of *licuados* less popular but still common enough are made with walnuts, oatmeal, or seeds like amaranth or flax.

Besides *aguas frescas*, *licuados*, and juices, two other traditional drinks are popular in Mexico, although they seem to be in decline: *horchata* and *tepache*. *Horchata* is a drink made with rice and cinnamon mixed with water, sugar, and ice. There are many variations of the drink not only in Mexico but all through the Hispanic world, including Spain, where it is made mostly with *chufa* (nutsedge plant), although rice, barley, and almonds are also used. In Mexico, the most traditional *horchata* is made with rice and a stick of cinnamon soaked in water for a few hours or overnight, then blended and mixed with sugar and water; it is served over ice and sprinkled with powdered cinnamon. Another popular version includes milk, which could be condensed or evaporated, vanilla extract, and sometimes chocolate or even almonds. For this version of *horchata*, the soaked rice, almonds, and cinnamon are blended with chunks of chocolate and mixed with equal amounts of milk and water, sweetened with sugar, and served on ice with sprinkled cinnamon on top. There is yet another version popular in the region of the Gulf of Mexico made with coconut and considered one of the most delicious *horchatas*.

Tepache is a fermented drink made traditionally with the peel and pulp of the pineapple and *piloncillo*. The *piloncillo* and the pineapple peel and pulp are placed in water and left to ferment for several days at room temperature. Once the fermentation has happened, the drink is sometimes mixed with a little water, resulting in a beverage of lower alcohol content; sugar may be added, depending on preference, to sweeten it. The drink is then served over ice, making it a very refreshing beverage, perfect for hot summer days. Like most traditional foods and drinks, there are many variations of *tepache*, according to personal taste or regional traditions. In some places it is made with spices like anise, cinnamon, and clove; in other regions, fruits like sugarcane, apple, quince, or tamarind are also used instead of or in combination with pineapple. Certain variations include sweet corn, and others increase the alcohol content by adding *pulque* or the bark of the *palo de timbre* tree (prairie acacia) to the drink while it ferments. Most of these variations are often used by local or indigenous communities in ancient rites or celebrations.

But the *tepache* made with pineapple and *piloncillo* is the traditional one, the one that most people still buy in popular markets and other fruit and juice stands. Due to its low alcohol content, it is considered a family drink and it is also served in food stands to accompany tacos, *sopes*, *quesadillas*, and other street foods. The drink is very traditional, although its popularity is in decline. It was a very popular drink up to the middle of the twentieth century, but *tepache* had a long history, including its prohibition, all through the colonial period; however, it was common to find establishments dedicated exclusively to selling the drink with a higher alcohol content called *tepacherías*, particularly in neighborhoods on the outskirts of the cities, and some of them were considered refuges of criminals of all kinds. This was the case of the barrios of La Palma and Santa Cruz in Mexico City, where *tepacherías* abounded, creating all sorts of problems due to public intoxication, lewd dances, and gambling, prompting some concerned neighbors to write to the viceroy of New Spain to complain about this problem and demand a solution (Guedea, 23).

A letter was sent to the viceroy in 1812, when Mexico was already in the war of independence and it complained of clandestine taverns and *tepacherías*, disguised as cafés with names such as Little Hell and Pass of Lucifer that gave away their true nature, making "the entire population tremble when they hear of them" (Guedea, 65). These places were, the concerned citizens added emphatically, the refuge of prostitutes and deserters; one imagines they made this accusation with the intent of prompting the authorities to act quickly. The relationship of colonial Mexico with alcoholic beverages was a complicated one, particularly because it was mediated by issues of race, class, and gender. It was also an economic issue. The colonial authorities had established early on strict control over what kind of drinks and spirits could be produced and commercialized in New Spain, and by suppressing and condemning local and native beverages and by not allowing the production of European wine and spirits, they were seeking to promote the consumption of those produced in Spain and brought to Mexico on long journeys that more often than not affected the quality and price of the products, mostly wine and sugarcane liquor.

But perhaps no other alcoholic beverage was more emblematic of Mesoamerican Mexico than *pulque*; it is a drink with a long and complex history. *Pulque* has deep roots in Mesoamerican cultures; it was considered a ritualistic drink by the Aztecs, a drink that could be dangerous if not controlled; it was a beverage associated with drunkenness and sexuality, since, according to the legend, it had caused the exile of the god Quetzalcoatl, who embarrassed himself due to the effects of intoxication with *pulque* and had to abandoned Tula, the city he founded, in shame. *Pulque* is a fermented beverage produced from the sap of the maguey plant called *aguamiel* (honey water), an agave plant that grows abundantly in central Mexico and the arid northern regions. *Pulque* is a white, viscous beverage with an alcoholic content similar to that of beer and that has a mildly acidic taste. The Aztecs consider it medicinal and sacred, and it was reserved for priests, the sick, and elderly; for the rest of the people it was forbidden under penalty of death. It was, as Clendinnen writes, "a coveted beverage in Tenochtitlan, hedged by rules and restrictions" (*Aztecs*, 195).

After the conquest of the Aztec Empire, the rules surrounding *pulque* were relaxed, but the drink was still controlled. Nonetheless, it became one of the most popular drinks among all classes, ethnicities, and genders, so much so that the authorities expressed concern about the number of Spaniards and Indians who abused it, and had to tighten the regulations of its production and commercialization. *Pulque*, however, continued to be one of the most popular drinks in New Spain all through the colonial period and beyond. In fact, it has remained popular even today. *Pulque* can be drunk white, that means pure with nothing added, or *curado* (cured), that is, mixed with fruits like strawberry, guava, pineapple, orange, or even celery or oatmeal. And if pulque was accepted by all classes, at first, towards the end of colonial times and the first decades of independence, it became synonymous with the populace, mostly Indians and the poor. While the upper classes adopted traditional dishes to European and cosmopolitan techniques and ingredients, or simply adopted European cuisine and drinks as their preference, the people continue to eat traditional foods and drink *pulque*. In fact, *pulquerías* were popular in Mexico City and other cities and towns in central Mexico until the late twentieth century, often with the same stigma attached. Recently, however, there has been a revalorization of the drink by younger generations.

Fermented beverages based on fruits, plants, or grains, particularly corn, were not unusual during Mesoamerican and colonial times, especially in specific regions and among indigenous communities. However, none had the reach and captured the imagination of the Mexican people more than *pulque*. Still, some of these other beverages remained popular in different regions of Mexico. Some of the most common are *potzol*, a fermented drink of corn diluted in water and sometimes sweetened with sugar or the pulp of some fruits. It is very traditional in the southern states of Veracruz, Oaxaca, Tabasco, Chiapas, and the Yucatán Peninsula. *Tesgüino* is another drink made with fermented corn and sometimes other ingredients like oatmeal, the bark of local trees, or even peyote. It is traditional among the indigenous communities of the northern states, particularly Chihuahua and Sonora, but also Durango, Nayarit, Colima, and Aguascalientes. *Tejuino* is the name given in the state of Jalisco to a drink similar to *tegüino*, prepared also with fermented corn dough and *piloncillo* or sugar and served over ice and sometimes with a squeeze of lime. Although some people considered both drinks the same, there are specific characteristics to each drink, and some people consider *tejuino* different from *tegüino* because in some versions it is not prepared with fermented corn.

Tejate is a drink, like *pozol*, made with corn and cacao, popular in Oaxaca. Not necessarily fermented, this drink is similar to the other ones described here because it uses corn or corn dough as well as cocoa beans; in the case of *tejate*, as described by Alex Whitmore in *The Atlantic*, it also includes *mamey* seeds and the flowers of a tree called *flor de cacao*. *Colonche* is another ancient drink still found in some regions of Mexico, mostly the arid regions of the states of San Luis Potosí, Zacatecas, Aguascalientes, and Guanajuato; *colonche* is prepared with the fermented fruit of the *nopal* cactus, known as *tuna* (prickly pear) in Mexico. It is a sweet, refreshing, low-alcohol drink that is usually available during the rainy season when the *tunas* are abundant; in some regions it is considered medicinal. A particularly interesting drink is *tuba*, a beverage made with the fermented sap of the coconut tree and it is sometimes mixed with other fruits. According to the dictionary *Larousse of Mexican Cuisine*, it was brought to Mexico from the Philippines in the seventeenth century, when the Philippines was under the control of New Spain and there was regular traffic between Acapulco and Manila.

Alcohol was discovered early by most societies, and it was immediately appreciated because of its mind-altering properties and because it was often safer to drink than water. Its discovery, however, was simply a matter of time, since alcohol is omnipresent in nature. So alcoholic beverages were known by Mesoamerican cultures, who had a variety of fermented drinks with different degrees of alcohol. No one knows for sure if they were familiar with distillation, but if they were, it was not a widespread technique. What is clear is that with the arrival of the Europeans, distillation became a practice familiar in New Spain, and by the seventeenth century it was a widespread activity. The agave plants, already a source of fermented drinks for indigenous cultures, were used for the production of a spirit called *mezcal*. The process was simple: the heart of the agave plant, also called *piña* (pineapple) because it resembles that fruit, was cooked in underground pits and fermented, then the fermented juice was distilled into wood-fired stills.

The more advanced technology required to produce spirits cause *mezcal* to be considered less primitive than the product of the fermentation process used in the making of *pulque*; this as well as the association of *pulque* with the masses, with Indians, and with disorderly conduct, made *mezcal* more popular as the alcoholic beverage of choice in the New Spain. *Mezcal* was also easy to transport and lasted longer than *pulque*, which helped it to spread through the colony and to eventually became the de facto national alcoholic beverage. The limitations of cultivating grapes in Mexico, first, and the need to protect wine and spirits produced in Spain, later, made wine consumed in the colonies very expensive and often of bad quality, since it had to go through a long journey across the Atlantic to reach New Spain. That favored the continued production of spirits with local ingredients and made the *vino mezcal* (*mezcal* wine, as it was originally known) a truly national favorite. As the technology evolved, and as the production and distribution became common practice, different regions specialized in their own version of *mezcal*. Many attempts to suppress and to implement very strict regulations on the production and sale of *mezcal* were in the end unsuccessful, and towards the end of colonial rule, *mezcal* was omnipresent in all of New Spain.

These attempts to restrict its production, ironically, made it possible for *mezcal* to spread to other parts of Mexico in an attempt to escape administrative control; it also created different regions specializing in particular types of *mezcal*, using the distinctive types of agave available to them. One of those regions was Nueva Galicia, today the state of Jalisco, where a particular type of *mezcal* was produced in a small, picturesque town called Tequila. With time, this *mezcal* became so popular and started to differentiate itself from other *mezcals* to the point that was referred to simply as tequila, the name of the town where it was first produced. By the end of the 1800s, the name had become standard and an industry had grown out of the spirit; all that made it easier for tequila to become its own spirit and, with time, the spirit of Mexico. Popular culture and patriotic attempts to create a national image and a unified culture after the revolution contributed to cement tequila's predominance in the popular imagination as the

> Tequila usually comes in three modalities: silver, gold, and aged. But is diamond a fourth? In 2008, scientists Javier Morales, Luis Apátiga, and Victor Castaño from the National University of Mexico discovered that the chemical composition of tequila was similar to that of diamonds. They decided to try to create diamonds from tequila . . . and succeeded. After heating a bottle of tequila into a gas, and then heating the gas to almost 1,500 degrees F, they ended up with a fine film of miniscule diamonds. Not impressive enough for an engagement ring, but useful for other applications.

Mexican spirit per excellence, aided mainly by mass media, particularly movies, that popularized the image of the quintessential Mexican man celebrating his triumphs or lamenting his love tragedies at a cantina, with a bottle of tequila and a mariachi band surrounding him.

This was a powerful cultural tool, since Mexico developed a very important film industry in the early decades of the twentieth century that was often utilized by the government to promote social initiatives. The Mexican film industry lasted until the so-called Golden Age of the 1950s and 1960s. Just about the same time the Mexican government and the tequila industry were attempting to regulate the production and commercialization of tequila worldwide, something that was finally accomplished by the 1970s, when tequila became the first non-European spirit to be given the label of denomination of origin. As result, strict norms for the production, the labeling, and the commercialization of tequila around the world were created and put in place. Tequila has since seen an increase in popularity, becoming in recent years one of the favorite spirits in the world, one that has also been described as having "surprising health benefits," according to reports from Rachel Hosie of *The Independent*. And if tequila became the first spirit to be given denomination of origin outside of Europe in the 1970s, 20 years later, *mezcal*, the other popular spirit made with agave, had the same consideration, and its recent popularity with younger consumers seems to indicate that it will go, presumably, through the same process as tequila and perhaps will become as popular and trendy as its brother.

Although tequila and *mezcal* are by far the most recognized spirits from Mexico, the list is actually a bit longer. Other *mezcals* are *raicilla*, *sotol*, and *bacanora*. *Raicilla* is produced like *mezcal*, but is less industrialized and continues to use more traditional and artisanal methods. *Sotol* is another *mezcal* that originated in northern Mexico, in the state of Chihuahua, and that is produced with the *sotol* (desert spoon) cactus; it is similar to *mezcal*, but can be a little smokier and often is mixed with herbs and fruits. Like *sotol*, *bacanora* is originally from northern Mexico, in particular the state of Sonora, where it was produced illegally for a long time, becoming legal only in the 1990s. It offers also a smoky, earthy, distinctive flavor that makes it perfect for cocktails mixed with fruits and herbs. Lesser known *mezcals* are *tuska* from Jalisco and *sikua* from Michoacán, but it is practically impossible to obtain them outside of these regions. Besides these *mezcals*, other spirits from Mexico that, although traditional, are lesser known outside of the country, or sometimes even the regions where they are produced, are *charanda*, a spirit made from sugarcane, similar to rum, that often comes in *plata* (silver), *reposado* (rested), and *añejo* (aged) modalities. It is traditional of the state of Michoacán and in the early 2000s was also given the label of denomination of origin. *Pox* (pronounced posh) is another spirit made with sugarcane, wheat, and corn; it is traditional of the southern state of Chiapas and other Maya regions, including Central America, where it is still used in religious ceremonies.

A review of traditional beverages from Mexico would not be complete without talking about bottled drinks that dominated the Mexican market for a large portion of the twentieth century, mainly beer and sodas. Even though beer was produced in Mexico since the sixteenth century, the poor quality and high price of the product made it impossible to compete with other drinks more accessible and traditional like *pulque* or *tepache*. For most of the colonial period, however, beer continued to be exported to Mexico for those who could afford it, and after the country's independence there was an attempt to establish a beer industry. A few English and Mexican nationals were the first to start the production of beer in a more systematic way, but still in relatively small quantities. It was not until the nineteenth century, particularly during the years of the Mexican Empire of Maximilian of Habsburg (1863–1867), that Mexico started industrial production and commercialization of beer. Many Swiss, Austrian, French, and German immigrants came to Mexico during Maximilian's reign and established themselves in the country. They produced industrial quantities of quality beer, particularly a brewer named Santiago Graf.

Graf was an Austrian immigrant who bought small breweries established years earlier in Mexico and consolidated and modernized them by bringing machinery and ingredients from Europe. The type of beer he produced, lager, became very popular in Mexico and it is still even today. His most celebrated beer, Victoria, can be found in *taquerías* and restaurants all over Mexico. Graf's brewery continued to produced quality beer until it was bought by the conglomerate Modelo in the early twentieth century, becoming one of the most important beer producers in Mexico.

The other major brewery is Cervecería Moctezuma, a company founded in Veracruz that later merged with the brewery Cuauhtémoc from Monterrey in the state of Nuevo León, becoming the Cuauhtémoc-Moctezuma Brewery. Moctezuma presented Dos Equis to the world in 1897. Originally this beer was called Siglo XX (twentieth century) in honor of the new millennium, but later was renamed simply XX (Dos Equis). Negra Modelo followed in 1935, a beer that remained relatively close to the original Vienna style beer of the 1800s. For most of the twentieth century, Moctezuma and Modelo dominated the market in Mexico before going international. Today the most popular Mexican beers still belong to either one of these breweries, with Corona, Negra Modelo, Modelo Especial, Pacífico, and Victoria being from the Modelo Group, and Dos Equis, Sol, Indio, Noche Buena, Tecate, Carta Blanca, and Bohemia from Cuauhtémoc-Moctezuma Group.

As popular as beer was, the other success story is sodas. The soft drink industry took off in the twentieth century and has become popular not only in Mexico but in many taco stands and taco trucks as well as Mexican restaurants and supermarkets all over Mexico and the United States. *Jarritos* is probably the best-known Mexican soda. *Jarritos* was born in the 1950s as a way of competing in a growing market with a uniquely Mexican flair; not only does the name proclaim its nationalism (*jarrito* is the traditional clay cup people use in Mexico to drink *atole*, coffee, or water) but the flavors of the soda are all based on Mexican fruits and the traditional flavors of *aguas frescas*: tamarind, mandarin, pineapple, hibiscus, guava, mango, grapefruit, strawberry, and lime. However, before *Jarritos*, there was another company that started producing soft drinks in the 1930s; when in 1947 it introduced a soda called El Naranjo, which came in a small roundish bottle, people called it *chaparrita* (shorty) and the name stuck. A noncarbonated drink flavored with fruit juices, it became a favorite of children because of its size and colorful appearance. Sidral Mundet, another popular Mexican soda, started production in the first decades of the twentieth century as an attempt to make bottled cider, but the result was a refreshing soft drink that started to sell as apple-flavored soda. It was so popular in Mexico that it was even considered a healthy option to hydrate sick children.

Many other soft drinks were produced and sold in Mexico, some known all over the country, like Sangria Señorial, a sangria-flavored soda, or Tehuacán, originally mineral water that later produced flavored sodas, to more local brands like Tonicol from Sinaloa; Topo Chico, also a mineral water company originally from Nuevo León; and Yoli, a lemon-lime soda from the state of Guerrero. But the major soda company is Cooperative

Pascual, producer of the Pato Pascual and Lulú sodas, a favorite of Mexican tables since the 1950s. Pato Pascual sodas were promoted with the slogan "fruit in your soda," again making a vague reference to the *aguas frescas* with the traditional flavors: pineapple, guava, tamarind, strawberry, mango, and orange. In the 1930s, the Refrescos Pascual Company started selling ice pops, bottled water, and finally carbonated sodas. In the 1960s the company introduced Boing! a noncarbonated juice drink iconic in its slim, modern bottle and its Tetra Classic Aseptic package, a fun tetrahedron-shaped carton made by the Swedish company Tetra Pack, for which Refrescos Pascual acquired the exclusive rights in Mexico.

This distinctive packaging was part of the charm of the company, as well as the claim that the drinks had real fruit pulp in each bottle, something you could actually see in some of the bottles, they said, which you had to shake before opening. What makes this company special in the Mexican context is the dramatic challenges it went through in the 1980s. In March 1982, the Mexican government approved a law that would raise workers' salaries nationwide between 10 and 30 percent, but Refrescos Pascual refused to do so, forcing its workers to go on strike. On May 31, the owner of the company tried to break the strike, walking into one of the plants with a group of armed men who started to shoot at the workers on guard, killing two and injuring seventeen of them. The struggle continued in court, and in the end the workers were successful against a company now in disarray with their boss in jail; rather than closing the factory and becoming unemployed, they decided to restructure the company as a cooperative, continuing with the production of sodas, but with the company now owned and run by the workers under the name Sociedad Cooperativa Trabajadores Pascual. The support of most Mexicans was evident not only during the months of struggle but once the cooperative started to sell its products, which includes now carbonated sodas, fruit juices, bottled water, and even flavored milk.

Atole de Fresa (Corn Dough Strawberry Hot Drink)

Yield: Serves 6

1 cup masa harina
6 cups water
½ cup piloncillo, chopped
1 small cinnamon stick
1 cup fresh strawberries
2 teaspoon vanilla extract
2 teaspoon powdered cinnamon, optional

Equipment: medium pot, mixing spoon, food processor or blender, measuring spoons

1. Bring 5 cups of water, cinnamon, and piloncillo to a boil in a medium pot. Meanwhile, dissolve the masa harina in the remaining cup of water and mix well.
2. When the water begins to boil, add the masa harina and water mixture to the pot. Simmer for a few minutes, whisking constantly, until the liquid thickens, about 10 minutes.
3. Place strawberries in a food processor or blender and puree. Add the strawberry puree and vanilla to the water mixture, mix well, and simmer for another minute or two.

Serve the atole hot in clay cups (jarritos) and sprinkle with cinnamon if desired.

Horchata (Rice Drink)

Yield: Serves 6

2 cups rice
3 cups water
2 cinnamon sticks
5 cups milk
1 teaspoon vanilla extract
¾ cup sugar
Ground cinnamon to taste

Equipment: large bowl or pan, strainer, pitcher, measuring spoons, measuring cups, mixing spoons

1. Soak rice and cinnamon sticks in 3 cups of water for a few hours or preferably overnight.
2. Drain the rice and place it in a blender with 1½ cups of the soaking water and cinnamon sticks; blend until smooth; add sugar and blend for a few more minutes.
3. Strain the rice puree into a pitcher and dispose of the leftover rice and cinnamon; add the milk and vanilla extract. Chill in the refrigerator for a couple of hours.

Serve the horchata in tall glasses over ice; if preferred, sprinkled with ground cinnamon on top.

Agua de Alfalfa (Alfalfa-Flavored Water)

Yield: Serves 1 to 2

¼ cup alfalfa leaves
1 lime, quartered
1 tablespoon *pingüicas*
3 chunks pineapple
2 tablespoons sugar
2 cups water
Ice

Equipment: blender, measuring cups, measuring spoons

1. Wash and disinfect the alfalfa, if necessary.
2. Place alfalfa in a blender with *pingüicas*, sugar, water, and pineapple.
3. Blend for 20 seconds; add lime (skin and all) and blend for 10 seconds more.
4. Strain into a glass with ice.

Serve the alfalfa water over ice and decorate with a slice of lime. Drink immediately, since it will become bitter over time.

Licuado de Plátano (Banana Smoothie)

Yield: Serves 1

1½ cups ice-cold milk
1 large banana
1 tablespoon sugar
1 teaspoon vanilla extract
Powdered cinnamon to taste
Ice, optional
1 egg, optional

Equipment: blender, measuring cups, spoons

1. Place the milk, banana, vanilla, and sugar in a blender.
2. Blend for a few minutes until smooth. Add ice and egg if using.

Serve in a tall glass; sprinkle the cinnamon on top. You may use ½ cup of strawberries, papaya, guava, mango, or mamey instead of bananas if you wish to try other flavors.

Paloma de Troy (Troy's Paloma)

Yield: Serves 1

2 ounces tequila
1 ounce fresh squeezed lime juice
4 basil leaves
3 ounces grapefruit soda (Jarritos, preferred)
1 slice of lime

Equipment: cocktail shaker, double jigger, muddler, highball glass

1. Gently muddle 3 basil leaves in the shaker.
2. Add the lime juice and the tequila to the shaker and mix well or give it a quick shake.
3. Strain the tequila and lime juice into a highball glass with plenty of ice.
4. Add 3 ounces of grapefruit soda, or enough to top the glass.

Serve garnished with a slice of lime and a basil leaf and enjoy on a hot summer day.

CHAPTER SEVEN

Holy Days and Special Occasions

A Year in Food

The celebration of the New Year in Mexico actually begins the year before; more precisely the last night of the year, or *noche vieja* (old night), as New Year's Eve is sometimes called. The festivities commence with an elaborate dinner and peak the very last seconds of the year, when everybody welcomes the New Year with a bunch of grapes. It is customary in most parts of Mexico to wait, grapes in hand, for the usual 12 tolls of the clock marking the end and the beginning of the year, right at midnight. The tradition of eating a grape for each chime of the clock is relatively new and probably came to Mexico from Spain at the beginning of the twentieth century, but it has become an indispensable part of the celebration. Thus, Mexicans begin a year of celebrations marked by food and drinks. Cider or champagne are the drinks preferred for the toast of the New Year, but beer, wine, tequila, *charanda*, *mezcal*, rum, or brandy are part of the celebration. January 1 is a day spent at home, with family, sometimes recovering from the festivities of the previous night, taking care of the *cruda* (hangover) with a traditional plate of *chilaquiles*, *birria*, or *menudo*, and relaxing at home. It could also be the day of the *recalentado*. *Recalentar* means to reheat in Spanish and it is how people jokingly refer to the gathering of friends and relatives the day after a big celebration to eat the leftovers of the feast.

Traditionally, people visit close friends and relatives on that day to wish them Happy New Year and are, in turn, invited to *el recalentado*. Families may also get together to eat leftovers and talk about the holiday and to relax and prepare to face one more year. The *fiestas de fin de año*, end-of-the-year holidays, conclude not after New Year's, but on January 6, the feast of Epiphany or Three Kings' Day. The evening of the feast, children spend the afternoon and evening shinning their shoes and writing their letters to the Three Kings, asking for presents. Before going to bed on the

January 5, children place their shoes by a window and stick their letters in one of the shoes. In the morning of January 6, children wake up early to find their presents, usually toys and lots of candies and chocolates; then in the evening, families get together to eat the traditional *rosca de reyes*. The *rosca* is a yeast-leavened cake in the shape of a circle or oval with a hole in the center, which is precisely what *rosca* means, any object shaped in that way. The shape of the cake is supposed to resemble a crown, and it is decorated with dried and crystalized fruits that represent the jewels of the crown. In Mexico in particular, a traditional decoration used to be *acitrón*, a candy made with the *biznaga* cactus. However, the *biznaga* has been declared a protected species, and the Mexican government no longer allows its commercialization. *Acitrón* is also the name given in Spain to the candied citron fruit, which is not traditional in Mexico.

Around dinnertime, Mexican families get together to cut the *rosca* and eat it with *atole* or hot chocolate. Baked inside the *rosca* there is one or more little plastic or ceramic dolls representing baby Jesus. According to tradition, whoever gets one of those little dolls has to offer a dinner with *tamales* and *atole* on the Feast of the Presentation of the Lord, or Candlemas, on February 2. On that day, people bring to the church the image of the infant Jesus that had laid in the nativity scene on Christmas to be blessed. After Mass, the images are blessed and families gather to eat *tamales*. This traditional feast is very old in Mexico and most likely originated in the late colonial period when ancient pagan traditions got mixed with the new Christian holiday and farmers would attend Candlemas bringing baskets with ears of corn to be blessed by the priest. These corn kernels were later used when it was time to plant the new crops, so it is not hard to imagine why foods like *tamales* and *atole* became associated with the feast of Candlemas. Although some traditions have changed and attending Mass on this day is no longer required for Catholics, the feast remains an important one in the country.

Not exactly a traditional holiday, Valentine's Day, known in Mexico as *día del amor y la amistad* (day of love and friendship), is nonetheless celebrated, particularly by younger people. A couple of weeks before the holiday, many department stores, restaurants, and other businesses start advertising the day, targeting adolescents and young adults. Often, besides giving candy and chocolates, they attend parties or go to a restaurant. The holiday has grown in popularity recently, such that according to a poll by the daily *El Excelsior* ("Todo lo que debes saber"), 50 percent of Mexicans said they celebrate the holiday because it is an excuse to be more romantic, with the vast majority of the women interviewed preferring to go out for dinner rather than receiving chocolates or candy.

Holy Days and Special Occasions

Towards the end of February, there is another holiday, *carnaval* (Mardi Gras), that few would associate with Mexico, but that is celebrated all around the country and boasts some of the most colorful and festive parties around the world. *Carnaval* was celebrated, traditionally, the day before Ash Wednesday; today, however, it is a popular celebration used by some local governments to promote tourism, so most *carnavals* start earlier, usually a week or so before Mardi Gras. Originally the celebration was all about the flesh before entering the 40 days of penance of Lent, so people would indulge themselves with dancing, music, love making, drinks, and, of course, food, since all meat had to be consumed before Lent. Most cities and towns in Mexico celebrate *carnaval*. There are therefore some elements common to all of them, like dances, parades, floats decorated with flowers, and the burning of *El Mal Humor* (Mr. Bad Mood), usually a controversial or infamous character burned in effigy. The celebrations are accompanied by food in restaurants, seasonal markets, stands, and street sellers offering all kinds of typical dishes, usually the most famous dishes of the region, including traditional drinks and sweets.

Among the most popular *carnavals* in Mexico are the *carnaval de Campeche,* considered one the oldest in the country; some of the dishes typical for *carnaval* are *manitas de cangrejo* (crab legs), *panuchos, pan de cazón* (a kind of enchilada of several layers of tortillas and dogfish), *cholombo* (a soup made with cow's tripe), and *torta de jamón claveteado.* The *carnaval de Mazatlán,* also one of the oldest in the country, offers a gastronomic festival as part of the celebration, with traditional dishes like *aguachile* (a type of shrimp *ceviche* with lime juice and *chile piquín* peppers), *pescado zarandeado* (a fish marinated in spices and grilled whole), *asado* (grilled steak and fried potatoes smothered in a tomato sauce), or seafood tacos. The *carnaval de Veracruz* is also popular and it offers everything in excess, including food and drinks. The cuisine of the state is vast and diverse, and most restaurants offer versions of regional cuisines for national and international tourists to enjoy. The same is true of the *carnaval de Mérida* in the Yucatán Peninsula or the *carnaval de Oaxaca*, states with an important cuisine that is on display for all tourists during *carnaval*.

If *carnaval* is all about excess, *cuaresma* (Lent) is all about abstinence. Ash Wednesday is at once the end of *carnaval* and the beginning of Lent. As such, according to Catholic mandate, it is a day of fasting and abstinence. So are all Fridays of Lent as well as Maundy Thursday. Fasting has evolved from not eating at all in the past to restricting the intake of food; in modern terms it means that most people between 14 and 59 years of age are mandated to have only one full meal that day and up to two snacks;

abstinence means that they cannot eat any meat of any kind, including chicken and other meat products, on those days. Because of this restriction, Mexican cuisine has developed various dishes without meat that are traditional for Lent. Meatless meals are not unusual in a typical week in most Mexican homes; however, some dishes are considered part of the tradition of the season. Some of the most popular are vegetarian, and many are based on legumes like beans, fava beans, garbanzo beans, lentils, and whole yellow or split peas.

Habas con nopales, a soup of fava beans with cactus, is one of them. This soup is popular in most of the country, with some regional variations, like the spices and the type of herbs used to flavor it. In places like Hidalgo, Tlaxcala, and Zacatecas, for example, mint or even saffron is added, but the most traditional herb used is cilantro. Regardless, all follow the same basic steps—first the fava beans and the *nopales* are cooked, separately, in water with salt; meanwhile, some chopped onions and tomatoes are sautéed in oil; and finally, all ingredients are mixed until the flavors combine. Another way of serving this soup is with guajillo or ancho chile peppers crumbled and fried in oil and sprinkled on top of the soup.

Other soups made with legumes that are traditional for Lent are *sopa* or *caldo de lentejas* (lentil soup), which is somehow different from its American counterpart. Mexican lentil soup is prepared by cooking the lentils in water and then adding to it sautéed diced onions, tomatoes, and garlic; sometimes a sprig of cilantro or parsley is added to enhance the flavor. Depending on the region, different ingredients are customary, like red wine or chopped vegetables, and in some regions, like Oaxaca, even plantains and pineapple are added. Garbanzo beans are sometimes cooked in a similar way to lentils, making a hearty soup that is served as a main dish for Lent. Yellow peas (called *arvejones* in Spanish) are cooked in a similar way to fava beans, including the *nopales* and cilantro. These soups are often served accompanied with warm tortillas or slices of toasted bread.

Nopales are a favorite food for Lent, particularly in central and northern Mexico; they can be cooked in a *chile*, in soups, or in salads. Some of the most common dishes are *nopales navegantes*; for this dish, the cactus leaves are cleaned, cut in small strips, and cooked in water and salt; once they are done, they are added to a sauce of tomatoes, *pasilla* peppers, onions, and *epazote*; other versions use *guajillo* peppers instead of *pasilla,* and some even add *charales* (a tiny fish from the lakes of central Mexico usually sundried and salted to be preserved); they are then called *nopales con charales*. In other parts of the country, a similar dish is simply called *nopales con chile*. *Nopales en salsa verde* is another favorite dish for Lent. As discussed in Chapter Four, there is a long tradition of making vegetarian meals a few

Holy Days and Special Occasions

times a week in many Mexican households. A traditional way of preparing them is in *tortas* or *tortitas* (patties). Some of the most traditional are *tortitas de papa* (potato patties), *de huauzontle* (huauzontle patties), *de coliflor* (cauliflower patties), *de espinaca* (spinach patties), *de ejote* (green bean patties), *de acelga* (chard), *de zanahoria* (carrot patties), and *de verduras* (mixed vegetables).

Any vegetable can be used, and the process for all of them is similar: the vegetables are cooked, formed into patties, sometimes with a piece of cheese in the middle, rolled in flour, covered in an egg batter, and fried in hot oil. Often they are covered in a tomato or a chile sauce and served with tortillas and beans on the side.

Another classic dish for Lent is *tortitas de camarón* (dried shrimp patties). In this case, the dried shrimp is pulverized (most markets in Mexico sell the shrimp already pulverized) and added to an egg batter; a spoon of the batter is fried in oil in the shape of a patty and cooked on both sides. Another traditional way of serving the *tortas de camarón* is with *romeritos* (seepweed), an herb resembling rosemary, but softer and smaller (hence the name, since *romerito* means little rosemary). *Romeritos* are often served during Lent, and they are cooked in water and then mixed with a *mole* sauce, small potatoes, and the shrimp patties.

Potatoes, a South American staple, came to Mexico early on and were immediately adopted and incorporated into the traditional cuisine. Many Mexican dishes are prepared with potatoes, and because of its versatility and because they are not too expensive, they are a favorite food for Lent. Potatoes are also a main ingredient in a variety of meatless dishes, mostly cooked in boiling water, mixed with other ingredients, and sautéed in oil. Some of the most traditional are *papas con acelgas* (potatoes and chard), *papas con espinacas* (potatoes and spinach), *papas con nopales* (potatoes and cactus), *papas con huevo* (potatoes and eggs), or *papas a la mexicana* (with tomatoes, onions, and jalapeño peppers). More elaborate potatoes dishes that are frequently served at this time of the year are *quesadillas de papa*, *enchiladas de papa y calabacita* (potato and zucchini enchiladas), *tamal de papa*, *flautas de papa* (rolled and fried corn tortillas filled with mashed potatoes), or a traditional *sopa de papa norteña* (northern potato soup), with potatoes, onions, tomatoes, strips of poblano or Anaheim chili peppers, cream, and cheese.

Capirotada is a Mexican bread pudding that is traditional for Lent. There are several variations of the dish, corresponding to the different regions of the country; however, the most common is prepared with slices of old bread fried in oil and covered in a *piloncillo* and cinnamon syrup, with peanuts, raisins, almonds and other dried fruits, and topped with cheese, either fresh or *añejo*. It can be prepared with milk (*capirotada de leche*) or just with the *piloncillo* syrup (*capirotada de agua*); sometimes anise seeds and clove are added to the syrup in addition to cinnamon; it is served warm or at room temperature. *Capirotada* is the only traditional dessert or sweet dish of the season, from Lent to Easter, included. However, there are other less known versions of the dish that are actually savory or semisweet, which include different ingredients like onions, tomatoes, even chicken in some parts of Oaxaca. They resemble the Spanish *capirotada*, which is always a savory dish prepared with old bread, garlic, onions, eggs, cheese, and sometimes game like deer or partridge.

The mandate of not eating meat allows for fish and seafood, which makes them very popular for Lent. Fish and seafood, however, are reserved most of the times for special days, like Good Friday or Maundy Thursday, when traditionally families get together to go to church and remember the Passion of Christ. Since fish and seafood can be very expensive in cities and towns far from the coast, some people prefer only vegetable dishes, since eating expensive fish and seafood may be contrary to the spirit of the holiday. So, if eating fish, simple dishes are preferred, mostly soups (*caldo de pescado*) prepared with smalls chunks of fish, including the head and tail, and some vegetables, as well as inexpensive fish fillets. *Pascua de resurrección* is the culmination of the festivities of Holy Week. It could be argued that this is the most important holiday of the Christian calendar, following St. Paul's proclamation that if Christ had not been resurrected, people's faith would be in vain (1 Corinthians 15:14). Surprisingly, however, in Mexico it is almost an ordinary day for most people. Besides going to Mass, Easter is basically just another Sunday. No feast, no glazed ham or eggs; no chocolate, no cakes, no buns. No hats, bunnies, chicks, or flowers. No Peeps!

For Mexicans, the big day of the celebration is not Easter, but Good Friday (*Viernes Santo*). It is the same for most Hispanic societies, where the mystery of Holy Week seems to be centered on the death of Jesus much more than on his resurrection. Consequently, there is no particular dish traditional for Easter. Most families would probably have a dinner like the customary Sunday family meals, which consist of large and more elaborate dishes than during the week with three or four courses, including fruit and dessert. Usually people eat meat on that day, since they have abstained from having any for several weeks (or at least several Fridays). These traditions are changing, and more and more people are familiar with other traditions and celebrations, and it is not uncommon to see advertisements in department stores, restaurants, bakeries, and even supermarkets for chocolates or decorations with the same motifs—chicks, bunnies, and flowers—of the celebration in other countries.

A relatively new, yet important, celebration in Mexico is Children's Day. This celebration started in 1925, when Mexico adopted the Geneva Declaration of the Rights of Children on April 30. Since then, the day has been devoted to making children feel special. Although not a statutory holiday and therefore children have to go to school, that day instead of classes, teachers organize festivals with music, plays, games, little toys, and lots of food. Most of the foods offered that day are sweets, cakes, chocolates, and candy, but some schools offer other types of food. A favorite treat for this day is *melón con nieve de limón* (half a cantaloupe with the seeds spooned out and a couple of scoops of lime ice placed inside). Some schools offer savory treats as well, mainly traditional snacks like *quesadillas*, *tostadas*, corn on the cob, and tacos. Some cities and towns also organize activities and festivals in the plazas and parks to celebrate children.

A bigger celebration happens 10 days later. On April 13, 1922, the daily *Excelsior* published on its front page a convocation to all sons and daughters to "extol in life or in memory that whom gave them life" on May 10. This initiative was devised by Rafael Alducin, the founder of the paper, following a celebration already popular in the United States. That year there was not a single person, reports *Excelsior* on May 11 who was not carrying flowers to honor their mothers. Ever since, the holiday has been celebrated in Mexico, and more and more it is celebrated by eating out. For breakfast, lunch, or dinner, it is one the most difficult days to find a table at a restaurant. Like many other celebrations in Mexico, Mother's Day is centered on food; however, there are not specific dishes that are traditional for this day. Even families who do not go out to a restaurant most likely organize a family *comida* or dinner at home to celebrate their mothers with lots of special dishes and sweets. If May 10 is Mother's Day in Mexico, regardless of what day of the week it is, Father's Day is always celebrated the third Sunday of June. There are some similarities between the two holidays, but the origin of Father's Day in Mexico is a little more obscure; it probably was created as a response to the popularity of Mother's Day. Food is also part of the celebration; it is common, for example, to have a *parrillada* or *bisteciza*, but, like in the case of Mother's Day, there is no particular dish that is traditional for Father's Day.

Between May and August, there are some popular holidays, mostly religious, that used to be celebrated with widespread festivals always involving traditional foods. Today they are less popular, but still celebrated in parts of the county. Some of the best known are Corpus Christi (also known in Mexico as the Day of the Mules because of an old legend about a miracle involving an incredulous man and a mule); the Feast of St. Peter and St. Paul, Ascension Sunday, Feast of the Holy Cross (the day when construction workers are celebrated often with tacos and beer); St. John the Baptist (a very ancient celebration related to the Summer Solstice, in which according to tradition it has to rain); or St. Cecilia, the patron saint of musicians, celebrated particularly by mariachi bands and other popular musical groups. However, after Mother's Day, the next big national holiday happens in September, on the eve of Mexican Independence Day, which is commemorated on September 16 usually with political speeches and a massive military parade through the streets of downtown Mexico City and other cities and towns. But the real popular festivities happened the night of September 15, while people in plazas, streets, and gardens all over Mexico await *El Grito*.

Early in the morning of September 16, 1810, the priest of the town of Dolores in the state of Guanajuato, Miguel Hidalgo y Costilla, rang the church bell calling people to Mass. Instead of Mass, however, he summoned all who responded to the call of the bell to revolt against the Spanish Crown. To the cry (*grito*) of "death to bad government," the process of independence from Spain had started. Today, every September 15 since the 1820s, an hour or so before midnight, the president of the nation tolls the same bell hanging in the central balcony of the National Palace and reenacts that cry of freedom, praising the country, the people, and the heroes of Mexico; meanwhile thousands of people repeat the cry in the Plaza de la Constitución, the main square in Mexico City. The ceremony of *El Grito* is followed by fireworks and different concerts of traditional and folk music, while the president, his family, and his cabinet offer a banquet to special guests and foreign dignitaries present at the ceremony.

The festivities the eve of Independence Day, however, are quite popular. Early in the day, as people gather in the plaza, waiting for the ceremony to start, musicians play popular songs while traditional dances are performed by groups from the different regions of the country. Street sellers offer souvenirs with patriotic motifs and countless food stands serve everything from *quesadillas*, tacos, *tamales*, or *elotes* to drinks, fruit salads, and ices. It is traditional to eat popular snacks or dishes on that day at home or even in some restaurants or bars. It is not uncommon for people to organize parties called *Noche Mexicana* (Mexican Night), where houses are decorated with Mexican flags and the national colors (green, white, and red), while attendees dress in traditional attire, dance to folk music, and eat typical dishes and drinks. The tradition is so popular now that most restaurants, hotels, clubs, and bars usually celebrate a *Noche Mexicana* on September 15 as a way of attracting customers. The origins of the *Noche*

Mexicana go back to 1921, when President Álvaro Obregón decided to celebrate the centennial of the Mexican independence, consummated in 1821, as a way of unifying the country after a bloody revolution. The new government wanted to portray itself as a government of the people. So, a *Noche Mexicana* was organized.

But *Noches Mexicanas* or street foods are not the only ways of celebrating the holiday; many families, even if they do not go to a plaza or a restaurant, may still celebrate *El Grito* by preparing traditional foods at home and getting together with friends and relatives. One of the most traditional dishes is *pozole*, a soup prepared with hominy and pork (or pork and chicken), cooked in a clear broth for *pozole blanco* (white *pozole*) or with dry chili peppers for *pozole rojo* (red *pozole*); these are the most traditional, but there is another version, with tomatillos and chili peppers, called *pozole verde* (green *pozole*). Traditionally pork is used to flavor the soup and for the meat, so many parts of the pork are used, including the head and feet, which once the soup is cooked are removed. Other meats, including fish or seafood, are common in coastal areas, like the traditional *pozole de camarón* (shrimp *pozole*) from Colima or *pozole con sardinas* (sardine *pozole*) from Oaxaca. Regardless of the type of *pozole*, the soup is usually served in a deep clay bowl called a *cajete* or *plato pozolero* (plate for *pozole*) and garnished with shredded cabbage or lettuces, sliced radishes, chopped onion, and oregano, as well as a spicy salsa and lime juice. All these ingredients are place on the table in small plates so people can add them to their plate as they like.

Pozole is popular for celebrations because it is an elaborate dish, very tasty, easy to serve and satisfying as a full meal. Other dishes popular for Independence Day, particularly for large crowds, are *tamales*, *tostadas*, and tacos. *Tostadas* are easy to prepare because the toppings are made ahead and the tostadas can be assembled right before serving, placing them in large trays, buffet style, so people can help themselves. *Tostadas* are flexible, since apart from two or three traditional recipes, you can use any topping you want. But the classics are *tosatadas de tinga* and *tostadas de carne*, which use shredded beef (ground beef is not very popular in Mexican cuisine), refried beans, lettuces, cheese, and cream. The *tostada* is prepared by spreading the refried beans on the toasted tortilla, then the beef, and shredded lettuces, crumbled fresh cheese, and Mexican or sour cream. Similar to *tostada* de carne is *tostada de salpicón*; a *salpicón* is a sort of salad made with shredded beef, chopped tomatoes, onions, and radishes, sometimes cucumbers, dressed with vinegar and oil. *Tostada de pata* is another traditional *tostada* popular in Mexico City and central Mexico. It is prepared with cow's feet cooked and chopped and dressed with vinegar and oregano. The feet are cut into small bite sizes and are spread over a toasted tortilla with shredded lettuce or cabbage, cream, crumbled cheese, and salsa. *Tostadas* are also common with fish and particularly with *ceviche*; they are prepared basically in the same way with the fish on the tortilla and similar toppings.

After Independence Day, the next big holiday in Mexico is what is known popularly as *Día de los Muertos*, or the Day of the Dead. In reality it is the Catholic feast of All Saints and All Souls, celebrated on November 1 and 2, respectively, at least since the ninth century CE. A holiday that in recent years has been considered unique to Mexico is really a holiday with direct connections to pagan Europe; supposedly of pre-Hispanic origin, it is more related to medieval traditions brought by the Spaniards to their colonies in the New World, according to historian Elsa Malvido ("Día de los Muertos no tiene origen preshispáncio"). Nonetheless, the European tradition did mix with and was complemented by some traditions of the Maya, Aztecs, and other American cultures, who like the Celts, Romans, and Greeks, included food in their funerary rituals. On November 1 and 2 people would go to churches to attend Mass. After that, they would go to the cemetery to clean the tombs of their loved ones, sometimes bringing food for the trip; a piece of bread or a sweet usually bought in the atrium of the church was sometimes placed on a table in memory of the departed loved ones. With time, this developed into home altars (*ofrendas* or offerings) in honor of the dead, adding more and more elements as time went by. As the tradition of the *ofrendas* grew, it became a tradition for most families.

However, in the second half of the twentieth century it became a public event promoted by the government as an authentic Mexican tradition. The transformation of this holiday continues today, and since 2016 a large parade is held in the streets of downtown Mexico City with gigantic papier mâché skulls, masks, people dressed up as skeletons and other related motifs. This parade was originally created for the opening scene of *Spectre*, the 2015 James Bond movie directed by Sam Mendes and filmed in Mexico City; after that it has been repeated every year by the people of the city. Mesoamerican or not, the holiday is celebrated today. And the real star of the celebration is food. The essence of the *ofrendas*, since its origins, has been food and drinks presented to dead relatives. They were typically family altars with candles; flowers; incense; seasonal and regional fruits like oranges, mandarins, *tejocotes*, guavas, or *jícamas*; sometimes drinks like tequila or *mezcal*; and, of course, *pan de muerto* (bread of the dead)—a round loaf of sweet bread with some decorations resembling bones and usually covered with sugar or sesame seeds.

This tradition continues, and depending on the region or the family tradition, some special dishes could be prepared for the *ofrenda*, such as turkey or chicken in *mole*, *tamales*, or some other foods, as well as desserts like *camote* (sweet potato) or *calabaza* (pumpkin) in a *piloncillo* syrup. The *calabaza en dulce, calabaza de todos los santos, calabaza en piloncillo, calabaza en conserva,* or *calabaza en tacha* are some of the names given to the most traditional dessert associated with *Día de los Muertos*. The pumpkin could be cut in big chunks and cooked in a syrup of water, *piloncillo*, and cinnamon or used whole with little holes all over it and covered it in the syrup to cook there. Sometimes other spices like anise, clove, or star anise are added, as well as fruits like guavas, oranges, and *tejocotes*. Contemporary chefs have tried to update this dessert by turning it into cheesecake and other elaborate concoctions with exotic ingredients and techniques. But the traditional, and extremely simple way of cooking pumpkin in *piloncillo* and cinnamon remains a favorite for most Mexicans.

Prepared in a similar way and also traditional for *Día de los Muertos*, *camote en dulce* is a traditional sweet dish that, like *calabaza en piloncillo*, is eaten as a dessert, as a snack, or for breakfast with milk. The most common way of making this dish is by washing the *camotes* (sweet potatoes) and cutting them in big chunks, then cooking them in a syrup of water, *piloncillo*, and cinnamon, with some other spices or fruits added, depending on the region. Other sweets popular for this holiday are sugar skulls, a tradition that goes back, according to some, to colonial times, but that most likely is a century or so old; the sweet is made with sugar, lime juice, and water cooked into a thick syrup and then molded into skulls of different sizes; once dried, it hardens and can be decorated with sugar paste of different colors. Often the name of a loved one is written on the top of the skull; these candies are used for *ofrendas* or as presents for friends and relatives. Although the traditional ones are made with sugar, in the past few decades, they have also been made with chocolate.

The year ends with what Mexicans called traditionally the *fiestas decembrinas* or December holidays, also known as *fiestas de fin de año*, festivities of the end of the year. The first big celebration of the month is the Feast of Our Lady of Guadalupe, a commemoration of the apparition of the Virgin Mary to an Indian, Saint Juan Diego, in 1531, who promised him to help all Mexicans if they would build her a temple right on that spot. Today the Basilica of Our Lady of Guadalupe is the most visited Catholic church in the world, receiving pilgrims all year round, but particularly on and around December 12. Although there is not a traditional food associated with the holiday, being an eminently popular holiday and attracting tens of thousands of pilgrims, it is a holiday full of the smells and the flavors of all the popular street dishes sold on the streets adjacent to the Basilica, as well as the routes most pilgrims take to the Basilica; the same happens in thousands of churches all over the country. Even entire blocks gather to hear a Mass and sing religious hymns to the images of the Virgin Mary, having a feast afterwards often with *tamales* and *atole*.

December 12 is also the unofficial start of the Christmas holiday since only four days later *Las Posadas* commence. *Las Posadas* mark officially the start of the Christmas holiday in Mexico. From December 16 until Christmas Eve, people get together every day to sing carols, drink punch, eat sweets and other foods, and break piñatas full of fruits like oranges, apples, peanuts, sweet limes, *jícamas*, *tejocotes*, sugarcane, and sometimes a traditional candy called *colación*. Originally a religious ritual, the *Posadas* included processions with candles carrying an image of Mary and Joseph and praying and singing carols, after which everybody sings and is offered food and drinks, which are enjoyed while children go outside to break a piñata. In most parts of Mexico, this is the only time when piñatas are broken. The food offered traditionally is fruits and candies, as well as *ponche de navidad*, a punch made with seasonal fruits, spices, *piloncillo*, and boosted with rum or tequila. The celebration in recent times, however, although the holiday still maintains some of the original elements, it has evolved into a popular festivity, and *posada* is the term used for most Christmas parties.

The *posadas* end on December 24, Christmas Eve. This is actually the main celebration of the season. More than Christmas Day, it is the eve of the feast what most people celebrate. In the past, families would go to midnight Mass, called *misa de gallo* (or rooster Mass), and after that, or right before it, they would have a large and special dinner, *la cena de noche buena* (the dinner of the good night). To make it easier for people to attend Mass and still celebrate a *cena* with family, the time of the Mass has changed, and today it is celebrated earlier than midnight. The celebration is a big deal, and people put on their best clothes and prepare a special dinner with a variety of dishes. Although there are some dishes that are traditional, the main rule is that it has to be a special meal with more than one special dish. One of the most traditional dishes for Christmas is turkey. Similarly to the way it is prepared in the United States, Christmas turkey in Mexico is roasted whole with a stuffing of bread, spices, and fruits or with a special *picadillo*. Often it is also seasoned with spices and even some dry chili peppers. Turkey prepared this way is called *pavo*. This *pavo* is served with several side dishes, particularly potatoes, a salad called *ensalada rusa* (Russian salad), which is prepared with vegetables potatoes, onions, carrots, peas, sometimes apples, and even raisins mixed, with

Holy Days and Special Occasions

mayonnaise. Other similar salads include apple and cabbage salad, green beans and potatoes salad, or simply a beet salad. Other vegetables are also common as a side dish for the *pavo*; however, most people prefer one of the mentioned salads.

Also traditional for Christmas is *bacalao a la vizcaína* (cod fish). Although the name implies that it is cooked Biscay style, it is really a Mexican dish; this is why also some people prefer to call it *bacalao a la mexicana*. The dish is prepared with dry, salted cod fish covered in water and soaked for a day, changing the water a few times to get rid of the salt; once the fish has rehydrated and softened, it is rinsed and shredded. A sauce is prepared with roasted tomatoes, garlic, onion, and parsley sautéed in olive oil. The sauce is left to simmer for a few minutes, then sliced olives, capers, raisins, cubed potatoes, and roasted peppers are added. Finally, the cod fish is simmered with the vegetables for a few more minutes. It is usually served in a large plate decorated with pickled *chiles güeros* (small, yellow peppers) and chopped parsley, as well as slices of bread or toasted corn tortillas. Equally traditional is *romeritos* or *romeritos con tortas de camarón*, a dish common for Lent. Usually, particularly if the entire family gets together, more than one dish is served during *la cena de Navidad*, with dishes like *pozole*, special stews, or a roast like *pierna de cerdo adobada* (leg of pork in adobo sauce), a pork loin, or a rack of pork. Less traditional, but also common are lamb, veal, or even goat; chicken cooked in special ways, with ingredients that are not ordinary, like mushrooms, wine, or dried fruits is also served for *la cena de Nvidad*.

Regardless of how fancy or humble the main dishes are, two dishes are almost always present: *ensalada de nochebuena* and *ponche de Navidad*. The *ponche* is traditional during the whole season, and particularly for posadas and Christmas Eve. The *ensalada de nochebuena* (Christmas salad) is also known as *ensalada de betabel* (beet salad), since this is the main ingredient. The salad is a combination of a variety of fruits like oranges, sweet limes, apples, *jícama*, mandarins, sugarcane, and peanuts. The beets are cooked in water and sugar; once they are done they are cooled and cut in cubes; the other fruits are also cut in bite-size pieces and all the ingredients, except the peanuts, are placed in a bowl. They are mixed together with some of the water in which the beets were cooked, sometimes combined with orange juice. It is garnished with the peanuts and allowed to rest for several hours before serving. The *cena de nochebuena* generally ends with the salad or with fresh fruit in lieu of dessert. However, some families do include desserts as part of their dinner, and one of the most traditionally desserts is *buñuelos*.

Buñuelos are discs of fried dough made with flour, lard, and sugar; usually very light and crisp, the size of a corn tortilla; they are served covered in sugar, a *piloncillo* syrup, or sometimes honey; there are other variations of *buñuelos*, including some balls similar to the beignets of New Orleans. Other conventional desserts could be served during the *cena de nochebuena*, like cakes, candied fruits, *flan*, jams and cheese, custards, sweets, chocolates, or cookies, depending on the region or, most likely, the family traditions. The celebration of the New Year in Mexico begins the year before, on December 31, with an elaborate dinner. *La cena de año nuevo* is traditionally very similar to *la cena de Navidad*; the dishes described as customary for Christmas are the same for New Year's, alternating between holidays and from year to year with very little variations. For example, the fruits traditional of *las posadas*, *jícamas*, *tejocotes*, sweet limes, or peanuts are not that traditional past December 25; instead, pears, oranges, and particularly grapes become the centerpiece for the New Year's feast. New Year's is more of a secular holiday, and therefore dancing and heavy drinking are more probable than in Christmas.

The holidays described here are important not only for reinforcing communal believes and traditions centering on food but also because they are central elements of the formation of a national identity. To end this chapter, however, it is important to mention holidays that although important from a cultural perspective, belong more to the private sphere, marking important events in the life of individuals. Of these celebrations, the first one is *bautizo* (christening). An important holiday, not only from a religious perspective but social as well, since it cements one of the most enduring relationships outside the family, *compadrazgo* (the relationship between the father and godfather of a child). Similar to *bautizo* is confirmation, a ritual that in Mexico happened surprisingly early in a child's life until recently, followed by first communion, which can be taken when a child reaches nine years of age.

These are the first three major events in a person's life in Mexico, since the country remains traditionally and culturally Roman Catholic, and there are always big celebrations, with a traditional *comida*. The most common dishes are the traditional party dishes in Mexican cuisine: *pozole*, *moles*, and particularly *carnitas*, *birria*, or *barbacoa*. *Barbacoa* is the name of a dish, but really refers to a process of cooking meat, traditionally goat or lamb, in a hole dug in the ground, where burning wood or coals have been placed at the bottom, and where the meat, wrapped in maguey leaves, is placed on bricks or rocks, then covered with more coals and the soil. The meat is left there to slowly cook overnight. Although lamb and goat are the traditional meats used for the dish, pork, beef, or even chicken

Holy Days and Special Occasions

could also be used. A very similar dish, *birria* was originally cooked like *barbacoa*; however, today is made in large pots, sometimes sealed with corn dough, that allow the meat to cooked in its own juices, slowly, for several hours. Like *barbacoa*, *birria* could be made with beef and pork, as well as other meats including chicken and even fish; it is one of the most traditional dishes from the state of Jalisco, but it is known all over the country.

Carnitas (literally "little meats") is pork meat cooked in the lard of the pig in a large caldron, usually made of copper, with oranges, beer, brandy or other liquor, until it is soft in the inside and crisp in the outside. For this dish all the parts of the pig are used and served separately or mixed. Like *barbacoa* and *birria*, authentic *carnitas* are best prepared by someone who specializes in preparing the dish with the traditional methods, using the traditional utensils and techniques. Some lighter versions of these three dishes can be prepared at home for special meals or more family-oriented celebrations, for example, birthdays. In fact, birthdays are the next in this list of personal celebrations. Birthdays are always big events in most Mexicans households. All birthdays are celebrated similarly, with a big family meal with traditional dishes and seldom a cake. Children's birthdays always include a cake, either bought at the local bakery or a *rosca* (Bundt cake) made at home. Recently, more and more people opt for meeting at a restaurant to celebrate a birthday, but even in those cases, often there is a special dish prepared at home for those unexpected guests that may come to wish people a happy birthday.

A very particular celebration related to birthdays is the celebration of a girl's birthday when she turns 15 years old. The *fiesta de XV años* is a tradition in many Mexican families and it is celebrated with a Mass, a banquet, and a choreographed dance with the *quinceañera* (the birthday girl). The food offered at this celebration is, particularly if the party is at home, the same party foods mentioned earlier in the chapter. Other family celebrations, usually including a big meal at home, occur when a young man or woman reaches benchmarks of their education, starting with *salida de sexto* (or finishing sixth grade), *salida de la secundaria* (finishing secondary school), or *salida de preparatoria o bachilleres* (finishing the school that prepares students to attend college). After *preparatoria*, the parties tend to be more organized and include eating and dancing at a venue selected and paid by the students and their families. Another important celebration is a wedding. Until recently, it was not unusual to celebrate a wedding with a large party organized in the house of either the groom or the bride. The traditional dish at the center of the banquet was almost always *mole*, particularly the *mole poblano*.

Mole is without a doubt the most iconic Mexican dish. According to tradition, the sauce was invented by a nun who wanted to impress the viceroy of New Spain when he visited their convent; other versions, said *mole* was invented when a nun, in rush to finish the dish before the viceroy's visit, accidently spilled all the spices in the rack over the sauce she was preparing; with no time to make the sauce again, she served it to the viceroy as it was, who loved it. There is no historic basis for these legends, and there are endless variations for the dish depending on the region, town, neighborhood, and even family, but they are illustrative of the love for the dish and the ways of explaining it. The *mole* described by the legends is *mole poblano*, a sauce with lots of ingredients including different chili peppers, chocolate, peanuts, almonds, pecans or walnuts, pumpkin seeds, sesame seeds, raisins, garlic, onion, and served with turkey, sprinkled with sesame seeds. Rice and tortillas are served alongside the *mole*. *Mole* and turkey in Mexican slang stand, even today, for a celebration.

> Another legend about the creation of *mole* attributes it to San Pascual Bailón, a Franciscan monk, considered the patron saint of cooks, who needed to make a special dinner for the Archbishop of Puebla visiting his convent. Under pressure to impress the prelate, he was so nervous that he tripped and spilled all the spices he was putting away into the pan with the dish he was making. With no time to make another dish, he served this sauce to the bishop, who loved it. In truth, Pascual Bailón lived and died in Spain and never visited Mexico.

Rosca de Reyes (Three Kings' Cake)

Yield: Serves 10 to 12

For the cake
1 envelope dry active yeast
½ cup warm water
3½ cups all-purpose flour
1 cup sugar
¼ tsp salt
3 large eggs
3 egg yolks mixed with 2 tablespoons of milk
1½ tablespoons orange extract [I used orange liquor: orange liquor/
   1 teaspoon of orange blossom essence (optional)]
1½ sticks of butter (12 tablespoons), softened
The zest of 1 medium orange

For the toppings
¾ cup flour
½ cup powdered sugar
1 egg yolk
6 tablespoons margarine
Assorted dry or candied fruits
6 to 8 maraschino cherries

Equipment: electric mixer, mixing bowls, measuring cups, measuring spoons, spatula, zester, baking sheet, 2 ceramic or heat-resistant plastic baby Jesus figurines

1. Dissolve the yeast in the warm water and let sit for 5 to 10 minutes.
2. Add ½ cup of flour and mix well; cover with plastic and let rest while preparing the rest of the ingredients.
3. Put 3½ cups of all-purpose flour, 1 cup of sugar, ¼ tsp of salt, 3 large eggs, 3 egg yolks mixed with 2 tablespoons of milk, 1½ tablespoons of orange extract (I used orange liquor), 1½ sticks of softened butter, and the orange zest in a large bowl and mix well.
4. Add the yeast mixture to all the ingredients and combine until incorporated.
5. Knead the dough for 20 minutes on a hard surface sprinkled with flour, working it uniformly in folding movements. Place the dough in a greased bowl and cover with plastic. Let rest for 1½ hours.

6. Take the dough out of the bowl and roll and shape as an oval on a hard surface spread with flour. Insert the figurines in the dough, hiding them in two extremes of the oval.
7. Prepare the sugar toppings by combining ¾ cup of flour, ½ cup of powdered sugar, 1 egg yolk, and 6 tablespoons of margarine; mix all ingredients well and make a paste. Roll the paste into a rectangular sheet of about ½-inch thickness and cut it into 4 large ribbons or 8 smaller ribbons.
8. Decorate the oval of dough with the ribbons of sugar and flour paste, spaced out symmetrically though the entire oval; place the cherries and pieces of candied fruits all over, simulating colorful jewels (you can substitute the candied fruits with any fruits in syrup.
9. Brush the oval of dough with an egg and bake in a preheated oven at 375 degrees for 20 to 25 minutes.

To serve, let it cool down and slice in individual portions; serve with hot chocolate or atole. Keep in mind, and remind your guests, that here are hidden figurines in the rosca.

Tamales de Dulce (Sweet Tamales)

Yield: Makes 12 tamales

¾ cup of lard or vegetable shortening
½ cup sugar
2¼ cups masa harina
1½ teaspoon baking powder
½ cup raisins
2 cup warm water
8 to 10 drops red food coloring
12 corn husks, soaked

Equipment: a large pot, a steamer basket, mixer, mixing bowls, mixing spoon, measuring spoons, measuring cups

1. Combine the masa harina and water in a large bowl and mix well to form a soft dough. Add more or less water to obtain the dough.
2. In a mixer beat the lard with baking powder until it is white and fluffy; add sugar and continue beating until it is all incorporated.
3. Add the dough to the mixer and beat until it acquires a light consistency; add the food coloring. To know if the dough is ready, drop a small ball into a glass of water, if it floats, it is ready, if it sinks to the bottom, continue beating. When it is ready, add the raisins and incorporate into the batter.
4. Spread about 3 tablespoons of dough in a corn husk and wrap the *tamale*, overlapping the ends then folding it in half to close. Tie the *tamale* if you want with strips of corn husk. Do the same until you run out of dough.
5. Place the steamer basket in the large pot and add enough water to reach the bottom of the basket. Place the *tamales* in the steamer, standing up, cover the pot with a lid, making sure it is tight; cover the pot first with aluminum foil if needed.
6. Steam the *tamales* until done, about 1 hour or until the husks separate easily from the tamale. *Make sure the water does not run out, and if it does add more.*

To serve, place the tamales on a large serving plate and place in the center of the table so people can help themselves; accompany with atole or hot chocolate. These tamales can also be made with blackberries or strawberries instead of raisins; just add generous amounts of chopped berries when spreading the dough on the husk.

Pozole de Camarón (Shrimp *Pozole*)

Yield: Serves 12

4 pounds hominy, precooked
2 medium onions, halved
2 heads garlic
2 teaspoons dry shrimp powder
3 pounds fresh shrimp
1 pounds dry shrimp
10 guajillo peppers, seeded
3 ancho peppers, seeded
2 tablespoon vegetable oil
2 teaspoons Mexican dry oregano, plus more to serve
1 teaspoon cumin
Salt to taste
Cabbage, shredded
Sliced radishes
Limes cut in wages

Equipment: a large pot, a medium pot, *comal* or cast-iron griddle, small pot, blender, strainer, deep sauté pan

1. Place the hominy, one halved onion, one whole head of garlic, and 4 quarts of water in a large pot. Bring to a boil, add dry powdered shrimp, reduce heat, and simmer until the grains of hominy open.
2. While hominy is simmering, peel, devein, and clean the shrimp and reserve heads and tails.
3. Place the dry shrimp with the heads and tails of fresh shrimp, the other halved onion, and the remaining head of garlic in a medium pot. Add 2 quarts of water. Bring to a boil, reduce heat to medium low, and simmer for about 20 minutes. Let cool.
4. In a *comal* or cast-iron griddle roast the guajillo and ancho peppers until fragrant and slightly toasted. Be careful not to burn them or they will become bitter. Place peppers in a small pot with enough water to cover them and bring to a boil. Turn heat off and leave them in the water until they are soft, about 5 minutes. Let them cool.
5. Transfer the dry shrimp to a blender with the guajillo and ancho peppers, the water where they rehydrate, 2 teaspoons of oregano, and the cumin; blend until smooth.
6. In a deep pan heat the oil and strain the contents of the blender; sauté for a few minutes until it forms a thick sauce.

7. Add the sauce to the large pot with the hominy; bring to a boil, reduce the heat and let simmer for a few minutes, letting all the flavors mix. Season with salt, if needed.
8. Turn the heat off and add the fresh shrimp, letting them cook with the heat of the *pozole* for 5 minutes.

To serve, place a generous portion in a deep bowl or a cajete (Mexican clay bowl); place serving bowls with shredded cabbage, sliced radishes, lime wedges, and oregano on the table so people can help themselves.

Birria Tatemada Estilo Jalisco
(Slow Cooked Beef Jalisco Style)

Yield: Serves 6 to 8

3 pounds beef short rib
1 pound beef shank
2 large ancho chili peppers
4 large guajillo chili peppers
5 garlic cloves
4 cloves
1 teaspoon cumin seeds
10 whole black peppers
1 tablespoon oregano
1 cinnamon stick
1 medium white onion
½ cup white vinegar
Salt to taste
3 medium tomatoes
4 *chile de árbol* peppers
1 bunch cilantro
2 limes, quartered

Equipment: large baking dish, tin foil, *comal* or griddle, small pot, measuring spoons, mixing spoon

1. Seed chili peppers and toast them in a *comal* or griddle for only a couple of minutes on both sides, just until fragrant (do not burn them). Place peppers in a pot with boiling water and soak them for 15 minutes.
2. Place chili peppers, garlic, cloves, cumin seeds, black peppers, oregano, cinnamon stick, ½ onion, and vinegar in a blender. Blend until all the ingredients form a silky paste (add some of the water from the chili peppers if necessary, one tablespoon at a time, just enough to help the blender run smoothly). Season with salt to taste.
3. Place meat in a large baking dish and cover with the chili pepper mix. Cover with foil and refrigerate for several hours or overnight.
4. Preheat oven at 325 degrees and cook the meat, covered with the foil, for about 5 hours or until the meat is very tender. Check meat every ½ hour and baste it with the juices.

Holy Days and Special Occasions 143

5. Once the meat is done, prepare a salsa by roasting the tomatoes and *chile de árbol* peppers in a *comal* or griddle, then blend them with 1 cup of the meat juices.

Serve a generous amount of meat in a plate; top it with chopped white onion and cilantro. Accompany with warm corn tortillas, lime wedges, and the chile de árbol *salsa.*

Ponche de Navidad (Christmas Punch)

Yield: Serves 12

6 gallons water
1 cup dry hibiscus flowers
½ pound *piloncillo*, chopped
3 cinnamon sticks
12 prunes
6 guavas
6 tamarind pods
2 apples
12 *tejocotes*
3 chunks of sugarcane stalk of about 5 inches each
Rum or tequila, optional

Equipment: Large pot, mixing spoons

1. Bring water to boil in a large pot. Add the hibiscus flower and boil for 10 minutes.
2. Fish the hibiscus flower out of the pot and add the cinnamon and the *piloncillo*. Simmer for 10 minutes or until the *piloncillo* dissolves.
3. Meanwhile, prepare the fruit. Wash and rinse all the fruits, then quarter the guavas, peel the tamarind pods, cube the apples, and cut the sugarcane stalk into 3 or 4 sticks for each chunk.
4. Add the fruit to the pot, starting with the sugarcane and the tamarind and let it simmer; after a few minutes, add the *tejocotes* and apples, let them simmer for a few minutes; add the prunes and guava and cook the fruit for about 30 to 45 minutes or until fruit is soft and the flavors are combined.

To serve, pour the punch in individual clay cups (jarritos), making sure you include pieces of all the fruits and a stick of sugarcane. Add a splash of rum or tequila to spike the punch if you want or enjoy it by itself.

CHAPTER EIGHT

Street Food and Snacks

Mexico has a long tradition of eating out; for generations, eating out meant mostly eating in *puestos* (stands) of pretty much any food imaginable. From a *puesto de tacos, de carnitas, de barbacoa, de quesadillas, de sopes, de tortas* to a *puesto de jugos, de atole* or *tamales* these establishments can be found in any city, town, or village in the nation. As their name indicates, each *puesto* specializes in one or maybe two items, and they could range from an improvised table and folding chairs with a grill, outside of a house, to metal stands fixed to the ground at a corner, or carts circulating the streets. Eating in markets is also traditional, and most markets have a section dedicated to *cocinas* (food stands). Street food is omnipresent in Mexico and follows the daily routine of the people, from breakfast to lunch to dinner. But many *puestos* are open all day selling food for after school, for coffee breaks, or for whenever the cravings hit. In fact, the generic name given to foods you can buy on the street in Mexico is *antojitos* (from *antojar*, to crave). Weekends and evenings are often days for families, couples, or groups of friends to gather in parks and plazas, particularly in smaller cities and towns, where they can sit on a bench, watch people, and enjoy some snacks.

Likewise, national and popular holidays see a proliferation of seasonal *puestos* that accompany whatever festivities people celebrate, with foods associated with the occasion. Traditionally, these *puestos* appear in popular markets called *romerías* that offer merchandise and food related to the most traditional holidays: Independence Day (from the end of August through September 16), *Día de Muertos* (from mid-October through November 3), and Christmas and Three Kings' Day (from mid-November through January 7). Other *romerías* may also be popular in different towns, cities, or neighborhoods, depending on local traditions and civic or religious celebrations particularly important for them; most recently there has been *romerías* for celebrations introduced in the country in recent decades, like Valentine's Day or Mother's Day. State and regional fairs centered on showcasing the goods produced by a region are also often centered on food, since many of these events are dedicated to agricultural or gastronomic products, like *feria del mole*, *feria de la piña*, *feria del maíz*, or *feria del nopal*. Some of these festivals celebrate beverages, rather than food, like *feria del tequila*, *feria del mezcal*, or *feria del pulque*, and some combine gastronomy and imbibing, like Guanajuato's *feria del pulque y las carnitas*.

For generations, Mexicans have loved eating out, particularly on the street; street food is a very popular tradition in the country because it is an inexpensive and convenient way of eating in busy urban centers, but also because it is a way of socializing that goes back to colonial times and even before, to the time before the arrival of the Europeans. When Cortés and his men entered the capital of the Aztec Empire, they marveled at the size and abundance of the products sold in markets, including all sorts of prepared food. Today, according to a poll conducted by Nielsen of Mexico, 40 percent of Mexicans eat out regularly and 30 percent of the interviewed people admitted that they enjoy eating on the street. So, every morning it is common to see, on any given weekday, large numbers of people gathering around food stands on street corners or outside subway stations in Mexico City, grabbing a quick bite to eat on their way to work. One of the most popular items for breakfast is *tamales*, which can be served straight out of the special pot in which they were steamed and are kept warm, wrapped in a brown piece of paper, or can also be fried in oil for a few minutes, making them crunchy in the outside and soft in the inside, served in paper or Styrofoam plates sometimes topped with sour cream. *Tamales* are often sold accompanied with a cup of *atole* or *champurrado*. *Tamal* is also the main ingredient in the *guajolota* (female turkey), a monstrous sandwich made with the *tamal* inside a piece of bread, invented in Mexico City that recently has gain mythological status. Another version is the *guajolote* (male turkey), invented in the city of Tulancingo in the state of Hidalgo, which is a sandwich made with an enchilada and refried beans, instead of the *tamal*.

Popular for breakfast as well, and a food easy to find on the street, is coffee and sweet bread; often this coffee is *café de olla*, which is sweetened with *piloncillo* and spiced with cinnamon. The bread is usually a piece of traditional Mexican sweet bread popular all over the country, like *conchas*, *cuernos*, *chilindrinas*, *panqués*, or *piedras*. Less common but still visible in some cities and towns is pancakes. Hotcakes, as they are called in Mexico, are a traditional snack, sometimes sold in the evenings in mobile carts topped with honey, condensed milk, or, more traditionally, *cajeta*, Mexican goat milk caramel. However, more and more they can be seen also in the mornings offering their products for breakfast. Although not very common, healthier or specialized breakfast foods are also visible, like gourmet coffee or vegan breads as well as other options such as yogurt and fruit, *avena de sabores* (flavored oatmeal drinks), porridge, or *jugos* and *licuados de frutas*. In fact, *juguerías* (juice bars) are an institution in Mexico, but traditional *puestos de jugos* for breakfast are often improvised and specialize on orange juice. Orange juice is considered a nutritious way of starting the day, so it is easy to find street stands (often just a table and a juicer) selling freshly squeezed orange juice; to make it even more substantial, they often are served with one or two raw eggs. An even more "nutritious" beverage is prepared with the juice, the eggs, a little vanilla, and a shot of *jerez* (sherry); this drink called *polla* is also popular for breakfast.

A traditional Mexican breakfast is often more than just coffee and bread; and when people are not in a hurry, it is an elaborate affair that includes eggs, tortillas, beans, salsas, often fruit and juices, as well as coffee and bread. That is why, perhaps, when in a hurry, many people still try to eat something more substantial. So, another traditional breakfast one can find on the street is *sopes, huaraches, memelas, tlacoyos,* or *gorditas*—commonly called *garnachas*. Although their names are very different, all these foods are variations of the same basic principle: a soft shell or boat of various forms and sizes made with corn dough (*masa*), and stuffed or topped with different ingredients. *Sopes* are thick, round tortillas cooked in little oil, usually freshly made when ordered; once cooked, a bean paste is spread on the *sope*, followed by a good amount of salsa, shredded lettuce, onion, and crumbled fresh cheese. This is the classic *sope*, but sometimes chicken, *chorizo*, or grilled beef can be added; *huaraches* (named after the traditional Mexican sandals) are similar to *sopes*, except that they are bigger, thinner and more often than not topped with a meat cooked in different sauces, from chicken and pork, to steak, *longaniza* or *chorizo*; for breakfast, however, the topping is traditionally one or two eggs.

Memelas are also traditional for breakfast and sometimes are confused with *quesadillas*; they are long, thin tortillas folded in half and stuffed with cheese, meats, or vegetables, often topped with shredded lettuce and grated cheese. *Tlacoyos*, on the contrary, are thick elongated or diamond-shape small cakes made usually with blue corn masa and filled with a paste of fava beans, split peas, or beans; they are cooked on a *comal* and then topped with salsa, crumbled cheese, and sometimes *nopales*. Like *tlacoyos, gorditas* (literally fatties) are round, thick cakes made with regular masa and filled with *chicharrón prensado* (pressed pork with skin) or a bean paste. They are cooked on a *comal* with little lard or oil and once they are done, they are open and filled with shredded cabbage, salsa, and crumbled fresh cheese. These foods are familiar to most Mexicans all around the country with small variations; *gorditas* are particularly popular and the variations could be significant. There are sweet and sour *gorditas*; *gorditas* made with corn or with flour; filled with meats, herbs, vegetables, stews, or cheese. The sweet *gorditas* are often made with flour, eggs, milk, *piloncillo*, cinnamon, or cream. The combinations are many, depending on the region and the local ingredients and traditions.

As mentioned before, the main meal of the day in Mexico is *la comida*, and it is served around two in the afternoon. Since most people have an hour or so to eat at work, the majority of Mexicans go to a *cocina económica* that offers *comida corrida*, a restaurant, or even a *cocina de mercado*—which is not really eating on the street. However, a large number of people rely on *puestos de comida*, particularly if they have little time for lunch or there are no markets or *cocinas* near the place where they work. Some of the foods described before could also be sold for lunch, particularly *gorditas* and *huaraches*; however, *quesadillas* are also popular. Mexican *quesadillas* are very different from those consumed in the United States. To start, *quesadillas* are made with corn tortillas, and contrary to what the name proclaims, they are not made only or exclusively with cheese. In fact, in Mexico the redundancy of ordering a cheese *quesadilla* makes sense, since cheese is just one of the many possible fillings. Other options are chicken, *chorizo*, mushrooms, zucchini blossoms, pressed pork, *cuitlacoche* (corn smut), or even potatoes. There are two main types of *quesadillas*, one is made with the masa shaped into a regular tortilla, stuffed with the filling of choice, folded, sealed, and fried in abundant oil. The other follows the same process, except that instead of frying the quesadilla, it is cooked on a *comal* with very little oil or lard.

No other street food is more traditional and beloved than *tacos*. *Taquerías* are ubiquitous in the nation and are emblematic of Mexico within as well as abroad, so much so that hundreds of books are dedicated to the food, and even Netflix has created a documentary called *Las crónicas del taco* (*Taco Chronicles*, 2019). But tacos are generally consumed in the evening, for dinner or as an evening or late snack. Some *taquerías*, however, open "early" so they can start serving people a late lunch in preparation for the night crowds. There are many types of tacos—and incidentally none of them is in a hard shell or uses ground beef. But there are two types of tacos that are almost exclusively for lunch—*tacos de guisado* and *tacos de canasta*. These tacos do not have the same appeal that the traditional tacos have, but they are also an institution, particularly for a quick *comida* on the go. The humblest of them is *tacos de canasta*; these tacos are often sold in the late morning or early afternoon and come prepared already,

Street Food and Snacks

> Tacos are the quintessential Mexican street food—some may say the quintessential Mexican food. No trip to Mexico City is complete without trying the famous *tacos al pastor* (tacos shepherd style); however, these tacos are actually a Mexican adaptation of shawarma, the Middle Eastern dish brought to Mexico by Lebanese immigrants and adapted to the local taste. Instead of lamb, for example, it is slices of pork stacked in in the shape of a *trompo* (spinning top), marinated in local spices, and roasted slowly in a revolving spit; the meat, thinly sliced, is served in a tortilla with grilled pineapple.

assembled inside a big wicker basket (hence the name, since *canasta* means "basket" in Spanish) covered with brown paper and a big sheet of blue plastic; then a kitchen towel is put over the tacos to keep them warm.

They are very simple, made with a folded tortilla and a single filling. Once prepared, the tacos are place in the basket in layers until it is full and hot oil or a thick sauce is poured over them. This method adds extra flavor and keeps them warm for hours; also, it keeps them soft, without becoming mushy. There are three traditional fillings: potatoes and chorizo, refried beans, and *chicharrón* in green sauce. In recent years, some innovators have tried to "improve" the street food culture in Mexico with variations of its traditional staples, and the *tacos de canasta* are no exception. Recently, more and more vendors are seen on the streets of many cities with untraditional variations of *tacos de canasta*, like sausage, *cochinita pibil*, or even regional delicacies, or gourmet tacos, like the ones a famous transgender woman, Lady Tacos de Canasta, offers through the streets of Mexico City with ancient ingredients from her native Oaxaca, iguana in green sauce, *chapulines* (grasshoppers), and *al pastor*. Tacos de canasta are accompanied always by a salsa, red or green, but the green traditionally has avocado blended in it, a salsa commonly known as *guacamole taquero*.

Like *tacos de canasta*, *tacos de guisado* are corn tortillas filled with different stews; usually these stews are presented in big clay pots in fixed stands or markets, and people can choose the fillings they want for their tacos. The *tacos de gusido* are traditional for *la comida*, and the fillings are limitless. Some of the most traditional are *chicharrón*, pork, or chicken in green sauce, beef or ribs in *pasilla* sauce, chicken in pumpkin seed sauce, *chiles rellenos*, chicken in *mole* sauce, Mexican rice and beans, *papas con longaniza*, squash in tomato sauce, beef tongue in sauce, *picadillo*, *rajas con crema* (strips of poblano peppers cooked with onions and sour cream), even liver with onions, and blood sausage. The *tacos de guisado* are sometimes considered lesser *tacos*; however, they are a wonderful encyclopedia of Mexican cuisine because the *guisados* represent the most important and beloved dishes from all over the nation, in smaller quantities and served in a tortilla. So when eating *tacos de guisado*, you could actually sample the diversity of Mexican food in one meal. They are the closest a Mexican can get to home cooking away from home. In fact, when you visit a Mexican home and they invite you *un taco*, it does not mean is Tuesday or that they are having tacos for dinner; it only means that they are offering you something to eat, most likely a tortilla with some of the food prepared for the *comida* or *cena* that day.

The most traditional tacos, the ones that have jumped to international fame, are considered almost exclusively a night affair. These tacos are so popular that hundreds of books have been written in English and Spanish about this food, including *The Taco Tuesday Cookbook*, *Taco! Taco! Taco!: The Ultimate Taco Cookbook*, and *Tacos: 75 Authentic and Inspired Recipes*, as well as others with such provocative titles as *Tacos: Recipes and Provocations*, *Guerrilla Tacos*, *Love and Tacos* and the wacky *Dragons Love Tacos*, *The Taco Cleanse*, and the deliciously (pun intended) obvious *Tacopedia*. Tacos at their most essential are elegant and delicious; they combine the perfect balance of flavors of a few, simple ingredients, usually a grilled meat, a small corn tortilla, chopped onions and perhaps a little bit of cilantro, as well as a few drops of lime juice, and, of course, a hot salsa. *Taquerías* usually open in the evening and stay open until the early morning, to serve those working late or those who get hungry after leaving the bars or nightclubs; they could be simple stands on a corner or restaurant-like establishment. They are often considered a treat for special occasions or just the perfect way of ending a night out.

They could also be a dinner choice for those nights when nobody is able to cook at home or when one is in a hurry and needs to eat something quickly. They are also a perfect option for friends who want to go out to eat, but in a more informal way. That does not mean that tacos could not be consumed in fancier *taquerías* or restaurants in more formal situations. But the traditional *tacos* are eaten on the street, standing, and in a very informal setting. A clarification is important to make here, and it is that although in the United States tacos are often hard shells filled with ground beef seasoned with a combination of different spices, Mexican *tacos* are never made with ground beef, except *tacos de picadillo*, but those tacos belong to the *tacos de guisado* category and do not include any special mixture of spices. A *taco* is traditionally food rolled in a tortilla; *taco* actually means a cylindric object, often hollow, that can be used for different

Street Food and Snacks 151

purposes; it can also be a cylindrical piece of wood or metal (think the high heel of a shoe, which is also called *taco* or *tacón*). Because of this, a rolled tortilla with nothing inside can also be called taco.

So, a taco is a rolled tortilla with some filling in it. As mentioned before, very few or no spices are used for the filling, which is most commonly a grilled meat; at most it may be seasoned with salt and pepper or a light marinade of garlic and peppers. The purists, however, prefer their tacos grilled, steamed, or cooked in their juices and fat; once a generous amount of the meat is place in two small tortillas (these tortillas are called *tortillas taqueras* and are at least a third smaller than the regular tortillas), the customers have the choice of adding toppings to their tacos or not, but their choices are limited to chopped onions and chopped cilantro; the customers then could add salsa to their tacos from the two or three available to them, as well as lime juice if desired. These are some of the most popular tacos in Mexico—and the most traditional: *tacos de bistec* (beef tacos), *tacos de suadero* (the part of the cow that is between the breast and the back leg of the cow; it is very tender), *tacos de cabeza* (a combination of all the edible parts of a cow's head), *tacos de tripa* (tripe), *tacos de cecina* (salt-cured, naturally dried beef), *tacos de longaniza* (sausage made with ground pork and spices, sun-dried or sometimes smoked), *tacos de arrachera* (skirt steak sometimes mixed with flank steak), *tacos de tuétano* (marrow), and of course *tacos al pastor*. Tacos al carbón are called that because they are made with steak grilled with charcoal, which is what *carbón* means.

But like everything, some other fillings are traditional in different parts of the country, like grilled or battered fish in Tabasco, Veracruz, and the peninsulas of Yucatán and Baja California; *cabrito* (baby goat) or *machaca* (dry beef) in the states of Nuevo León, Coahuila, Tamaulipas, and other northern states; or *mixiote* (barbecued meat marinated with *axiote* also known as annatto) and *sesos* (brains) in central states. A variety of vegetarian tacos is also popular, but mostly as *tacos de guisado*; these tacos are rarely sold in *puestos*, being more common in restaurants or *cocinas*. Some of the most traditional vegetarian tacos are *tacos de hongos* (mushrooms), *tacos de rajas* (grilled poblano peppers), *nopales con queso* (cactus and cheese), or *tacos de papa con chorizo*. Anything edible can be turned into a *taco* by simply placing it in a tortilla. Traditionally, *taquerías* specialize in two or three types of *tacos*, as described earlier. However, there are two popular kinds of tacos that are usually considered separately—*tacos de carnitas* and *tacos de barbacoa*. Typically, the places where they are sold are called *puestos* rather than *taquerías*, since they are often portable stands, and they tend to be more popular on weekends; *carnitas* and *barbacoa* can be served all day, but they are more common in the morning or during the day.

Early in the morning, the *taquero de carnitas* arrives to the place where he is going to set his *puesto* and begins assembling it, firing the burners, and setting the *cazo* (a large copper cauldron) where he will cook the pork. Customarily, *carnitas* are prepared by cooking very slowly chunks of different cuts of the pig in lard until the meat is very tender. There are small variations on how to prepare it, for example some people add beer or brandy to the cauldron or sometimes even brown sugar or Coca-Cola. But the most authentic method of cooking *carnitas* calls for nothing except the meat cooked in lard. *Carnitas* (which literally means little pieces of meat) is the generic name for the dish, but when ordering, customers usually ask for specific parts of the pork, with ribs and *maciza* (the lean white meat) being the most popular and the most expensive, followed by *surtida* (mixed), which combines bits and pieces of all parts, including the skin and stomach. Other popular parts are *buche* (the throat and stomach), *cueritos* (the soft skin), *trompa* (snout), *oreja* (ear), *lengua* (tongue), or *menudencias* (which is a mix of heart, kidney, and sometimes even feet).

Taqueros who sell *barbacoa* also arrive early in the morning to wherever is that they are going to set their *puesto*, which often consist of large wood containers, a table to chop the meat, and occasionally a folding table and chairs for the customers. However, unlike the *carnitas*, *barbacoa* is already cooked and ready to serve. The name *barbacoa* refers to the process of cooking meat in an oven dug in the ground, filled with hot rocks at the bottom and firewood on top of the rocks; the meat then is wrapped with agave leaves and placed in the pit in a large pot, which is subsequently covered with soil to create a seal. The meat is cooked for several hours until it is very tender. The most popular meats for the classical dish are goat and lamb; however, other meats are used in different regions, including beef, chicken, and even fish in some coastal areas. There are several versions of the origin of the word *barbacoa*, but the most accepted is that it came to Spanish form the Taino language of the Caribbean, who took it from the Maya, who still practice a similar way of cooking called *pib*. From Spanish it passed to English, where it became barbecue.

As mentioned earlier, it was common to find *puestos de jugos* in the mornings offering orange juice, a popular item for breakfast, particularly if a couple of eggs are added. But a traditional street food you can find all day in many Mexican cities is *puestos de jugos y licuados*. Like other street foods, these *puestos* could be metal stands fixed to the ground on a street corner, establishments opened in the first floor of a house or building, or in popular markets; like *cocinas*, markets have a few stands dedicated to selling *jugos y licuados* and other related foods; they are called *juguerías*. These establishments are an institution in Mexico and very much part of the urban landscape of most cities. But what are *jugos y licuados*? It is probably easy to guess what *jugos* is—the word refers to fruit juices from orange, grapefruit, carrot, and beet. *Licuados* refers to fruits and sometimes other ingredients like nuts, vanilla, cinnamon, and raisins, mixed in a blender with milk and sugar. The word *licuado* literally means "liquified," which is what a blender (*licuadora*) is supposed to do in Spanish. *Licuados* are not the same as smoothies or shakes, since the only ingredients are one type of fruit, sugar, and milk. Some fruits, like bananas and *mamey*, are only blended with milk; some, like pineapple, cantaloupe, or watermelon, can only be blended with water, and therefore they are called *aguas*, rather than *licuados* (e.g., *agua de piña*, *agua de sandía*). However other fruits, like papaya, guava, or strawberry could be mixed with water or with milk, and they can be made into *licuados* or *aguas*, as in *licuado de fresa* or *agua de fresa*.

These establishments are popular for breakfast and lunch, and usually open early in the morning and close in the late afternoon or early evening; they are considered healthier than other street foods. Because of this reputation, some *puestos* offer, in addition to *jugos y licuados*, more substantial foods, mainly fruit salads, called *cocteles de fruta*. These salads include bite-size pieces of different fruits such as pineapple, papaya, watermelon, cantaloupe, orange, and other seasonal fruits. Smaller stands usually sell these *cocteles* in large plastic cups ready to go; they are usually a combination of two or three fruits, although cups filled with only one fruit are also common. Often these salads are natural or dressed with lime juice, salt, and powdered chili pepper. Larger and more formal *juguerías* offer *cocteles de frutas* made with a larger variety of fruits. Usually they pile the pieces of fruit in layers on a plastic or paper plate, starting with the watermelon, pineapple, cantaloupe, and papaya; followed by chopped oranges, apples, and other fruits like guava or mango and strawberries, then slices of banana are arranged all around the fruit and everything is covered with honey, sprinkled with granola, and topped with whipped cream.

Not all street food is offered exclusively for breakfast, lunch, and dinner; there are other types of food, usually snacks, that could be offered all day or at any time of the day. These foods are traditionally sold in plazas, parks, and—this may surprise some people—outside of schools. The kind of food you are likely to find outside of many schools is generally sweets and small portions of salty foods, of which some of the most traditional are *chicharrones* or *churritos*. These are snacks made with flour fried in oil, flavored with salt and lime shaped as pork rinds or sometimes as little wagon wheels; when they are made with corn flour and shaped like little sticks are called *churritos*. Usually they are served with lime juice, salt, and, chili pepper powder. Other traditional snacks sold outside schools are *nieves* (ices), *paletas de hielo* (popsicles), *merengues* (meringues), and *gelatinas*, as well as traditional candies like *cocadas*, *alegrías*, or *palanquetas*. Today, those traditional candies are less visible and more and more industrially prepared and prepacked chocolates, cakes, cookies, and other sweets are more in demand.

Small cities and towns still maintain a tradition of relaxing and socializing on evenings and weekends by going to the *plaza* or main square. The traditional design of towns and cities all through Mexico is the same as in Spain and most Hispanic countries, with life revolving around the central square or main plaza, where there is usually a church, offices of the local government, and two or three major businesses, a bank, a restaurant, a general store. Many plazas have a *kiosco* (bandstand) for performances by local bands and several benches around for people to sit and enjoy themselves. On most evenings, but particularly on weekends and holidays, the plazas are full of people and consequently lots of sellers offering all kinds of snacks. Many of these snacks are the same ones already mentioned, like *chicharrones de harina*, *nieves*, *churritos*, fruit, *merengues*, *paletas*, and other regional candies and local specialties. However, there are two that are expected when visiting a park or a plaza in Mexico, and they are *esquites* and *elotes*.

Elotes, as prepared in parks and plazas in Mexico, are well known in the United States since many Mexican restaurants offer their own versions of these popular street foods as appetizers. *Elote* simply means a tender corncob, and the *elotes* people buy on the street are prepared in two ways. One is by cooking them in boiling water, then covering them in mayonnaise, sour cream, grated cheese, salt, lime juice, and chili pepper powder. They are served with a long stick at the bottom so it can be hold like a popsicle and eaten while walking around or sitting on a bench. Another way of preparing *elotes* is by grilling them on a brazier, then preparing them, most likely, with lime juice, salt, and chili pepper powder, which really enhances the roasted sweet kernels marvelously, giving them a smoky, slightly acidic taste. These traditional snacks are popular all over the country, particularly in the plazas and parks, of most cities and towns. For most Mexicans, an *elote* evokes a stroll through a Mexican plaza, while listening to a local band playing traditional music on a Sunday afternoon.

Esquites, the other traditional snack, is tender corn kernels cooked in a stock made with the corn, salt, and *epazote*. The kernels are cooked in a big pot and kept warm in a brazier; the *esquites* are usually served in plastic cups topped with lime juice and chili pepper powder; alternatively, they are also served, like *elotes*, topped with mayonnaise, grated cheese, and chili pepper powder. Some modern versions of *esquites* have appeared experimenting with different flavors, but they all are centered on the corn. Another traditional way of preparing *esquites* is by toasting the corn in a large pan or a *comal* and served it with salt and lime juice. Although less common on the streets, this method is most likely the original way of preparing *esquites*, as its name reveals—the word *esquite* comes from the Nahuatl *itzquitl*, derived from the verb *ihcequi*, that literally means "to toast corn." In some rural parts of Mexico *esquites* are still prepared toasted rather than boiled, particularly at home or when they are intended to be served as part of a meal, rather than as a snack. *Elotes* and *esquites* are not the only foods sold in parks and plazas, but they are the ones that most people would associate with them.

There are some seasonal street foods that can only, or mostly, be found at specific times of the year, for specific holidays. One of the most popular celebrations is the season called *fiestas de fin de año* or *fiestas decembrinas* (the December or end of the year holidays); these festivities are celebrated from early December through January 6, Three Kings' Day. During this holiday street markets are popular in many cities around the country. These markets include stands with Christmas decorations, Christmas trees, lights, glass balls, ornaments, Nativity scene figures and sets, and piñatas, etc. They could include crafts and other presents as well as toys, and, of course, food. The food is usually the traditional fare for winter like *ponche*, *buñuelos*, *tamales*, *atole*, coffee, and candy, in addition to many of the foods already mentioned. Because piñatas are traditional for the season and usually they are filled with fruits like sugarcane, peanuts, *tejocotes*, oranges, small *jícamas*, as well as a type of candy called *colación*, many stands sell the fruits for the piñatas and the *colación*.

Romerías are also traditional for another major holiday, the Day of the Dead; for this holiday, the street markets happen from early October to early November and sell allusive objects and products, mostly decorations for the altars in honored of the departed loved ones, like candles, incense, and flowers, including *cempasúchil* (marigolds), the traditional flower of the dead, as well as small skeletons and skulls made out of sugar, *pan de muerto* (bread of the dead), pumpkins, sweet potatoes, and other fruits like oranges, mandarins, and guavas. Like other *romerías*, food is also something that can be sold at these markets, like pumpkin and sweet potatoes in *piloncillo* syrup and other traditional street foods, like *sopes*, *quesadillas*, or *tamales* and *atole*. Traditional candies and bread—especially the sweet rolls adorned with "bones" and rolled in sugar or sprinkled with sesame seeds—are also visible in these markets, and people buy them to consume them for breakfast or supper or to placed them in the family altars for a couple of days in honor of dead family members.

The other major celebration with *romerías*, these traditional street markets, is Independence Day, which is celebrated on September 16. These markets offer Mexican flags of all sizes, as well as other decorations and trinkets with patriotic motifs and the national colors, green, white, and red; they usually happen from mid-August until the night of *El Grito*, the official ceremony that starts the festivities on the night of September 15. That night, Mexicans gather in the main plazas of their towns, cities, and municipalities to witness the local authority reenact the call (*grito*) for independence that the Father of the Nation, Miguel Hidalgo, gave the early morning of September 16, 1810. The *Grito* is followed by fireworks and popular music, while the people gathered in the massive square echo the shouts of their leader while celebrating an authentic popular fiesta. Among the thousands of people in the plaza, there are hundreds of food vendors offering the same traditional snack described all through this chapter, from *sopes* and *tamales* and *atole*, to *quesadillas*, *tortas*, *elotes*, *esquites*, as well as traditional candies like *alegrías*, *cocadas*, or *merengues*. The scene is repeated in all the cities and town in the country.

Although not official, other big holidays, civil or religious, could also be celebrated by large numbers of people and therefore it is not uncommon to have *romerías* around the time of those holidays, albeit for a shorter period of time. Some of these are February 2, Candlemas Day; February 14, St. Valentine's Day; or the Feast of Corpus Christi on a late Thursday in June. All these holidays are associated with food and with popular festivities; Candlemas Day and the Feast of Corpus Christi used to be very traditional and large street markets were common. Candlemas was associated with *tamales* and *atole* eaten after presenting the image of the baby Jesus in church to be blessed; Corpus Christi was associated with mules and the fruits and vegetables they carried into the city in colonial times; until recently, that day children were dressed in traditional indigenous attire and brought to church with offerings, usually flowers and food. The celebration is not as big a holiday as it used to be, however it is still possible to see *puestos* with little mules made out of corn husk, candies, bread, and other traditional foods. Valentine's Day is a more recent holiday, celebrated, like in many other countries, with flowers, candy, and chocolates. So, a few days before, some street markets appear here and there selling all sorts of stuff animals, balloons, and sweets.

Finally, this chapter would not be complete without mentioning the numerous food festivals that happen in Mexico all through the year. Most of these food festivals are popular and they celebrate traditional foods and drinks. Recently, however, there has been a trend of more upscale festivals in luxurious hotels, restaurants, or cultural and convention centers, but the most traditional food festivals continue to be street affairs. Because of their popular nature, some of them have been happening for decades, some are new, and some happened ones or a few times and then disappeared. Some, like the ones dedicated to *mole*, *tamales*, enchiladas, and strawberries have become institutions. The most popular festivals (called *ferias* or fairs) are the ones dedicated to specific dishes, like the *Feria del Tamal*, which happens every year in Mexico City, in the southern district called Coyoacán. Also in Mexico City, people get together every year around the *puestos* of enchiladas in the popular *barrio* of Iztapalapa to celebrate the *Feria de la Enchilada*. The *Feria del Mole*, one of the most beloved ones, happens every October in the outskirts of Mexico City, in a town called San Pedro Actopan; it has been happening uninterrupted since the early 1970s. The *Feria de la Torta* (sandwich) is organized every year the first week of August in Mexico City, while the *Feria del Chile en Nogada* is celebrated in the town of San Andrés Calpan in the state of Puebla.

Other festivals center on specific ingredients or products, trying to promote the local economy through gastronomy. Some of the most popular are *Festival del Chocolate*, celebrated in late November in the state of Tabasco; another festival dedicated to chocolate, along with the bread of the dead, is the *Festival del Chocolate y Pan de Muerto*, which happens in Mexico City. In Mexico City as well, in the southern district of Xochimilco, there is an annual *Feria de la Nieve*, dedicated to ices, ice cream, and all kinds of frozen desserts, celebrated in April. Similarly, the *Noche de los Rábanos* in Oaxaca celebrates radishes. The festival happens on December 23 when farmers and sellers display intricate scenes, including Nativity scenes, made with carved radishes. The *Feria del Elote* is traditional in the town of Jala, Nayarit every August, and it centers on corn; it is usually combined with the religious feast of the Assumption of Mary. Because corn is so important in Mexico, many more festivals dedicated to corn take place in the country, but one of the most traditional is the one from Jala. Wild mushrooms are an important part of traditional Mexican cuisine as well, so the town of Cuajimoloyas, Oaxaca, has organized every July the *Feria de Hongos Silvestres* for almost 20 years.

Known for its strawberries, the city of Irapuato, Guanajauto, celebrates every March one of the most beloved ferias in central Mexico, the *Gran Feria de las Fresas*, which has existed for over 100 years. Also with a long tradition, the *Gran Feria de la Manzana*, celebrates apples, and it happens every August in the town of Zacatlán, or Zacatlán de las Manzanas, in the state of Puebla. In August as well, but in the town of San Miguel de las Pirámides, near the archeological site of Teotihuacán, the locals celebrate prickly pears in the traditional *Feria Nacional de la Tuna*. The three national beverages, *pulque*, tequila, and *mezcal* each have a festival dedicated to them, in which food is offered along with different types of spirits and cocktails. There are actually several festivals dedicated to *pulque*, mostly in Hidalgo and the Estado de México states, as well as local gastronomic specialties like *sopes*, *quesadillas*, and *barbacoa*. The *Feria del Mezcal* is celebrated every July as part of the larger celebration of the famous Guelaguetza Festival of the state of Oaxaca; traditional foods and different cocktails made with *mezcal* are part of the celebrations. And, finally, for almost 50 years, the town of Tequila in the state of Jalisco has been celebrating the spirit that carries its name and gave it world fame: tequila. The *Feria Nacional del Tequila* is celebrated at the end of November and the beginning of December for a couple of weeks of music, drinks, and local specialties like *pozole*, *birria*, or seafood enchiladas to celebrate perhaps Mexico's most famous export the world over, *el vino tequila*.

Street Food and Snacks

Esquites (Street Corn Kernels)

Yield: Serves 6 to 8

4 tablespoons unsalted butter
½ small white onion, finely chopped
3 cloves garlic, minced
6 cups fresh corn kernels
1 cup water
3 sprigs *epazote*
Salt to taste
¼ cup mayonnaise
½ cup cotija cheese
1 jalapeño chili pepper minced
Chili powder to taste
Wedges of lime

Equipment: medium pot or skillet, mixing spoon, measuring cups and spoons

1. Heat the butter in a large pot or skillet over medium heat; add onion and garlic. Cook for a few minutes, until onion becomes translucent, stirring occasionally.
2. Add the corn kernels and jalapeño, and cook for a few minutes.
3. Add water, epazote, and salt; cook for 15 minutes or until corn is done.

To serve, place a generous amount in a cup or a glass and top with mayonnaise and crumbled cheese; sprinkle with the chili powder and squeeze the lime.

Fruta de La Calle (Street Fruit Salad)

Yield: Serves 4 to 6

½ cantaloupe
½ medium papaya
½ pineapple
¼ watermelon
1 large *jícama*
1 green mango
2 limes
Salt to taste
Ground *chile piquín* pepper

Equipment: cutting board, sharp knife

1. Peel all the fruits.
2. Cut all the fruits lengthwise in thick sticks of about the same size.
3. Arrange an assortment of fruit sticks in individual large glasses.

To serve, cut limes in half and squeeze them over the fruit, covering all the fruit with the juice. Sprinkle with salt and the chile piquín.

Tamales Verdes (Green Tamales)

Yield: Makes 12 tamales

¾ cup of lard or vegetable shortening
2¼ cups masa harina
1½ teaspoon baking powder
2 cups warm water
12 corn husks, soaked
1 large chicken breast
¼ white onion
6 tomatillos
1 jalapeño pepper
Salt and cumin to taste
1 tablespoon of oil

Equipment: a large pot, a steamer basket, mixer, mixing bowls, mixing spoon, measuring spoons and cups, blender, sauté pan, mixing spoon

1. Combine masa harina and water in a large bowl and mix well to form a soft dough. Add more or less water to obtain the dough.
2. In a mixer beat the lard with baking powder until it is white and fluffy.
3. Add the dough to the mixer and beat until it acquires a light consistency. To know if the dough is ready, drop a small ball into a glass of water; if it floats, it is ready, if it sinks to the bottom, continue beating.
4. Spread about 3 tablespoons of dough in a corn husk, add the filling and wrap the *tamals* surrounding the filling and overlapping the ends then folding it in half to close. Tie the *tamales* if you want with strips of corn husk. Do the same until you run out of dough.
5. Place the steamer basket in the large pot and add enough water to reach the bottom of the basket. Place the *tamales* in the steamer, standing up, and cover the pot with a lid, making sure it is tight; cover the pot first with aluminum foil if needed.
6. Steam the *tamales* until done, about 1 hour or until the husks separate easily from the *tamales*, making sure the pot does not run out of water.
7. To make the filling, place the cooked chicken breast in water with onion. Then make a sauce by blending tomatillos, jalapeño pepper, clove of garlic, a pinch of cumin, salt, and couple of tablespoons of water. Cook the sauce in the oil and add the shredded chicken. Mix well and simmer until the sauce thickens.

To serve, place the tamales on a large serving plate and place in the center of the table so people can help themselves; accompany with atole *or hot chocolate.*

Cocktail de Frutas de Mercado (Fruit Salad Market Style)

Yield: Serves 2 to 3

½ cup papaya, cut in bite-size chunks
½ cup pineapple, cut in bite-size chunks
½ cup watermelon, cut in bite-size chunks
½ orange, cut in bite-size chunks
½ sliced mango
3 strawberries, quartered
1 banana, sliced
1 tablespoon honey
Whipped cream
1 tablespoon granola

Equipment: cutting board, knife, individual bowl or plate

1. Cut the fruit into small cubes of about ½ inch, except the banana.
2. Place the fruit in a bowl and mix in layers, starting with watermelon, pineapple, papaya, and orange, forming a pyramid; be careful not to smash it.
3. Arrange the mango and strawberries on top.
4. Slice the bananas and arrange them around the bowl in a row of quarter-size bites.

To serve, drizzle the honey evenly all over the fruit and top with whipped cream and sprinkle with the granola (optional). Alternatively, this salad could be made savory by squeezing a lime over the fruit and season with salt and pepper or chili powder instead of the honey.

Quesadillas de La Esquina (Street Corner Quesadillas)

Yield: Serves 4 to 5

1½ cups masa harina
1¼ cup warm water
½ cup vegetable oil
½ pound Oaxaca cheese
2 sprigs fresh epazote

Equipment: *comal* or griddle, mixing bowls, measuring cups

1. In a large bowl mix the masa harina and water until forming a soft dough. Add more water if needed. The dough should be soft and malleable. Cover with a wet kitchen towel.
2. Divide masa dough into 8 or 10 pieces of the same size. Roll the pieces into balls; place balls, one at a time, between two sheets of plastic and form thin circles using a tortilla press or a rolling pin. Wet the dough if it cracks.
3. Place enough cheese and a couple of epazote leaves in the circle of dough and fold it in half.
4. Heat the oil in a frying pan; when very hot, place 1 or 2 *quesadillas* in the pan and deep fry for a couple of minutes, until golden brown. Transfer to a plate with paper towels to drain excess oil.

To serve, place a couple of quesadillas on a plate and add salsa de molcajete *if you want.*

CHAPTER NINE

Dining Out

There is an established tradition of eating out in Mexico, from the occasional treat at a taco stand or a *puesto de quesadillas*, to a breakfast or lunch on the go, to a healthier fruit salad or a piece of candy or an *elote* on a Sunday afternoon at the main plaza of any traditional town. Tacos are almost always synonymous with eating out and typically consumed standing at a street corner, surrounded by people you do not know. Although many of the street foods can also be found in small establishments called *taquerías*, *fondas*, or *cocinas*, they are also included in most restaurants today, from the moderate to the elegant. Since the 1920s, right after the revolution, Mexican traditional food started to be accepted and valued as a symbol of national identity and pride by the middle and upper classes, and since the second half of the twentieth century its popularity and prestige have only increased thanks to numerous projects, public and private, aimed at documenting and promoting the sophistication, variety, and uniqueness of Mexican cuisine, efforts that were rewarded with the declaration by UNESCO of Mexican food as an intangible heritage of the world.

However, this is a new phenomenon, since for decades, starting in the late nineteenth century, most elegant restaurants in Mexico served international cuisine, with French cuisine being the most popular among the aristocracy and upper classes. A quick review of the history of restaurants in México starts early in the sixteenth century when inns and other establishments that provided lodging and food to travelers appeared in the roads and cities of New Spain. The clientele usually was composed of travelers, merchants, or newcomers to the New World who had not stablished themselves in the colonies yet. These establishments offered rudimentary services and their owners often had a bad reputation as thieves and dishonest people. Besides the inns, people could eat and drink in taverns and *puestos* on the road and streets. It was not until the mid-1800s that some rudimentary restaurants appeared, often next to inns or other places offering lodging. All this changed after the second French invasion of Mexico (1861–1867) and the establishment of the Mexican Empire with Maximilian of Habsburg as the emperor, which ended with his deposition and execution on June 19, 1867. While emperor of Mexico, Maximilian tried to modernize the country and brought cooks and other staff from Belgium and Vienna, as well as other countries, to replicate a European court in the Mexican capital.

Once the French army left Mexico in defeat and Maximilian was executed, many cooks and bakers decided to stay in the country to start their own businesses. Many cafes and bakeries began to appear not only in Mexico City but in other large cities, where the local middle and upper classes started to frequent them to enjoy modern, European foods. But flourished during the dictatorship of Porfirio Díaz, who dominated the political scene of Mexico since 1876 when he became president for the first time. In 1884, he again was elected president, but this time he managed to stay in power until 1911. This period of Mexican history is considered the most *afrancesado* (frenchified), and Díaz's administration promoted that image, imitating everything French, from music, theater, and language, to architecture and, of course, cuisine. In addition to cafés and bistros, more refined restaurants started to appear displaying the elegance of any French restaurant with the added ostentation of the Mexican *nouveau rich*. For who would dare to ask for a chicken broth with vegetables, like the ones they enjoy at home—conjectures ironically Salvador Novo, a famous Mexican poet and gourmet aficionado who did a lot for the vindication of Mexican food—when they could order a *petite marmite,* or who would ask for poultry when they could have *volaille* or request cheese instead of *formage*?

A menu written in French, continues Novo, would have confer a "clear superiority to those who could read it" ("Incursión," 46), providing also a sense of distinction and worldliness. However, not only the elite frequented these places, but also politicians, military people, bullfighters, actors, dancers, poets, and artists of all types, as well as bohemians and *bon vivants*, creating in the process an urban culture that revolved around French-like cafés and bistros right before the revolution. After the Mexican Revolution, some of these establishments continued operating modifying their menus to include a new clientele of intellectuals, politicians, artists, and the administrators of a new political class emerging from the bottom of the pyramid. However, for most of the first three or so decades of the twentieth century, elegant restaurants continued to serve mostly European food, with French being the most sought after. Spanish, Italian, German, and Chinese foods were also present, some of them as the result of people of these ethnicities migrating to Mexico. With the changes that the revolution brought to Mexico, including an official project of developing a national identity to unify the nation, based on popular and autochthonous cultures, some traditional foods and techniques were slowly incorporated in high-class restaurants, which included "refined" versions of Mexican dishes in their offerings. Since the revolution had renewed a patriotic sentiment, restaurants offering exclusively Mexican food started to appear in larger numbers. Although some, like Hostería de Santo Domingo, had started actually in the nineteenth century; others, like Café de Tacuba, saw an opportunity at the beginning of the new century.

From the late 1800s to about 1910, Mexican industry developed swiftly, establishing the productions of goods that represent the core of Mexican economy, some of which are still important today, such as steel, glass, paper, tobacco, textiles, soap, or beer. At the end of the revolution, in the 1920s, there was a consolidation of these industries, and in the 1940s and 1950s there was a second wave of industrialization, taking advantage of the opportunities that World War II offered to emergent economies; as a result, there was a massive migration from the countryside to the cities. Mexico intensified its industrialization and diversified the production of goods; that in turn favored the creation of a considerable middle class formed by government officials, administrators, professionals, teachers, and workers in the service, commerce, health, and other white-collar occupations. Consequently, the traditional working hours were modified accordingly and since the mid-1940s most companies, offices, stores, and other places of employment established work shifts on fixed schedules. With cities growing rapidly and the continued industrialization of the nation, combined with the steady but persistent incorporation of women to the workforce, people started to go out to eat more out of necessity, but also because many now could afford it. And that is, of course, reflected in the number and kind of restaurants that started to appear and multiply in the second half of the twentieth century.

First, to attend the demand of a new working class, some companies offered cafeterias in their places of employment, but that was rare; therefore, a proliferation of the *cocinas económicas* mentioned in previous chapters and small *fondas* grew up around work areas. However, the biggest change was the establishment of American-style eateries with booths, as well as soda fountains, and a large bar where people could seat to eat something relatively simple, relatively fast, attracting mostly the new type of urban workers in clerical and administrative positions. The idea was not new, and in fact the first, and one of the most famous of these restaurants was Sanborns, which was the first American-like cafeteria to open in Mexico and the first one to have a soda fountain. The original restaurant opened in 1903 in downtown Mexico City, and in 1919 it moved to one of the most emblematic buildings of the city, *la casa de los azulejos*, or the House of Tiles, the eighteenth-century palace of the Count of the Valle of Orizaba. The building had actually housed the Jockey Club, the most exclusive in the city, in the decades previous to the revolution. The beautiful palace was turned into a restaurant by covering the courtyard with a glass ceiling and placing booths along the walls as well as tables and chairs in the center. It also included a pharmacy, making it a very convenient place to eat and pick up a few items needed for personal grooming. It was in the 1940s, when the restaurants were sold to Charles Walgreens of Chicago, that Sanborns became a chain of American-like restaurants.

The other important restaurant of this type is VIPS, which was established in the early 1960s and followed the same model as Sanborns, therefore becoming its biggest competition. Both restaurants grew into large chains in the second half of the twentieth century, covering most of the country, and in the case of VIPS, also Spain. Today, these restaurants continue to be very popular among people of all walks of life, but particularly white-collar workers and students. Their menu, however, has changed from exclusively American to Mexican with an international flair; while it is possible to order smoothies and shakes, pancakes, burgers, and French fries, they are offered alongside Mexican and Mexican inspired dishes. For breakfast, for example, they offer many of the traditional Mexican egg dishes, such as *huevos rancheros*, *huevos a la albañil*, or *huevos divorciados*, but also the traditional American combination of scrambled eggs with ham, bacon, and pancakes, as well as fruit and yogurt, cereals, and porridges. Lunch and dinner, likewise, can be of traditional Mexican dishes like enchiladas or *chilaquiles*, but also club sandwiches, burgers, and other combinations a little more international, like *milanesa de pollo con ensalada* (chicken Schnitzel and salad), pasta, or *enchiladas suizas*. Some of their dishes change regularly to keep their menu interesting and often include seasonal and regional cuisines.

With the increase of the middle class and urban populations, as well as a youth more in tune with the world, mostly through the influence of American media and entertainment, other American and American-like restaurants, diners, and cafés started to appear in most cities in Mexico staring in the 1970s, 1980s, and 1990s, a trend that continues until today. Most of the standard American coffee shop chains have become part of the Mexican urban landscape, in the case of Denny's at least since 1967, with most of them, like Applebee's, Chili's, and T.G.I. Friday's, becoming omnipresent in most urban centers in the 1990s, and their popularity continues to grow. But besides these chain restaurants, other more specialized such as IHOP, California Pizza Kitchen, P. F. Chang's, and Cheesecake Factory have also been very successful in Mexico in recent decades. There are even some unexpected surprises like Magnolia Bakery, the Greenwich Village institution of *Sex and the City* fame, which opened a café in Mexico City in November 2014, and the popularity of Starbucks, with over 750 stores in Mexico, more than in any other country outside the United States. The fascination of Mexicans, particularly the young and the middle class, with American eateries is not unique, as the proliferation of fast-food chains like McDonalds and KFC all over the world testify. However, it is surprising in a country that so zealously guards its culinary traditions.

All these restaurants mentioned so far are related to urban life and to the subsequent creation of a middle class with a more international aspiration. The American influence in the way Mexicans eat, as in many other aspects of modern life, is categorical and should not surprise anybody, considering the proximity of both nations and the fluidity of their economies and populations—large numbers of Mexicans came to the United States during the twentieth century, but also Americans have moved to Mexico in larger numbers than to any other country on Earth. So logically the abundance of American and American-like restaurants in Mexico mirrors the number of Mexican and Mexican-like restaurants in the United States. But the influence of other foods has always been inevitable in Mexico and pretty much every other country; Mexican food itself is by definition the combination of at least two cuisines and as it progresses it borrows and mixes different traditions. From an ordinary Mexican meal of lentil soup, meatballs and pasta, and oranges or mangoes for dessert, to a typical Tuesday taco dinner in an average American household, what is consider "everyday" food is anything but pure.

But going out to eat is also a luxury, a way of marking a special occasion or to treat oneself and one's loved ones. Dining out in Mexico in particular is synonymous with a celebration; it is also a matter of economics. Traditionally, Mexicans have been less inclined to go out just for going out's sake, compared with Americans. And when eating out for no particular reason, usually an informal event, the majority of the people would choose a taqueria or a café or a chain restaurant, like VIPS and Sanborns, depending on the traditions, culture, and budget of each person. But this has been changing in the past decades, and more and more Mexicans, particularly of the middle and upper classes, dine out at more proper restaurants with some regularity. Again, this is not entirely different from what happens in the United States where a similar trend has been observed, since according to recent research, in 2019 more than half a dollar spent in food went to eating at restaurants, compared to 25 cents in the 1950s. The increase is motivated by a relatively stable economy and a more dynamic social mobility but also to "two important drivers for the industry from a consumer perspective—convenience and socialization" (Rogers). Likewise, an improvement in the economy and a desire for "convenience and socialization" are important aspects in the increase of numbers of Mexicans going out to eat with friends and family.

According to a recent poll, 40 percent of Mexicans eat out at least once or twice a week; of the people who answered the poll, 46 percent said that they prefer a formal restaurant, and more than half take into consideration the price but also the service and quality of food ("40% de los Mexicanos"). What this poll suggests is that people eat out not just for necessity, but also for pleasure, so much so that the web page of one of the largest banks, BBVA Bancomer, posted a blog entry warning its costumers that dining out is the enemy of their paycheck and gives them some tips on how to save money if they must eat out. Although many polls make little or no distinction between eating out at a formal restaurant, a café, diner, or even at a *puesto*, there are indications that Mexicans are dining out in larger numbers, and that they are doing it in ways different than the traditional ones. According to the association that represents the restaurant industry, for example, today this industry is the second employer in the nation, with a high percentage of female workers and administrators (Asociación Mexicana de Restaurantes). There has been also an increase in the number and variety of options, with some Mexican restaurants recognized all over the world among the best and other opening branches in other countries, like Cosme in New York City, owned and operated by the chef of what most consider the best Mexican restaurant, Pujol, or Cala, the San Francisco restaurant of Mexican chef Gabriela Cámara, whose Contramar is one of the most beloved seafood restaurants in Mexico City, as well as numerous other Mexican chefs bringing traditional flavors and techniques to the United States.

> Gabriela Cámara, the chef and owner of Contramar in Mexico City, is as passionate about cooking with local and seasonal ingredients as she is about social causes. She sees her business as an opportunity for social justice. She felt that her restaurants attracted rich clientele who came to eat food that less privileged people cook and get very well paid for, that farmers grow and get very well paid for, and that fisheries provide responsibly and get very well paid for. This commitment was noticed, and she was invited to be an advisor to the president of Mexico in matter of food and nutrition.

Dining Out

And the diversity and number of formal restaurants and restaurants of international cuisine, as well as Mexican *haute cuisine*, continues to grow. The restaurants included in these pages are by no means an exhausting review of all that Mexico has to offer (how could it be in country with more than 428,000 eateries nationwide, according to the National Restaurant Association?), but rather a sample to pique your curiosity about the diversity and richness of the restaurant culture in Mexico. The best way to approach this task is to divide the restaurants discussed here in two large categories, Mexican and international cuisine, and to focus only on restaurants that offer full, formal service—the kind of restaurant that Mexicans would go to for a special occasion. French cuisine has been present in Mexico since the 1800s, and at the end of the nineteenth century was synonymous with dining out; however, as Marcela Suarez Escobar points out, the sophistication of the French cuisine was often combined with Mexican dishes, as the recipes in a couple of early cookbooks testify by offering dishes like *pato en pepian* (duck *pipian*) or *conserva de xoconoxtle* (preserve) next to *consomé à l'infante*.

Some of the most popular restaurants of the second half of the nineteenth century were La Bella Unión, La Maison Dorée, Recamier, Café Iturbide, and Café de Fulcheri. Fulcheri is considered the one that introduced Chantilly cream, cream cheese, and Neapolitan ice cream to Mexico. Other cafés like Iturbide offered exotic drinks like gin cocktails and sherry cobblers to its discerning clientele. In October 1868, El Café de la Concordia announced that it would open a restaurant in November to serve the most select of Mexican society with enough china brought from Europe for 100 people and service and décor to satisfy the "most demanding gourmet" (Díaz y de Ovando, 82). And in 1875, Café del Progreso made history when, with the intention of attracting new patrons, it was the first to employ women as waitresses. When Café de la Concordia was closed and later the building where it was housed for decades demolished, intellectuals and journalists wrote of the end of an era. Most of these cafés and restaurants occupied a few blocks in downtown Mexico City, most notably the Calle de Plateros (silversmiths' street), today Francisco I. Madero Street. This street runs in a straight line from east to west, from Plaza de la Constitución, pass the Alameda Park and the Palace of Fine Arts, and from there, heads southwest on Paseo de la Reforma, the boulevard that leads to Chapultepec Park and to the castle that was the seat of Maximilian of Habsburg's court, and therefore it was one of the most aristocratic streets until the revolution.

But French food is not the only international cuisine Mexicans have had access to for most of the twentieth century. If the French cafés and restaurants were popular with the aristocracy and the frenchified intelligentsia of the late nineteenth century, it was because they were the best places to hang out after the opera or the different theatrical spectacles, as well as to meet other fellow poets and artists to discuss world news, or perhaps to conduct business meetings, or the ideal places to treat the several international professionals, consultants, and visitors, a more industrialized Mexico was attracting, with the administration's blessings since it favored its dream of a modern nation. A mix of pleasure and business, then, characterized these places and it was almost exclusively for the aristocracy. But as the country became more industrialized and trade with other nations intensified, the way business was conducted change, and more and more it became traditional to seal a deal or mark an important partnership by dining at a restaurant, preferably from the culture of the business partner, or one of the established business cuisines in the world. Spanish cuisine has always been present in Mexico understandably, so some of the first restaurants to open in Mexico were Spanish, like the traditional Prendes, which opened in 1912, or Casino Español, a social and cultural center of the Spanish community in Mexico founded in 1863 that later included an elegant restaurant.

In 1915, the first German restaurant opened; it was called Bellinghausen and was in the centric Colonia Juaréz neighborhood, later called the Zona Rosa. It is still very popular and it has since opened other restaurants associated with it in other parts of the city. In 1924, soon after the revolution, a café called Loma Linda that offered international dishes opened on Paseo de la Reforma; later, during the 1940s, it was converted into a restaurant that offered a new concept brought by its owner after a trip to Argentina: grilled cuts of meat over an open fire. It is considered the first steak house in the city and it is still a very popular place for business meetings or special occasions. Other places, like the still famous Café La Opera (1895) were a mix of French and international foods, that gradually included more Mexican dishes in its offerings. Places like the already mentioned Café de Tacuba and Hosteria de Santo Domingo and the humbler El Taquito (1923) and La Jalisciense (1875) specialized in Mexican food from the beginning. These restaurants are among the oldest in Mexico and they are still operating; for the most part, however, there are not many records of other restaurants; so the concept of an international cuisine was largely reduced to French and Spanish cuisines, with some Italian and German.

As Mexico grew, became more industrialized, diversified its economy, and strengthened its partnerships with international corporations and investors, the number of international restaurants also grew, mostly during the second half of the twentieth century. According to Julio Moreno, World War II was responsible for "the country's industrial and commercial growth" (81), particularly evident in advertising, which "allowed Mexican and American companies to market their products to a diverse audience and society where values, beliefs, and practices were rapidly changing" (151). America made sure that Mexico felt part of the alliance against Nazi Germany by aiding its industrialization in an effort to diminish German influence in the Mexican economy. This in turn favored urbanization. Cities became more and more influential, and for decades after that, the struggle for the "authentic" Mexican culture oscillated between the urban and the country. This was also reflected in the dichotomy of Mexican versus international restaurants. Different districts of the city—and in fact, other cities besides Mexico City—developed and became important and helped decentralize the monopoly on food and entertainment held by the historic downtowns (the *centros históricos*) of the nation's capital and other major cities.

Mexico came out of World War II as a modern nation with a stable, strong economy and a more cosmopolitan culture and population. Since then, Mexico has continued to do its best to keep up with the rest of the industrialized world, and it has not been that bad considering that Mexico's economy is among the strongest in the world (number 15 globally). Today, Mexican cities offer a variety of international restaurants suited for all tastes and for all budgets. Like in previous decades, most people go out mostly for special occasions. Birthdays, anniversaries, graduations, and other personal celebrations are popular, but also national celebrations, like Independence Day or New Year's. In fact, according to numbers by the Cámara Nacional de la Industria de Restaurantes y Alimentos (National Chamber of Restaurants and Food Industry) of Mexico, Mother's Day is the day when the most money is spent in restaurants in the country, followed closely by New Year's Eve. Also popular are Father's Day, Valentine's Day, and Sundays. This is in addition to the traditional business lunches and dinners and other social commitments. In the last few decades, however, going out just for the pleasure of experiencing different cuisines or new trends and to socialize with friends and relatives has become more common among younger generations. These are some of the most popular restaurants in the country, and some of the ones considered to be the best. However, it is important to mention that considering how important and strong tourism is and the number of resorts and world-class hotels all over the country, it is understandable that many cuisines appear and disappear regularly from the standard offerings. Nonetheless, this should provide a clear idea of what is like eating out in Mexico.

Mexico City, arguably, offers the most diversity and the best ranked restaurants. But not exclusively, since other regions, particularly larger cities and popular tourist destinations, have also developed a food and drinks industry catering to tourists and locals alike with high standards of quality. Restaurants of the most diverse cuisines are increasingly more regular in Mexico, serving an international, cosmopolitan, and curious clientele; nonetheless, restaurants specializing in Mexican cuisine, including regional cuisines, are equally or more popular and revered in the country. The first restaurant worth mentioning is considered the best restaurant in Mexico, and one of the best in the world: Pujol. Pujol is a restaurant of what could be described as modern or Mexican haute cuisine. It opened in 2000 by renowned chef Enrique Olvera, and in its almost 20 years it has become an institution and consistently ranked among the best world restaurants. The modern interpretations of traditional Mexican dishes is innovative and bold; there are two main tasting menus: one called corn (*maíz*), which includes a *tlayuda*, a *tamal*, and a *papadzul*, and as a main dish its famous *mole madre* (a *mole* sauce that has been reheated daily for months, adding some new batches regularly to develop interesting flavors), two delicate circles of two different *mole* sauces (one new in the center surrounded by a circle of *madre mole*) are placed in the middle of a huge plate with no other ingredient, vegetables or meat, served with freshly made corn tortillas; some of this *mole* has been aged for more than three years.

The other menu is called sea (*mar*) and centers on seafood, with *ceviche*, octopus, and sea bass in green *mole* as the main ingredients. There is also a menu of tacos to have with cocktails at the bar. The restaurant has two periods, the first one from its foundation to 2017 is marked for a sophisticated, sober presentations, with a relaxed yet formal atmosphere; the second, more casual and inviting, maintains an elegant and intimate atmosphere, albeit more Mexican. In an interview a few years ago, when Pujol moved to the new location in the same fancy Polanco neighborhood, talking to *The New York Times*, chef Olvera was categoric about his idea for the new Pujol, "We want to be the favorite restaurant of people, not the best restaurant," he told Shaun Pett, perhaps in response to the most commonly heard criticism of the restaurant in Mexico—it is too expensive for most people to visit, and the food is too "avant-garde" for them to leave fully satisfied. Pujol offers contemporary cuisine and goes back to the source by focusing on the flavors and the quality of ingredients, rather than the quantity of mediocre food. This concept, although, not new, is less common in Mexico and for the time being, at least, it is restricted to the adventurous gourmet travelers, the food writers, the pretentious bourgeoisie, the celebrities, the *nouveau rich*, the occasional discerning tourist, people related to the industry, and of course other chefs. That is, Pujos has its future secured. As per turning it into "the favorite restaurant of people," the chances of this happening are not good, unless, of course, one understands the claim literally as favorite of *people* as opposed to animals or vegetables.

Following the steps of Pujol, another important restaurant representing the modern cuisine of Mexico, Quintonil, opened in 2012 and since then it has also been included among the best restaurants in the world. Like Pujol, Quintonil offers a limited menu of inventive interpretations of traditional Mexican dishes, like *mole* Actopan-style, *barbacoa de pescado, huauzontles,* and *cola de res*. It also offers seasonal menus with several courses with a wine-pairing option. The winter version of this menu for 2019–2020 offered a selection of small dished like crab in *pipián* sauce, codfish, rice and duck, pared with national and international wines for about 200 dollars. Other restaurants in the same style are Dulce Patria, of chef Martha Ortiz, or Lur, a Mexican-Basque fusion, the resurrection of the famous Biko of chefs Mikel Alonso and Gerard Gellver. Fusion is also a trend in many restaurants in recent decades, so besides Lur, Rosa Negra offers a menu with influences of many Latin American countries like Argentina, Brazil, or Colombia, while Astried y Gaston, a Mexican version of the Peruvian restaurant in Lima, Peru considered one of the best in Latin America, offers traditional Peruvian dishes with a Mexican twist, including tacos and other Latin American dishes.

Interestingly enough, fusion with other Latin American cuisines is not that common in Mexico; the most common combinations, continue to be with European cuisines, like French and Spanish or, more recently, Italian. One of the best examples of the latter is the fashionable and romantic Rosetta. Housed in an old townhouse in the Roma neighborhood of Mexico City, with the tables arranged in the courtyard and the interior of the house, surrounded by lush plants and delicate flowers, which adorn also the comfortable tables, the restaurant is famous for its sophisticated, yet informal atmosphere and attentive service, but especially for the seasonal dishes and Italian adaptations of chef and owner Elena Reygadas; the menu is big enough to offer a variety of options, without being overwhelming. The restaurant has an Italian flair, but among the Italian specialties, sometimes dressed with local flavors, the menu offers Mexican delicacies like *mole de hoja santa* and *tamal de quelite, tamal de elote,* and gnocchi with *cuitlacoche*. All the dishes are made with fresh seasonal ingredients. Nonalcoholic drinks include some traditional Mexican flavored waters, like cucumber, basil, guanabana, and tarragon, while alcoholic beverages include artisanal beers, cocktails, and a good selection of Italian, French, and even Mexican wines.

Polanco is one of the most elegant neighborhoods in Mexico City; consequently, there is a high concentration of restaurants in that part of town. Besides the restaurants already mentioned, there are other important restaurants, a little more traditional in their food and service, that were, and have remained, important culinary points of reference for those looking for a place to celebrate a special occasion or to conduct a business meeting. Porfirio's is one of those restaurants, offering traditional Mexican cuisine. In an elegant and modern setting, the restaurant has become famous for its Mexican dishes—many of them interpretations of street food like *esquites*, *elotes*, and tacos. Another important restaurant in Polanco is Dulce Patria, as we mentioned, which like Pujol and Qunitonil, offers its own interpretation of Mexican traditional food. Martha Ortiz is a tireless promoter of Mexican cuisine in the world; not only she has an academic background on gastronomical history and has published several books on Mexican food, but she has brought that knowledge successfully to London, where she opened a restaurant, Ella Canta. So her culinary abilities are beyond reproach; but what distinguishes Dulce Patria is the playfulness of the whole experience, from the color scheme of the place to the whimsical presentation of the food and drinks, including flowers, dry ice, little mariachi hats, traditional candies, and artisanal toys.

Much more traditional but still excellent options to enjoy delicious Mexican food in Polanco are restaurants like Hacienda de los Morales, an elegant and spacious restaurant in what used to be a hacienda from the late 1600s. Since the 1960s, the place has been offering visitors the opportunity to enjoy a meal in a historic building, decorated in a way reminiscent of colonial Mexico, and to experience its old charm in the décor and the service, right in the middle of the city. Unlike restaurants serving modern versions of traditional Mexican food, the dishes at Hacienda de los Morales are the real deal, with *quesadillas*, *ceviche*, and *tacos* served as appetizers and *tortilla* soup or *caldo tlalpeño*, for example, as first course, as well as *pato en pepián*, *pescado a la veracruzana*, and chicken in *mole* sauce as main courses. Like most Mexican restaurants, Hacienda de los Morales includes international dishes such as onion soup, Cesar salad, shrimp in garlic and butter, grilled tuna, and beef steaks, but many of these dishes are combined with local ingredients. The restaurant has a small selection of wines and beers, particularly Mexican, and traditional cocktails like bloody Mary, margaritas, and mimosas, as well as sodas and old-fashioned *aguas frescas*; juices, tea, and coffees are also served.

Much more casual, but still a great place to eat out and celebrate, is Villa María. Unlike Hacienda de los Morales or Dulce Patria, the place is simple in its décor, which is borderline tacky with signs painted on the walls of traditional "proverbs" and quirky Mexican motifs. A huge, open restaurant, Villa Maria focuses on classical Mexican food without claiming innovative dishes or recreations of street foods; the restaurant offers a large list of the most traditional dishes like enchiladas, *quesadillas*, chicken in *mole*, filet mignon with tequila, *huauzontles*, chicken in *pipián*, and tacos in abundant portions. It also offers a long list of margaritas, tequilas, and *mezcals*, as well as Mexican beers and sodas. Less appropriate for business meals, formal lunches, or for romantic dinners, it is a perfect casual restaurant, ideal for families or for large groups of friends who want to go out and have drinks with some traditional Mexican dishes. The place has been around for over a quarter of a century and has established itself as an institution, popular with locals and tourists alike, particularly when there is mariachi bands playing or when it celebrates regional cuisines with special menus, including a pre-Hispanic menu offering guacamole and grasshoppers and ant larva or agave worm tacos.

Among other notable restaurants in Polanco is Jaso, an international restaurant with a modern American influence that offers quality food with fresh local products. It is a tastefully decorated and elegant restaurant with some of the best pastries and cakes in the city. Bros, another American restaurant, advertised as restaurant and oyster bar, offers standard American dishes and cocktails with a Mexican influence. The place is well decorated, elegant, yet casual, with a terrace that looks over at the Soumaya Museum, which holds a huge collection of Mexican and international art. Just off Polanco, on the spectacular Paseo de la Reforma, there is another American restaurant that has been very successful in bringing the classical dishes typical of an American restaurant to Mexico, the Capital Grill, which offers great cocktails, superb Prime-aged steaks, and a raw bar. Like Capital Grill, Morton's, an American steakhouse established in Chicago in 1978, with more than 50 restaurants in the United States and nine international restaurants, including the one in Mexico City, has helped expanded the idea Mexicans have of American food, taking it beyond hamburgers and beer, and offering excellent cocktails and traditional steaks and seafood.

Mexico City is a huge, modern city, so it is understandable that in the last four or five decades, as the rest of the country became more industrialized and urbanized, the restaurant scene changed accordingly not only in the city but the entire country. In Mexico City, besides Polanco there are several other neighborhoods with popular and award-winning restaurants.

One of these neighborhoods is Roma. A *colonia* that started at the turn of the twentieth century as an upper-middle-class neighborhood that allowed traditional families to move outside of the crowded downtown area, by the 1950 it had become overcrowded and more mixed, with poor planning and a construction boom of office spaces and apartment buildings that contributed to its decline; once more, the well-to-do families moved out, this time to new neighborhoods like Lomas de Chapultepec. Roma never lost its appeal, particularly when artists and students started to move into the neighborhood and more businesses and offices continued to thrive. It was in the late 1980s that Roma started to become trendy again, and today it is a hub for bars, cafes, and restaurants.

Some of the most popular restaurants are Nudo Negro, a self-described roller coaster of flavors, that offers a fusion of different cuisines, including Asian, Mexican, and Middle Eastern. The menu is innovative and eclectic, with fresh, local ingredients and a full bar that offers a variety of cocktails. Yuban is another popular restaurant in Roma that offers modern Mexican cuisine. More informal than the restaurants in Polanco, it is a hip, cool, fresh place with an old-world, rustic décor. The food is modern interpretations of traditional dishes like *mole verde*, *ceviche*, *salpicón*, corn soup, and roasted pumpkin. Macelleria is another popular restaurant; it offers traditional Italian food via the United States—the traditional Italian soups, salads, pasta, steaks, and fish of Italian Americans are as popular as the pastas, pizzas, and subs offered to go in the "NY Deli" section of the restaurant. All of the dishes, according to the restaurant's web page, are prepared according to the traditional Italian way, but with Mexican ingredients. The drink offerings are also plentiful with soft drink like sodas, *aguas*, juices, mineral water, as well as aperitives, Mexican and artisanal beers, as well as a wine list of mostly Italian and Mexican wines, and cocktails with names like Sinatra, sticky julep, or Mr. Pink.

Casa Virginia is another institution in the neighborhood, a restaurant of chef Mónica Patiño, Elegant and airy, Casa Virginia offers Mexican modern cuisine, in an elegant, yet casual restaurant. The food is simple and centered on Mexican dishes, but with a French influence. Also by Patiño, Delirio is another restaurant that makes Roma its home. Delirio is more casual and offers, like Casa Virginia, Mexican classics with a Mediterranean influence; yet, as they claim on their website, they cook with olive oil from Ensenada, sea salt from Cuyutlán, and specialties from all over the world. Other restaurants in Roma, like Matcha Mio, Sesame, Galanga Thai Kitchen, Mog, or Aoyama offer Thai, Japanese, and other Asian cuisines. Rosetta is also one of the culinary stars of Colonia Roma. In addition to these international cuisines, there are countless informal and casual restaurants offering traditional Mexican food, like Taquería Orinoco, El Parnita, Lalo!, or El Hidalguense. Being a hip neighborhood catering to a younger crowd, it is not surprising that there are also vegetarian and vegan options, like the famous vegan *taquería*, a fancy taco stand called Por Siempre.

Colonia Condesda, next to Roma, has a similar story, except that the neighborhood never really stopped being residential, despite the migration of businesses and offices to its ample, nice streets in the 1970s and 1980s. However, in the 1990s the neighborhood had a transformation with young people moving in and turning it into the hippest district in the city at the end of the last century. Bookstores, cafés, boutiques, art galleries, and of course restaurants followed, and even today, Condesa is one of the most active neighborhoods in the culinary scene. Among the best restaurants in Condesa are some institutions like Contramar, the seafood restaurant of renown chef Gabriela Cámara, who also opened Cala in San Francisco. Contramar is famous for its inventive but simple fish and seafood dishes like *tostadas*, tacos, and *sopes* with octopus, shrimp, tuna, or crab; its fish soups and seafood cocktails are popular also; as are its grilled octopus, fish meatballs, or pasta with clams in a garlic sauce. The ingredients are always fresh and seasonal so the menu is always changing depending on what is available. Lardo is a more casual version of Rosetta, the other restaurant of Elena Reygadas. Open and light, with a certain rustic feeling, Lardo is a bistro that offers dishes mostly to be shared—grilled octopus, squid, or chicken; lamb kebab or red snapper with couscous, as well as several salads. It also has a good list of wines mostly form Italy, France, and Spain, but also a couple from Mexico

Another popular restaurant is Sonora Grill. Sonora Grill describes itself as a contemporary Mexican steakhouse and promises a unique experience including the space, the meat cuts, the architecture, and the atmosphere, which is modern and elegant, with a mixed crowd. In addition to typical appetizers like *queso fundido* or octopus *tostadas* and soups like lentil or tortilla, the menu includes grilled octopus, burgers, and roasted chicken as main dishes. However, Sonora Grill is famous for its prime beef cuts, desserts, and a good collection of wines, including a respectable list of Mexican wines. But perhaps one of the best restaurants in the area is Azul Condesa, one of the three restaurants of award-winning chef, author, and advocate of Mexican cuisine, Ricardo Muñoz Zurita. Chef Muñoz Zurita is considered one of the best chefs in Mexico and in Latin America; his cuisine has remained consistently Mexican, in what he often describes as classical Mexican. That means that all his dishes are versions of the most traditional dishes from colonial times to contemporary creations, but unlike Enrique Olvera or Jorge Vallejo, for example, Muñoz Zurita's dishes are as close as possible to the original ones that have been passed from generation to generation, with a respect for tradition derived from his own research.

The other two of Muños Zurita's restaurants are located in sections of the city that are important as well as referents for a culinary culture. The Centro Histórico (historic downtown) and San Angel. Azul Histórico is located in the heart of the city, in the courtyard of a colonial palace, a few blocks from the main square, Plaza de la Constitución. The location is perfect for business people and politicians to conduct business meals, the younger professionals who have been rediscovering that part of the city in the last few decades, as well as tourists visiting the many colonial buildings, like the cathedral and the National Palace. There have always been restaurants in Centro Histórico, however most of them were consider traditionally more practical than real culinary experience. Some of them were very good, other simple or practical serving generic food for the many workers and bureaucrats in the area. But that has changed lately. Another recent restaurant that has been creating waves is Roldan 37, a restaurant in a house from the late 1700s, that has been in chef Rómulo Mendoza's family for over 100 years. The food is traditional Mexican, with *moles*, *sopes*, tacos, enchiladas, *quesadillas*, and all of the most traditional dishes, served in different rooms of the house charmingly decorated in an old fashion style. But the dish that has given the restaurant its fame is *chiles en nogada*; in fact, Roldan 37 has been voted as having the best *chiles en nogada* in Mexico.

Before Azul Histórico and Roldán 37, it was El Cardenal the restaurant that dominated the culinary scene in downtown Mexico City. Founded in 1969 and originally housed in the building of the first University of Mexico, it moved to its current location, a French-style house of the nineteenth century, a few blocks away from the original location, in 1984. The cuisine of El Carden is traditional Mexican, offering popular dishes from all the regional cuisines of the country, in addition to all the usual suspects, respecting the most traditional way of preparing and presenting these dishes; it has been consistently impeccable since the beginning. Elegant and comfortable, the restaurant is very popular with all types of people, including politicians, artists, and families from other parts of the city visiting the Centro Histórico. Besides the main restaurant on Palma Street, there is another one in the downtown area, at the Sheraton Hotel, across from the Alameda Park, and three more in other parts of the city, including San Angel in the south, Lomas near Polanco, and Nápoles, near the World Trade Center of Mexico.

San Angel and Coyoacán, in the southern part of town, are two neighborhoods that also have their own culinary scene and host some interesting restaurants going back to the nineteenth century. El Cardenal and Azul, for example have restaurants in that part of the city. It would be unfair to talk about the neighborhoods and the restaurants of one city without mentioning restaurants in other cities and other states across the country. For the purpose of this chapter, to offer an idea of what is like to go out to eat in Mexico, it seemed more appropriate to center on neighborhoods and restaurants that most people would visit. Most neighborhoods in the country, particularly if they are relatively far from the center of a city, tend to be mostly local, with people from other neighborhoods rarely traveling there to eat. It is, however, important to mention some of the restaurants considered the best in other Mexican cities to give a more complete idea of what are the options for most Mexicans when they go out to eat.

Guadalajara is the second largest city in Mexico; it is also a cosmopolitan city with national and international tourism all year round. It is not surprising, then, that its restaurants are also eclectic and innovative. One of the most popular and most interesting ones is Hueso; Hueso is a fun, modern, eccentric space with framed bones (*hueso* means bone in Spanish) of all types, painted white, covering its walls; it is described by the owner and chef, Alfonso Cadena, as a workshop, consequently, the food is more playful and experimental, prepared with fresh, seasonal ingredients. Mesa 1 is another restaurant serving urban food and cocktails in a modern space with a beautiful terrace. I-Latina is an eclectic restaurant that fuses Mediterranean, Asian, and Mexican cuisines, considered one of the best in the city. More traditional, with dishes inspired on authentic Mexican food prepared with seasonal ingredients, Alcalde is another favorite of the *tapatíos*. International cuisine is also popular. Nápoles and La Moresca, for example, are traditional Italian restaurants with classical dishes, pizza, pasta, fish, risotto, and other Neapolitan specialties as well as desserts. Anita-Li is recognized as a creative restaurant with Vietnamese and Thai inspired dishes served in a very colorful, bright, and modern setting, while La Matera offers steaks and other traditional dishes from Argentina.

Monterrey is the third city in Mexico, an industrial town, and like Guadalajara, it has become more cosmopolitan. The restaurants of the city confirm this. Some of the best restaurants in Monterrey are Krei, a modern restaurant with casual and refined atmosphere and a mix of contemporary Mexican dishes and grilled meats Brazilian style. Los Arcos and Mare del Zur are both seafood restaurants. Los Arcos is more family oriented with bright, colorful tables, table cloths, and chairs offering fresh seafood; Mar del Zur offers modern Mexican food with Asian influence, like grilled octopus, fish, or shrimp in an Asian-inspired sauce; tuna *tamales*, salads and soups are other of the popular dishes. Fornera Wine House offers a good selection of wines (mostly Italian and French) with chesses, meats, and pastas with a Mediterranean influence. Modern and eclectic food is the signature of El Lingote; they offer a complete menu with soups, salads, sandwiches, burgers, and all the standard international dishes to be expected, as well as a large cocktail menu. La Nacional is one of the most popular restaurants in Monterrey, offering Mexican and Latin food in general, with, tacos, sandwiches, grilled vegetables, roasted pig and goat, and specially steaks. They do have a good wine list and a variety of traditional desserts. San Carlos and El Gran Pastor, on the other hand, focus on regional cuisine with *cabrito* (roasted goat) at the center of the menu, but also grilled pork and other grilled meats.

With a long culinary tradition, Puebla is synonymous with *mole* and *chiles en nogada*, as well as a numerous candies and desserts created in its convents. However, besides the countless restaurants and stands in markets to enjoy the local dishes, Puebla offers a select number of first-rate restaurants. Among the most popular are Casa Reyna and El Mural de los Poblanos, which offer traditional regional cuisine in a refined and modern setting with classical dishes prepared in the most traditional way. *Moles*, *mancha manteles*, enchiladas, soups, and other regional dishes are prepared with time-honored methods and seasonal, fresh ingredients. Intro and Moyuelo, although still focused on regional cuisine, offer contemporary interpretations of these dishes that are fresh and innovative; with contemporary, minimalist décor, these restaurants aim at attracting the new generations of customers to one of the best regional (and most traditional) cuisines of Mexico. La Noria is another modern, more family-oriented restaurant that offers a mix of international and Mexican dishes with a local flavor; housed in an old hacienda charmingly decorated in a modern and elegant style, La Noria is one of the most popular restaurants of the city. Similarly, La Purificadora, a restaurant in the hotel of the same name, offers modern interpretations of traditional dishes in the ample, airy space of an old ice factory turned into a boutique hotel with a rustic charm.

Guanajuato, like Puebla, is a colonial city with a tradition of beautiful architecture, well-defined local culture, and an old culinary tradition. The state of Guanajuato is Perhaps more famous for San Miguel de Allende, a town with a tradition all of its own; but Guanajuato City, the capital city, offers some excellent restaurants. Casa Valdez is an institution in the state; it is a restaurant with international and regional cuisine that has been popular with locals since 1950. It is among the 50-best Mexicans restaurants and has an eclectic, ample menu with Mediterranean and Mexican specialties. La Virgen de la Cueva offers a more adventurous version of the dishes of Karen Valadez Burstein, the same chef at Casa Valdez, with a menu of Mexican dishes she describes as unique and exquisite, made with love and passion. La Taberna de Diego y Frida offers modern Mexican cuisine inspired by the art and recipes of Frida Kahlo and Diego Rivera, perhaps Guanajuato's most famous son. The space is decorated in a sober and modern Mexican style with reproductions of Diego and Frida's paintings and photographs of the couple. Finally, El Jardín de los Milagros is considered the first restaurant with a signature cuisine in the state; it is appreciated also because of its beautiful setting in a hacienda from the 1600s with a modern décor. Its menu is big enough to showcase a modern Mexican cuisine with a strong Spanish and Mediterranean influence.

Mexico is a vast country with multiple regional cuisines that have not finished evolving yet, particularly as they mix with and complement other world cuisines and get pushed to their limits by young, inventive chefs. The size of the country and the diversity of its towns and cities, make it impossible to describe the experience of eating out as if it were one and only one uniform experience for everybody, instead of what it really is: an experience as diverse as the nation's regions, climates, histories, ethnicities, and traditions. However, the truth is that Mexico City has been and continues to be the place that dictates fashions for the rest of the country. When it comes to eating out, what happens in Mexico City is a very good indicator of what is happening in the rest of the nation. This does not diminish the distinctiveness of cultural practices in other cities and regions, but underlines the social, political, and economic role of the nation's capital and enhances the sense of a Mexican identity centered on gastronomic practices. The diversity of food and venues for eating out in Mexico is literally endless and allows for all budgets and tastes. This gives the reader an approximation of the experience of eating out in Mexico, with the understanding that the reality is much more diverse.

Enchiladas Suizas (Enchiladas in a Creamy Sauce)

Yield: Serves 6

12 tomatillos
2 serrano or jalapeño chili peppers
1 garlic clove
½ small white onion
4 ounces cream cheese
1 cup whipping cream
3 sprigs cilantro
4 tablespoons vegetable oil
Salt to taste
12 corn tortillas
1 large chicken breast, cooked and shredded
8 ounces shredded manchego cheese, or Mexican cheese mix
6 tablespoons sour cream
Chopped cilantro, optional

Equipment: medium pot, blender, sauté pan, mixing spoons, frying pan, baking dish

1. Place the tomatillos and chili peppers in a medium pot, cover with water and bring to a boil; cook for 8 minutes.
2. Transfer tomatillos and chili peppers to a blender; add the onion, garlic, cream cheese, whipping cream, and the 3 sprigs of cilantro; blend all ingredients to form a smooth sauce.
3. Heat 2 tablespoons of vegetable oil in a sauté pan and add the sauce; cook for a few minutes and season with salt and pepper; simmer for a few more minutes.
4. In a frying pan heat 2 tablespoons of vegetable oil and slightly fry the tortillas one or two at a time; transfer tortillas to a plate, place a generous amount of chicken and roll them; place rolled tortillas in a baking dish and cover with the tomatillo sauce; top enchiladas with the cheese and bake in preheated oven at 350 degrees for 10 to 15 minutes or until cheese melts.

To serve, place two enchiladas on a plate and top with the sour cream and sprinkle with chopped cilantro if using.

Huachinango a la Vercruzana
(Red Snapper Veracruz Style)

Yield: Serves 4 to 6

1 3-pound red snapper whole, cleaned and scaled
3 tablespoons olive oil
3 garlic cloves, minced
½ medium white onion, finely chopped
4 large tomatoes or 6 medium tomatoes, chopped
1 teaspoon Mexican oregano
2 large bay leaves
2 tablespoons finely chopped fresh parsley
½ cup pitted green olives
2 tablespoon capers
15 baby potatoes, cooked and peeled
4 to 6 pickled yellow chili peppers or pickled jalapeño peppers

Equipment: large frying or sauté pan, big enough to fit the fish, measuring spoons, mixing spoon

1. Sprinkle the fish with salt and pepper and let it rest.
2. In a large sauté pan heat oil and add onion until it turns translucent; add garlic and cook for a few seconds; add tomatoes and sauté for 10 minutes.
3. Add oregano, bay leaves, and parsley and simmer for a few minutes.
4. Add olives and capers; season with salt and pepper.
5. Place the whole fish in the sauce and cover; cook for 8 to 10 minutes, or until it is done. Place the potatoes around the fish.

Serve the individual portions of fish with 3 or 4 potatoes. Cover with abundant sauce and slices of the pickled chili peppers on top.

Ceviche Contramar

Yield: Serves 6 to 8

Ingredients
1 small red onion, sliced lengthwise
2 tablespoons regular sea salt
2 pounds white fish (halibut, mahi-mahi, etc.), cut into bite-sized chunks
1 cup celery, chopped
3 serrano chili peppers, sliced lengthwise
2 manzano chili pepper, sliced lengthwise
½ cup lime juice
½ cup cilantro, chopped
Olive oil
Maldon sea salt to taste
Tortilla chips

Equipment: medium bowl, large bowl, mixing spoons

1. Place the onion in a bowl with cold water and 1 tablespoons of sea salt; let soak for 5 minutes, then drain. Reserve.
2. In a mixing bowl add the fish and sprinkle with 1 tablespoon of sea salt and let rest for a few minutes. Add *serrano* and *manzano* peppers, as well as celery; mix well.
3. Drain the red onion and add to bowl with the fish.
4. Pour lime juice all over fish and vegetables and mix well.
5. Sprinkle with cilantro and drizzle olive oil. Mix well, careful not to break the fish.

To serve, keep in bowl or transfer to a serving plate or bowl, sprinkle with Maldon salt and accompany with tortilla chips.

Recipe adapted from *My Mexico City Kitchen* by Gabriela Cámara, Lorena Jones Books, California and New York, 2019, p. 170.

Pollo al Oregano (Chicken with Oregano)

Yield: Serves 4 to 6

Ingredients
1 whole 3-pound chicken cut into 8 pieces
3 cups water
2 tablespoons salt
2 tablespoons lime juice
1 head garlic
¼ teaspoon peppercorns
1 tablespoon oregano
¼ teaspoon cumin seeds
1 pound Yukon Gold potatoes, cubed and cooked

Equipment: large pot, mixing spoons, measuring spoons

1. Season chicken with lime juice and salt; let rest for 15 to 20 minutes.
2. Grind garlic, peppercorns, cumin, and oregano in a mortar.
3. Place chicken in a large pot with 3 cups of water and bring to a boil; lower heat and cook for 45 minutes to an hour; remove impurities that surface to the top until the water evaporates.
4. Add ground spices and coat all the pieces of chicken.
5. Let the chicken brown, stirring constantly, until crisp.
6. Add cooked potatoes and let them crisp. Adjust salt.

To serve, place in a plate with a nopalitos *salad and warm corn tortillas.*

Recipe adapted from *Oaxaca: Home Cooking from the Heart of Mexico* by Bricia López, Abrams, New York, 2019, p. 192.

Codorniz a La Espinaca (Quails with Spinach)

Yield: Serves 4

2 tablespoons oil
4 quails
1 tablespoons salt
1 pound spinach
1½ cups chicken broth
½ cup of roughly chopped cilantro
3 garlic cloves
½ medium white onion
8 tomatillos
½ cup Mexican cream or sour cream

Equipment: heavy saucepan or Dutch oven, measuring cups, blender, mixing spoons

1. Place the heavy saucepan or Dutch oven on high heat; add oil, once oil is hot, add quails, sprinkle with salt, and brown on all sides.
2. In a blender, blend half the spinach with half the chicken broth, cilantro, garlic, onion, and tomatillos until very smooth.
3. Add contents of the blender to the pan with the quails and bring to a boil; lower the heat.
4. Simmer for 30 minutes; add remaining spinach and cream; let simmer for a few minutes over low heat. Remove from heat and adjust salt.

To serve, place a quail on a plate with abundant amounts of sauce and accompany with warm corn tortillas or white rice.

Recipe adapted from *Verde en la cocina mexicana* by Ricardo Muñoz Zurita, Fundación Herdez, Mexico, 1999, p. 160.

CHAPTER TEN

Food Issues and Dietary Concerns

During the last decades of the nineteenth century in Mexico, during the years when dictator Porfirio Díaz was in power, there was an important impulse to bolster the economy, but the models favored then were centered on foreign investment and incentives to rich landowners to promote production and exportation of natural goods in high demand in the world like coffee, cotton, oil, precious metals, and henequen. There was very little interest in state regulation of these activities and minimum efforts to fortify an emergent middle class formed by professionals, merchants, small farmers, and artists. It was not until the end of the revolution in 1921 that a new model was implemented, centered on state control of the natural resources and regulation of most business activities, as well as land distribution. Among these policies there were a series of measures to guarantee access to food and to improve nutrition for low-income families in urban centers and small rural communities.

These programs were intended not only to help feed the people but to provide access to better food to fight malnutrition; one way of doing this was through the administration of stores and milk distribution centers by parastatal companies like Diconsa, Liconsa, and the now-defunct Conasupo, as well as with subsidies to agriculture, which also helped small producers to get their products out into the market. The Conasupo stores were strategically located in low-income areas and offered all sorts of foods at lower prices; they were considered supermarkets for the poor, located mostly in urban communities. The same is true of Diconsa, dedicated to helping rural communities. Liconsa started processing and selling milk in the 1940s under a different name, but with the same mission of making sure people could get good quality milk at a lower price. Many similar programs and social policies were kept in place by the Mexican government for most of the twentieth century, at least until the 1980s and 1990s. As Julio Moreno observes, the "revolution trigged policies and regulations that promoted economic sovereignty and social democracy within the framework of industrial capitalism" (Moreno 18). In turn, these policies and regulations aimed at bringing the benefits of the revolution to the masses while maintaining social peace.

For the Mexican government after the revolution, food was seen as a right of all Mexicans, but also as an effective way of social negotiation to maintain the status quo, and in later decades as a way of maintaining in power the governing party, the PRI, which was only defeated in 2000. The formula was successful in keeping relative social peace. The programs established by the Mexican government evolved with time and adapted to the new circumstances and the nutritional needs of the people. However, in the end, they were not enough, and inappropriate nutrition and illnesses related to this problem continued to be a challenge for Mexico, aggravated by an increase in the population. Besides Conasupo and Liconsa, cities and towns promoted popular markets during the second half of the twentieth century in most neighborhoods, as well as a program of street markets called *mercados sobre ruedas* (markets on wheels) with the intention of improving the diet of the working classes; these itinerant markets made fresh produce available to a larger portion of the population, but still fell short.

Access to food, particularly healthy and quality food, and the redistribution of land were two of the reason the revolution had unquestionable popular support; therefore, providing enough food became a goal of the postrevolutionary government. However, as the country's population increased, Mexico found it harder and harder to produce enough food to feed all its citizens, and became dependent on other countries to provide enough food for all. As the administrative bureaucracy grew more complex, nutrition plans, created to support the dietary needs of the population, were handled by different agencies sometimes unrelated. This in turn provided the opportunity for corruption to infiltrate several levels of the government. In the end, it became practically impossible to maintain consistent and sustained food programs and strategies to help the people, particularly the poorest in cities and isolated rural communities, to have access to food.

Inconsistent and imperfect, many of these programs nonetheless continued with more or less success until the 1990s, when the priority of the government became negotiating free trade agreements and neoliberal policies, which were intended to reduce the role of the government in many industries, including agriculture and food distribution, culminating with the consolidation of NAFTA in 1994. As result, many of these social programs were dismantled and open to the free market. The cancellation of these programs had consequences not just for low-income families but the entire population, since many of these programs in addition to providing accessible foods and coordinate nutrition plans, helped to incentivize small and medium agricultural producers. One of the main challenges that the Mexican government has had to confront for most of its modern history is being able to guarantee access to food to all its citizens. And not just food, but nutritious food and, for low-income families, food at accessible prices. However, it has also been expected from the Mexican government to educate people and provide information about nutrition and good eating habits, which it has done with modest results.

From time to time, for example, federal and local governmental offices release campaigns to inform the population of good and bad eating habits, of ways of improving nutrition, or how to eat well and save money. A program that has been particularly successful is the one called *Canasta Básica* (literally "basic basket"), which provides a list of the necessary items (food but also other household goods) a typical Mexican family would need to subsist; then it offers incentives to making them available to most people at lower prices, sometimes in stores managed by the government. Programs like this, however, were affected with the creation of NAFTA, when under pressure to open the Mexican market to American discount stores like Walmart, the government diminished or disappeared some of them. According to James W. Russell, the "Neoliberal laissez-faire reforms associated with NAFTA greatly cut back Mexico's Canasta Básica" (141). The formation of the new Segalmex (Seguridad Alimentaria Mexicana, or Mexican Food Safety) in 2019, an organization associated with the Department of Agriculture and Rural Development, dedicated to coordinate the efforts of Diconsa and Liconsa, represents a return to such programs.

Today, Diconsa administrates some 27,000 communal stores in the entire country with the mission of guaranteeing "the distribution of foods with a high nutritional content at an accessible price to the marginalized population" (Diconsa), favoring, as well, local products, thus giving the opportunity to local farmers to sell their products at competitive prices. In addition, Segalmex revised the contents of the *Canasta Básica*, increasing the number of items in the official list from 23 to 40, all of which are sold at the Diconsa stores. Among these products, which are introduced by the statement that "Every person has the right to nutritious and enough food of quality" (Canasta Básica), are the expected items, namely corn, beans, rice, flour, milk, dairy products, eggs, bread, pork, beef, and chicken, but also toiletries like soap, detergent, toothpaste, and toilet paper. The list also includes chocolate, Jell-O, cookies, dried fruits, and, for the first time, amaranth and chia seeds. Without a doubt, one of the major food issues Mexico has faced is being able to provide enough food to the entire population. Despite the initial intention of the government that came out of the revolution of doing so, the lack of political and ideological consistency has caused that most aspects related to food production and distribution, and issues of public health in general, be administrated arbitrarily, favoring a climate of corruption.

Consequently, Mexico lacks long-term and consistent strategies to deal with the number-one food issue in the nation—making sure everybody has access to nutritious food. Now, making sure everybody has access to food brings us to the other big food issue in Mexico; and it is that to provide sustenance for all, someone has to produce that food. Unfortunately, as the population grew and farmers migrated to cities in search of other opportunities, agricultural production centered even more on industrial single-crop farming for export; this created a crisis in food production for internal consumption. That means that Mexico is no longer self-sufficient in food production and has not been since at least the early 1980s, relying instead on exports from other countries, like the United States, which is the main provider of grains, such as corn and wheat, as well as meat; or Chile, another important partner from which Mexico imports mostly fresh fruit and wine. This position is a curious one, since Mexico is at once the main exporter of vegetables and fruits to the United States, particularly tomatoes, avocados, chili peppers, cucumbers, strawberries, limes, watermelon, mangoes, and papaya. So, while Mexico sells all these products to the United States, it buys corn, wheat, rice, pork, beef, dairy products, and processed foods, including canned vegetables and fruits, from it.

Another food issue related to food production and distribution, as well as nutrition, is food safety. Although Mexico has very good standards for food safety, in many ways comparable to any other developed nation, there are from time to time problems with food contamination, both with foods intended for export and foods consumed at home, which makes it clear that safety measures can only be improved. However, considering the amount of food produced and exported by Mexico, that seems to be the exception rather than the rule. Both export and import of food are huge part of the economic partnership between Mexico the United States; therefore, improving food safety is a priority for both nations. In the case of Mexico, the government and the agricultural industry know that food safety is extremely important for the economy to compete globally. This is essential not only because governments have the responsibility to guarantee the safety of their citizens but also because consumers all over the world are now more educated than ever and very aware of their buying power. So, food safety standards are a priority for everybody, because otherwise customers simply would not buy the products.

Food safety at industrial levels is not a real problem, despite the occasional outbreak of salmonella or other bacterial infections of fresh vegetables or fruits; that is not to say that the system is perfect, but rather that considering the amount of goods processed and commercialized between Mexico and the United States, incidents of this kind are rare. A very different thing happens in the case of Mexico when it comes to production and especially consumption of food and drinks at a smaller scale; in this context it is not rare to get foodborne illnesses caused by contaminated food. This contamination is usually caused by bacteria, viruses, or even parasites that find their way into the food mostly as the result of carelessness handling food. Among the most common causes of food illness are contamination with *Salmonella enterica, Escherichia coli, Campylobacter, Mycobacterium bovis, Cyclospora cayetanensis,* and *Listeria monocytogenes.* In almost all of these cases, the contamination is often the result of inadequate facilities for food preparation, lack of or inappropriate hygiene practices, some environmental issues, and failure to monitor the preparation and handling of food by the corresponding authorities. Traditionally, food illnesses happen when eating out, rather than when eating at home.

Mexico is a country with a long and rich tradition of street foods. As noted earlier, many Mexicans eat most of their meals on the street at convenient stalls and improvised stands. In books, blogs, vlogs, articles, and other medium, professionals and aficionados alike, praise, explain, discuss, recommend, condemn, or deconstruct the different types of street food available in Mexico. Street foods (generally called *antojitos* in Mexico) are foods most Mexicans eat not for necessity, but for *antojo* (craving), for pleasure. And as convenient and delicious this tradition may be, it could also be a health problem, mainly because most of the *puestos* that sell street food are improvised, which means that the people who prepare and sell the food are usually not trained in proper ways of handling food and have limited or no access to running water and other basics for proper hygiene. In addition, these *puestos* are usually placed wherever there is a free space or where there is a lot of traffic (outside a subway stop, a busy corner, a bus stop, a business or a school), so not always in the cleanest of places.

Aware of the situation, the government often issues recommendations to the public and food vendors on how to prevent food contamination. To avoid this problem, it recommends preparing food hygienically, washing hands before eating and after going to the bathroom, and washing and disinfecting fruits and vegetables; in particular, however, it recommends people to "avoid eating in food stands or places with unsanitary conditions" ("Recomendaciones para prevenir enfermedades"). Many of the publications, announcements, and blogs from the Department of Health are related to gastrointestinal issues and recommendations on how people can protect themselves, which reveals a real problem. In fact, in one of these blogs from June 2016, "Medidas de higiene en la preparación de alimentos," it claims that about 200 million cases of foodborne diarrhea are reported every year in Mexico. And time and time again, the culprit is poor hygiene and inappropriate food handling. What is not mentioned, and clearly the real problem, is not so much that people disregard the authorities' advise to wash their hands, or to storage food properly, or to avoid cross-contamination by using different utensils for different foods, but that the majority of street vendors do not have access to running water or any system of refrigeration. The reality is that there is very little or no control of most of these operations.

For the most part, street vendors try to do the right thing; however, the biggest problem is that they do not have access to the proper accommodations. Since many street vendors are underemployed individuals or untrained citizens struggling to make some extra money, most of their *puestos* are usually improvised stands put together with whatever furniture they have at home. That means no running water and no refrigerator, which results in most salsas, meats, dairy, and other perishables being kept at room temperature sometimes all day in high temperatures. Things are better when the food is sold at specific times of the day and quickly (morning *tamales* or *sopes*, evening tacos, etc.), as well as when the food sold is cooked when ordered. But raw fruits and vegetables and freshly squeeze juices sold out of a table at some street corner are particularly problematic, especially considering that the Department of Health regularly recommends that people scrub and wash thoroughly all fruits and vegetables with purified water, even if they've already been disinfected. Also, these *puestos* are usually tended by one or two family members, which means that often people handling food is also handling money when clients pay for their food, increasing the possibility of cross-contamination.

It is important to mention also that most Mexicans are aware of the risk of eating on the street, but also consider it a tradition, part of their culture and even of their Mexican identity, since there is a "belief that only Mexicans have a strong enough stomach to eat on the street without getting sick" (Sanchez). However, according to the daily *Excelsior* ("Comer en la calle"), half of all Mexicans have gotten sick at some point from eating on the street, and yet they continue to do so for pleasure, because they crave the food when they see it, but also because it is fast, convenient, and inexpensive. Similarly, a study of the eating habits of students in many cities of Mexico found out that young people prefer the food sold outside their schools, which they consider flavorful and varied, despite the lack in most cases of proper equipment, or even the ignorance of the vendors on how their food can transmit illnesses (Loyola Moreno, 463). The study also found that students were aware of the risk that eating on the street posed for their health, but nonetheless continued to consume those foods because they were inexpensive, accessible, and better tasting.

Taste and tradition, besides convenience and prices, are some of the reasons more often given by Mexicans for eating on the street. But if eating on the street is an established institution in the country, connected to the culture and the identity of the nation, its economic importance is equally impressive since in the period between 2015 and 2017 it generated more than 11 billion dollars in sales, way above fast food restaurants like McDonald's and Burger King, and only slightly below full-service restaurants like VIPS and Chillis (Valadez). Nonetheless, some people have concerns that these unregulated activities may be hurting the economy in the long run. In general, most experts agree that street food in Mexico is part of the culture and it is not going anywhere, so the Department of Health and other institutions at the federal and state level, constantly put out recommendations to eat safely on the street, so, if not to eliminate, at least to reduce the possibilities of getting sick. Recommendations like washing hands, eating at the stands that appear cleaner, but also to make sure that there is running water and refrigeration in those *puestos*, are the most common. Critics of these measurers point out that is not enough to publish these recommendations in official websites and bulletins, since most likely will not reach the target audience, many of whom do not have access to the Internet at home or are even unable to read. So, by not addressing at the same time other issues like economic inequality and better education renders these efforts futile.

Food safety in general is a very important issue for Mexico, not only for the dangers it potentially could pose for its citizens, but also for the conceivable ways in which could affect tourism. Mexico represents one of the most attractive markets for food consumption, since the country has to feed every year not only its own population, but the millions of international tourists that rush to its beaches, cultural festivals, archeological centers, and colonial towns annually (45 million international tourists in 2019 alone). This places Mexico in a unique position when it comes to the intersection of food and the market. Mexico has one of the strongest economies in the world and a good number of trade agreements, including NAFTA, as well as strong ties to world commerce. The population of the country today is somewhere between 128 and 130 million people; however, agricultural production has not been keeping up with the pace; thus, Mexico faces enormous challenges related to food, from hunger and malnutrition of a portion of the population, to insufficient domestic production of food, and a street culinary tradition deeply rooted in the national subconscious. Add to this, the fact that some 40 percent of the population lives in poverty, and the challenges Mexico faces became clear to all.

So, maintaining high standards of food safety is vital. International food companies often collaborate with the Mexican government and maintain close watch of their own facilities throughout the country to keep their standards consistent with international expectations. Restaurants and bars all over the country, but particularly in highly populated areas and popular tourist destinations, also collaborate with the government and self-regulate with higher standards than the basic required by law. Related to this issue of food availability, there is another problem Mexico has had to deal with since the last decades of the twentieth century, a radical change in the traditional diet, with its subsequent battle between industrialized and natural food. This is a problem that has had already tremendous consequences for the population in general, but particularly children, and has contributed to the biggest problem related to food that Mexico faces today: obesity. Mexicans are proud of their cuisine and claim that it is the ancestral diet of the nation. It is a mantra for Mexicans and foreigners alike to proclaim every single dish a direct descendant of the Maya or the Aztecs; dishes, they say, that go back hundreds, if not thousands, of years, ignoring, of course, the large quantities of cream, cheese, or lard in them. In reality Mexican food today has very little to do with the original food of Mesoamerican cultures. Ancient Americans had no fats to fry their foods in, and dairy products and meat protein were rare and mostly came from hunting and from eating small animals, including insects.

Methods for cooking food were also rustic—grilling in an open fire, boiling, cooking tortillas, or roasting tomatoes and chilis on a clay griddle placed directly on the fire. One imagines they also ate some raw vegetables

> Mexico has an epidemic of obesity and noncommunicable diseases such as diabetes and high blood pressure. Many experts point to the increase of American fast food that threatens to replace the traditional diet, but others, like Dr. Enrique Morales Villegas from the Cardiometabolic Research Center in Aguascalientes, consider that today's diet is more dangerous than fast food alone, since in addition to the traditional fried foods, people consume more junk food and soft drinks that invaded Mexico after NAFTA. In addition, people maintain a philosophy of comfort, which leads them to eat too much and watch too much TV.

and fruits. So, *pozole* with pork, *tamales* filled with chicken or beef, prepared with lard, and *quesadillas* thick with delicious Oaxaca cheese and topped with sour cream, have absolutely nothing to do with original Mesoamerican food. Mexican food is the result of the combination of European and American ingredients in a holy (or unholy, depending on your own ideology) marriage, and it is anything, but pure. Pretending otherwise is simply not true and could be misleading if not harmful for a contemporary person's health. Idealizing this diet, by pretending to "decolonize" it, is problematic; to assume that all Mesoamericans ate a healthy diet of abundant vegetables and fruits, rich in fiber, and to claim that the same was true of Mexicans up to the twentieth century, who supplemented their diets of beans and tortillas with avocados, berries, papaya, pineapples, nuts, chia or amaranth seeds, is simply a myth.

The issue here, of course, is that this idealization ignores the fact that bad eating habits are often the result of poverty, in Mexico and elsewhere. Mexican food is a combination of European and American ingredients, but that fact does not necessarily condemn the European influence in the name of some obtuse idea of purity; neither does it minimize the value of the Mesoamerican diet. Mexican food as enjoyed today, the version that has been consumed in Mexico for centuries and is popular in the United States and many other countries around the world; the only food that, in fact, can be called *Mexican food*, is meat, and butter, and lard, and fats, and dairy products, and rice, and cumin, and cinnamon, and clove, and oh yes, beans, corn, squash, tomatoes, and chili peppers. This diet is the traditional Mexican diet and for the most part was able to keep people nourished and in good shape, partially, of course, because it was frugal and incorporated many of these ingredients in small quantities and not every day. Even street foods, so important in Mexican culture, were eaten until recently in rare occasions. The efforts of the Mexican government to educate people on nutrition were precisely because of the scarcity of nutrients in the limited diets of beans and corn most poor people could afford.

Historians and anthropologists have argued constantly over the precise diet of the Mesoamerican peoples, with some of them commenting on how scarce it was for the people, while the aristocracy would eat meats and fish, corn, vegetables, and fruits, as well as all sorts of sauces and condiments, while drinking chocolate and *atole*. Others, on the contrary, describe a more wide-ranging diet, including small animals and wild vegetables and fruits in addition to corn, beans, and chili peppers. Whatever the case may be, the reality is that once Mexico became a Spanish colony, the diet of both Americans and Europeans complemented each other. And this food over time became the traditional Mexican cuisine, with more or less meat, cheese, cream, beans, corn, or chili peppers depending on the preferences and possibilities of each family. Some of these foods were, of course, markers of race and class and remained as such until the revolution, but for the most part they combined over time and created a Mexican cuisine that depended on local, fresh products and minimum industrialization until well into the twentieth century. This traditional diet changed dramatically in the second half of the last century. As the country became more industrialized in the 1940s, eating habits changed. People had less time and more distance to travel between work and home to be able to have home-cooked meals every day.

Industrialization also meant the introduction of processed foods into the Mexican diet to capture a growing market, but also for pragmatic purposes to help mothers who were now working to prepare meals for their families in a faster, more convenient way. As the country became even more modernized, the traditional foods began to incorporate canned foods and other processed ingredients into a still more or less traditional cuisine; however more aggressive policies of modernization started in the 1980s. During the administration of Miguel de la Madrid, and from pressure of the industrial class, the Mexican government started to open the economy more to foreign investment, which demanded a drastic reduction of the government's involvement in regulation and subventions, paving the way for free market policies, which concluded with the signing of NAFTA in 1992, which entered into effect in 1994. Although there were some clear benefits for Mexico with NAFTA, the results were not as favorable as expected. The development of the country happened in an uneven way and unemployment grew because many small and medium businesses could not compete with large transnational corporations, leaving Mexico more dependent on the American economy than ever (Rouquié 441). NAFTA also meant that big discount stores like Walmart or Costco could operate aggressively in Mexico.

Independently of the economic benefits NAFTA brought to Mexico, the implications for the food and agricultural industries were huge and not particularly favorable. The arrival of American stores meant also the massive arrival, at low prices, of a series of food products that had never been part of the Mexican diet. Canned and process foods were always seen by most Mexican families as alien and not particularly nutritious or flavorful. They were, paradoxically, identified also as middle- and upper-class foods, mostly because of their association with industrialization and modernity, and because they were also more expensive than natural foods bought at the local market. To open a can of tomato soup or to prepare a sandwich with white bread, sliced ham, and Cheez Whiz was seen more

Food Issues and Dietary Concerns

modern and cosmopolitan than a *bolillo* (a piece of traditional Mexican bread) smeared with refried beans and topped with fresh cheese and salsa. This image spoke to a number of families that aspired to be more modern and to signal their becoming part of the growing middle class.

The convenience of processed foods made these items more and more indispensable in the pantries of families with both parents working, and gave them an aura of modernity. It is not that processed foods were not available in Mexico before NAFTA, but that they became suddenly omnipresent and that prices went down tremendously. Potato chips, cookies, chocolate bars, sodas, canned sardines, fruits in syrup, or granola bars were products that people bought for children or family members as a treat very rarely. However, as of 2017, according to the Universdidad Utónoma de Chapingo, the average Mexican diet includes a whopping 60 percent of processed foods ("Dieta de mexicanos"). This is more than half of the foods Mexicans consumed every day and represents a huge change from the traditional diet of the country, consisting of leafy greens, vegetables, corn, grains, and fruits, making the new Mexican diet high in sugars, fats, and preservatives, elements that, according to the experts, are the main causes of obesity and the epidemic of diabetes that Mexicans suffer today, where "more than four million people have been diagnosed with this illness" ("Dieta de mexicanos") and which is one of the main causes of death in the country.

So, the dramatic change in the traditional diet goes beyond just a matter of taste or a colorful dispute between tradition and modernity, and is identified by all experts as the cause of the number one food issue Mexico is facing right now—noncommunicable diseases. According to a report by Laura Vela, diabetes, obesity, and hypertension are the conditions that most affect Mexicans and that end up costing the health authorities about 124 billion pesos (almost 5 billion dollars) every year. The tragic aspect of this is that such illnesses are preventable, since they are caused by bad habits, namely high consumption of calories, lack of physical activity, and not knowing how to put together a balanced diet (Vela). Much has been written about this problem in the last decade or so, with all experts agreeing on the problem, summarized this way by Noel Eyres: although there are many possible reasons for these epidemics, including a more sedentary life and cultural changes on how food is perceived, "the main culprit is the changing eating habits. Mexicans are eating less traditional dishes made from fresh ingredients and far more commercial products and fast food, high in saturated fat. And far too much sweet drinks" (Eyres). Again, the change from a traditional diet to an industrialized one is seen as the problem. And it is. In Mexico, like in the United States, cheap food with low-nutritional content and high in sugars, salt, and other chemicals is widely available.

These foods are more visible in stores, supermarkets, kiosks, and schools and neighborhood stores, not to mention the billions of dollars spent by corporations in advertisement in mass media, including radio and television. Besides their convenience, these foods are also a "bargain" for low-income families because of their high content of empty calories—that means very little nutritional value with high contents of fats and sugars—that make people feel full and happy since sugar makes food taste good and is addictive. Their low price compared with fresh foods, and the somehow confusing labeling advertising added vitamins, minerals, and other "nutrients" to "fortify" them, helps create the illusion of a nutritious meal at bargain prices. Today, Mexico is considered number two behind the United States in adult obesity and number one in childhood obesity; diabetes is also an illness that has been increasingly present in children, with a report from the Department of Health in 2018 announcing that three out of ten children had diabetes (Miranda), and UNICEF declaring that obesity and diabetes in Mexican children were an "emergency that required immediate action" ("La obesidad infantil"). The problem is serious and the Mexican government is aware of it. In fact, many reports, studies, and programs addressing the issue of obesity and noncommunicable diseases appear regularly in the web pages of the federal and state governments, offering advice, information, education on nutrition and healthy habits, and facts to debunk old myths.

However, the real problem resides in the fact that using social media and other official means of disseminating information does not guarantee that this information, again, is going to reach their target audience, working-class and lower-income families, as well as farmers and country dwellers, simply because these families tend to be also families where the parents are less educated and sometimes unable to read or simply do not have either access to the Internet or time to go through all the research papers, newspaper articles, and official documents, some of which are highly specialized in their content and vocabulary, to find out how to eat. If it looks like the authorities are doing everything in their power to combat obesity and other illnesses in the population by putting out lots of information, there is no doubt, on the other hand, that the food industry has tremendous influence on the government's answer to this crisis. Not only is Mexico the largest consumer of processed foods in the world but also the third producer of these foods, with exports to North, Central, and South America as well as the European Union. Given this, and that this industry is a major generator of employment, is impossible not to wonder how much influence it has in shaping the response of the government.

To monitor children's eating habits, to go regularly to a nutritionist, to choose only healthy foods, to avoid or to consume in moderation processed foods, and to read labels to be informed on its contents and nutritional value are some of the suggestions that specialists repeat again and again. But to consider the job done by mentioning these wise recommendations often times is naïve, simply because, they are not very practical. Furthermore, it is not realistic to assume that parents have nothing else to do than follow their children everywhere at all times to monitor their eating habits and protect them from constant exposure to, and even predatory practices by, the food industry, which has so much more resources to advertise their products and in many cases to even obscure or distort information about them. Although the industry and the government have collaborated to combat obesity, it has not always been a smooth relationship, particularly in the battle for controlling information about processed foods, with the industry proposing a self-regulatory approach and the government siding with consumer and health advocacy groups who are pushing for clear and easy to read labels warning consumers of the risks of consuming these products.

When the Mexican government agreed to a more comprehensive labeling of processed foods, for example, the industry opposed the proposal arguing that warning people that a food item was high in sugar or fat or sodium was not enough since that would not inform consumers of all the nutritional ingredients in the food. This battle lasted for years, with the industry opposing several measures, including a modest proposal to increase taxes on sodas and other sugary drinks in 2016, which, *The Guardian* reports, has been effective in reducing the consumption of these products, according to researchers of Mexico and the United States who "found that the 5.5% drop in the first year after the tax was introduced was followed by a 9.7% decline in the second year" (Boseley). But more radical was the proposal of changing the labeling of processed foods to a clearer frontal warning of the dangers of these foods, introduced in 2019, which passed both chambers of the Mexican Congress and was signed into law in March 2020. According to this law that goes into effect on October 1, all processed food will have to have on the front of the product octagonal black stop signs with white, clear, large letters reading "high in sugar," "high in saturated fats," or "high in sodium."

Measures like this one, although may seem drastic to some, are a positive step towards addressing obesity and the noncommunicable diseases it causes by forcing the industry to disclose in a very clear way the dangers of consuming processed foods and sugary drinks in excess. This is a very different approach than posting information in the web pages of government agencies hoping that people may come across them; this approach brings the information right to the consumer in a clear manner and at the moment of purchasing these products. The fact that the information is presented in an octagon resembling a stop sign is likely to be understood immediately by people and hopefully make them think twice about buying the product. In an obvious recognition that the children are particularly vulnerable before the power of corporations and advertisement, the law also prohibits the use of cartoon characters to advertise what in Mexico is called *comida chatarra*—junk food. An ambitious and aggressive measure, the clear labeling requirement is a very good indication of how serious the problem is, but also of how serious the current Mexican government is about combating it. The law will be implemented in three phases that will take about five years to complete, and everything seems to indicate that it will yield positive results, just like a similar law, implemented in 2016, has already done in Chile.

Carlota de Limón (Lime and Cookies Dessert)

Yield: Serves 6 to 8

1 12 oz can evaporated milk
1 14 oz can condensed milk
½ 8 oz bar cream cheese
½ cup lime juice, freshly squeezed
1½ rolls *galletas marias* (Marie biscuits)
1 lime

Equipment: rectangular 11 × 7 baking dish, blender, mixing spoon

1. Place the evaporated milk, the condensed milk, and the cream cheese in a blender. Blend at medium speed.
2. While the blender is running, add the lime juice slowly and blend until the mix thickens.
3. In the baking dish place a layer of cookies at the bottom and pour a third of the milk mixture over it; spread the mixture uniformly. Place another layer of cookies and pour a third of the mixture and spread. Add another layer of cookies and pour the last third of the mixture and spread smoothly. Sprinkle the zest of 1 lime on top as decoration. Refrigerate overnight.

Serve chilled, topped with whipped cream.

Guajolota (*Tamal* Sandwich)

Yield: Serves 4

4 *tamales* with green sauce
4 large rolls
2 tablespoons vegetable oil
Shredded cheese, optional
Sour cream, optional

Equipment: knife, frying pan, plate

1. In a frying pan, add the oil and fry the *tamales* until crunchy and golden brown.
2. Cut open the rolls.
3. Place a *tamale* in the roll and top with cheese and spread bread with sour cream, if using.

Serve on a plate and accompany with a large cup of atole.

Dorilocos (Mexican Frito Pie)

Yield: Serves 2 to 3

1 bag Doritos (9.75 oz), nacho cheese flavored preferred
Shredded carrots
Shredded *jícama*
Peeled and chopped cucumbers
Cueritos (pickled pig skin)
Hot sauce, Valentina preferred
Chamoy (sweet and sour condiment often added to candy or fruit, considered a junk food)
Cacahuates japoneses (crunchy peanuts covered in flour and soy sauce)
Lime juice
Gummies, optional

Equipment: scissors, mixing spoon

1. Cut the bag of Doritos a little above half, fold the edges to form a "bowl."
2. Add the shredded vegetables to the "bowl" (all ingredients are added to taste).
3. Add the *cueritos*, chop them if they are too big.
4. Add *chamoy* and hot sauce.

Top with cacahuates japoneses, gummies if using, and squeeze half a lime to serve.

Tamales de Gansito (Tamales with Gansito Cake)

Yield: Makes 6 tamales

¾ cup lard or vegetable shortening
½ cup sugar
2¼ cups masa harina
1½ teaspoon baking powder
2 cup warm water
8 corn husks soaked (you need only 6; the other 2 are in case you need them)
6 Gansito cakes
Whipped cream

Equipment: a large pot, a steamer basket, mixer, mixing bowls, mixing spoon, measuring spoons, cups

1. Combine masa harina and water in a large bowl and mix well to form a soft dough. Add more or less water as needed.
2. In a mixer, beat the lard with baking powder until it is white and fluffy; add sugar and continue beating until it is all incorporated.
3. Add the dough to the mixer and beat until it acquires a light consistency. To know if the dough is ready, drop a small ball into a glass of water, if it floats, it is ready, if it sinks to the bottom, continue beating.
4. Spread a generous amount of dough in a corn husk, then place a Gansito cake in the middle; add more dough to cover the cake completely; wrap the *tamale*, overlapping the ends of the husk, then folding it in half to close. Tie the *tamale* if you want with strips of corn husk. Do the same with the rest of the Gansitos.
5. Place the steamer basket in the large pot and add enough water to reach the bottom of the basket. Place the *tamales* in the steamer, standing up, cover the pot with a lid, making sure it is tight; cover the pot first with aluminum foil if needed.
6. Steam the *tamales* until done, about 1 hour or until the husks separate easily from the *tamales*. Make sure the water does not run out, and if it does add more.

To serve, place one tamale on a plate, open the husk and top with whipped cream; accompany with atole or hot chocolate.

Higos en Almíbar (Figs in Syrup)

Yield: Serves 4 to 6

½ cup lime
3 cups water
2 pounds green figs
2 cinnamon sticks
3 cups sugar
4 fig leaves

Equipment: large pot, heavy pot or Dutch oven, mixing spoons

1. Soak figs in water and lime, stirring often so the lime does not sink to the bottom. Soak them for 20 minutes or so.
2. Drain figs and rinse in running water several times to get rid of all the lime. Pierce figs with a toothpick.
3. Place figs in heavy pot or Dutch oven; add 3 cups of water, cinnamon sticks, sugar, and fig leaves and bring to a boil.
4. Simmer over low heat for a couple of hours or until a thick syrup forms (check regularly and add more water if needed); figs should be soft, but firm and impregnated with the syrup.
5. When done, remove from heat and let cool.
6. Transfer to a jar or other receptacle with a lid and chill in the fridge.

To serve place a few figs in a glass with plenty of syrup. It could be accompanied with slices of Chihuahua cheese, whipped cream, or ice cream.

Glossary

Achiote
Seed of annatto used as condiment.

Acitrón
Candied *biznaga* cactus.

Agave
A succulent plant with long leaves of about four to five feet of a blue-gray color forming a rosette; it is used to make tequila.

Aguacate
Fruit native to Mexico with creamy and smooth flesh of a green color and dark coarse skin; it is used mostly in salads and sauces.

Aguas frescas
Traditional drink made with water, fruit, and sugar.

Antojitos (also *garnachas*)
Snacks, traditionally savory, eaten often on the street.

Ate
Fruit paste made with a variety of fruits, usually served as dessert or as a snack.

Atole
Drink made with water or milk, corn dough, piloncillo, or sugar and spices, often flavored with fruits.

Barbacoa
Meat cooked underground, wrapped in maguey cactus leaves; also, this process of cooking.

Betabel
Beets.

Birria
Meat, traditionally of goat or lamb, marinated in spices and chili peppers and traditionally cooked in *barbacoa*.

Blanco de Pátzcuaro
Small fish with soft, delicate flesh found exclusively in Lake Patzcuaro.

Bolillo
Traditional Mexican bread in an oval shape with tips on the extremes. It is soft with a crunchy crust.

Botana
Snacks often served at bars or cantinas with drinks, also served at home with drinks before a meal.

Buñuelo
A fried little cake made with flour, eggs, and sugar, usually covered in a piloncillo syrup.

Cacahuates
Peanuts.

Cajeta
Milk caramel, known in other countries as *dulce de leche*. Traditionally made with goat milk in Mexico.

Calabacita
Mexican squash, or zucchini.

Calabaza
Pumpkin.

Camote
Sweet potato.

Capirotada
Traditional bread pudding made with bread, milk or syrup, cheese, and dried fruits.

Capulín
Small fruit, the size of a blueberry, with a lustrous black skin and a large pit in the center surrounded by a sweet flesh that taste like cherries.

Carnitas
Traditional dish of pork cooked in lard and spices until tender; it is used to make tacos.

Cecina
Dry meat, sometimes cured with salt, spices, and chili peppers.

Glossary

Cena
Evening meal, traditionally lighter than the main meal of the day eaten in the early afternoon.

Ceviche
Fish, and sometimes other seafood, marinated and cooked in lime juice. It is served mixed with chopped onion, tomatoes, and chili peppers.

Champurrado
Atole made with chocolate, water, and piloncillo.

Charal
Small fish from lakes and rivers of central Mexico; it is eaten usually dry.

Chayote
Vegetable with the shape of a large pear with sweet, juicy flesh and covered in a smooth or thorny green skin.

Chia
Seed of the plant related to sage, native to Mexico, used often in drinks or sweets.

Chicharrón
Fried pork rind.

Chilaquiles
Traditional dish made with tortilla chips cooked in a thick green or red sauce and spices; it is traditional for breakfast.

Chile
A sauce made with chili peppers and spices used to serve with meats or vegetables as a main dish.

Chiles
Chili peppers, either dry or fresh, traditionally used in Mexican cuisine.

Chipilin
Aromatic herb with a green color and agreeable taste, popular in southern Mexican cuisine.

Chocolate
The cacao seeds or any product derived from it, whether liquid, powder, or paste. It was highly appreciated in Mesoamerica.

Chongos
Traditional dessert made with curds, cinnamon, and piloncillo or sugar.

Cilantro
Aromatic herb with green leaves and long stems, with a strong earthy taste often used in Mexican cooking.

Cocada
Traditional sweet made with shredded coconut, sugar, and sometimes milk or water.

Comal
Round griddle made of clay or metal used to cook corn tortillas and other foods.

Comida
Main meal of the day, traditionally served in the early afternoon.

Crema
Mexican cream, slightly tangy cream, lighter than sour cream, made with milk, salt, and other ingredients.

Cuitlacoche (also huitlacoche)
A fungus that affects corn when rain gets into the husk and it rots between the kernels. It is considered a delicacy in Mexico.

Dulces
Sweets. Usually the word refers to traditional artisanal candies made with candied fruits, pastes, or seed and honey, sugar, or piloncillo.

Ejotes
Green beans.

Elote
The ear of corn when young.

Enchiladas
Traditional dish made with tortillas covered in a spicy sauce and filled with meats, cheese, or vegetables.

Epazote
Strong, earthy herb very popular in Mexican cuisine.

Frijoles
Beans, one of the main staples of the Mesoamerican diet.

Guacamole
Traditional salsa made with avocado, tomatoes, onion, and chili peppers.

Guajolote
One of the traditional names given to a turkey in Mexico.

Huauzontle
A plant with a long, thin, fibrous stem with many bunches of very small green edible flowers; it is related to quinoa and amaranth and has remained an important food in Mexican cuisine.

Jicama
An edible tuberous root with a yellowish skin and white, juicy flesh; its flavor is sweet and refreshing. They are used mostly in salads or sliced with lime and ground chili pepper.

Limón
Traditionally in Mexico lime is called *limón*; a lemon, is known sometimes as *limón real*.

Machaca
Dry beef that has been seasoned, shredded, and dried (similar to beef jerky).

Maguey
A plant in the Aspargaceas family, with long, thin leaves of different colors from gray to green, gathered around a center, forming a large rosette, used to produce an alcoholic beverage called *pulque*.

Maíz
Corn, the most important cereal in Mesoamerica; it is a plant related to the grass family with tall, leafy stalks; it was first domesticated in Mexico. Its kernels were cooked with lime or ashes to make them edible. The main staple of the civilizations of Mesoamerica.

Mamey
The edible fruit of an evergreen tree native to southern Mexico, Central America, and the Caribbean. The fruit, with a rough brown skin and a creamy, sweet flesh of an orange color, is very popular in desserts and drinks or by itself.

Metate
A utensil made of volcanic stone tilted and supported by three feet, used to grind grains and spices.

Mezcal
Spirit made from a few varieties of agave.

Molcajete
A mortar made of volcanic stone.

Mole
Traditional sauce made with over 80 ingredients, including chocolate, chili peppers, and spices. Traditionally served with turkey for big holidays.

Nixtamal
Corn after it has been cooked with lime or ashes and is ready to be milled and made into a dough for tortillas and other foods.

Nopal
Prickly pear cactus. An edible cactus plant used in stews or salads.

Pan dulce
Any variety of sweet bread popular in Mexico for breakfast or supper.

Pejelagarto
A fish from the rivers of the state of Tabasco, which looks like a cross between a fish and an alligator and is considered a living fossil.

Piloncillo
Unrefined, brown sugar with rich caramel and molasses flavor, traditional in sweets and other desserts.

Piña
Pineapple.

Pipián
Dish made with chili peppers, spices, and toasted and grounded pumpkin seeds.

Plátano
Banana; in some regions plantains, also known as *plátano macho*.

Pozole
Traditional soup made with hominy, spices, and meat, especially pork, but also chicken or even shrimp.

Pulque
Traditional alcoholic beverage made from the fermented sap of the maguey plant.

Quelite
A generic name to refer to a variety of wild plants and herbs used in dishes and salads.

Quesadilla
Traditional snack or appetizer made with a small corn tortilla with cheese or other fillings, folded in half and either cooked on a *comal* or fried.

Queso
Cheese, a dairy product made primarily with cow milk, but also of other mammals like goat or sheep.

Salsa
A spicy fresh or cooked sauce of chopped or blended tomatoes, onions, and chili peppers served with most Mexican foods.

Sope
Traditional snack made with corn dough in the form of a thick tortilla topped with salsa, shredded lettuce, chopped tomatoes and onion, as well as shredded cheese and cream.

Taco
A traditional Mexican snack consisting of a small corn tortilla filled with meats, stews, or vegetables, rolled and served with salsa.

Tamal
Traditional snack made with corn dough in the shaped of a little elongated cake wrapped in a corn husk, filled with pork or chicken in a spicy sauce, and steamed; it can also be made sweet with raisins.

Tejocote
A small fruit native to Mexico, with the shape of a very small apple with yellow, smooth skin and flavorful flesh. It is used in drinks and sweets.

Tequila
Distilled spirit made from the blue agave plant; it can only be produced in specific areas of the country; it is considered the national spirit of Mexico.

Tomate
A popular vegetable in Mexican cooking traditionally used in salads, stews, sauces, and other foods; usually of a red color and round shape, was originally cultivated in Mesoamerica.

Tomatillo
Small fruit with a pale-green color, sometimes with a purple hue, covered by a dry husk; used in salsas and stews.

Torta
The name given to a sandwich in Mexico. Also it refers to a patty.

Tortilla
A thin, round cake made with corn meal and cooked over a *comal* or a griddle. It is the most important staple in Mexican cuisine and it is served with most meals. It can also be made with flour.

Tuna
The fruit of the prickly pear cactus; it is elongated in shape, the size of a large egg, with thorny skin and juice, sweet flesh, green or red, and lots of small edible seeds. It is eaten fresh or in sweets and drinks.

Vanilla
A climbing plant native to Mexico, related to orchids; its aromatic pods are harvested and the seeds extracted to be used in foods such as cakes, drinks, or candies.

Zapote
Name of a fruit of the Sapotaceae family with sweet, soft flesh, either black or white, with a round shape and regular size. These fruits are eaten fresh or in sweets, drinks, and other desserts.

Selected Bibliography

Abascal, Paulina. *Postres Mexicanos*. Mexico: Ediciones Larousse, 2009.
Agren, David. "Mexico City's James Bond-inspired Day of the Dead Parade Gets Mixed Reviews." *The Guardian*, 30 October 2016, https://www.theguardian.com/world/2016/oct/29/day-of-the-dead-parade-james-bond-mexico-city. Accessed 10 November 2019.
Agren, David, and Sam Jones. "Cursed Are the Cheesemakers." *The Guardian*, 15 January 2018, https://www.theguardian.com/world/2018/jan/15/spain-mexico-trade-deal-manchego-cheese-dispute. Accessed 18 December 2019.
Aguilar Rodríguez, Sandra. "La mesa está servida: comida y vida cotidiana en el México de mediados del siglo XX." *Revista de Historia Iberoamericana*, vol. 2, no. 2, 2009, pp. 52–85.
Baker, Lauren E. *Corn Meets Maize: Food Movements and Markets in Mexico*. Lanham, MD: Rowman & Littlefield Publishers, 2013.
Bayless, Rick. *Mexican Kitchen. Capturing the Vibrant Flavors of a World-Class Cuisine* New York: Scribner, 1996.
Benitez de, Ana M. *Pre-Hispanic Cooking/Cocina prehispánica*. Mexico: Ediciones Euroamericanas, 1974.
Bilger, Burkhard. "The Hunt for Mexican Heirloom Beans." *The New Yorker*, 16 April 2018, https://www.newyorker.com/magazine/2018/04/23/the-hunt-for-mexicos-heirloom-beans. Accessed 18 December 2019.
Boseley, Sarah. "Mexico's Sugar Tax Leads to Fall in Consumption for Second Year Running." *The Guardian*, 22 February 2017, https://www.theguardian.com/society/2017/feb/22/mexico-sugar-tax-lower-consumption-second-year-running. Accessed 15 March 2020.
Cámara, Gabriela. *My Mexico City Kitchen, Recipes and Convictions*. New York: Lorena Jones Books, 2019.
"Canasta Básica." *Official Webpage of the Mexican Government*, https://www.gob.mx/canastabasica. Accessed 10 May 2020.

Casas, Bartolome de las. *Brevísima relación de la destrucción de las Indias*. Madrid: Ediciones Cátedra, 2005.

Clendinnen, Inga. *Ambivalent Conquest. Maya and Spaniard in Yucatan, 1517–1570*. New York: Cambridge UP, 1987.

Clendinnen, Inga. *Aztecs. An Interpretation*. New York: Cambridge UP, 1991.

Coe, Michal D. *The Maya*. New York: Thames and Hudson, 1995.

"Comer en la calle, mal para más de la mitad de los mexicanos." *Excelsior*, 24 May 2014, https://www.excelsior.com.mx/nacional/2014/05/24/961136. Accessed 15 June 2020.

Cortés, Hernando. *Five Letters. 1519–1526*. Trans. J. Bayard Morris. Abingdon, Oxon: Routledge Curzon, 2005.

"Día de los Muertos no tiene origen prehispánico: historiadora." *Milenio*, 1 November 2017, https://www.milenio.com/cultura/dia-de-muertos-no-tiene-origen-prehispanico-historiadora. Accessed 8 November 2019.

Díaz del Castillo, Bernal. *The True History of the Conquest of New Spain*. Trans. Janet Burke and Ted Humphrey. Indianapolis: Hackett Publishing Company, 2012.

Díaz y de Ovando, Clementina. "El café: refugio de literatos, políticos y de muchos otros ocios." *La república de las letras. Asomos a la cultura escrita del México decimonónico*. Eds. Belem Clark de Lara & Elisa Speckman Guerra. Mexico: UNAM, 2005. Pp. 75–88.

"Dieta de mexicanos, con 60% de alimentos procesados." *Forbes*, 19 October 2017, https://www.forbes.com.mx/dieta-de-mexicanos-con-60-de-alimentos-procesados/. Accessed 19 March 2020.

"Diconsa." *Official Webpage of the Mexican Government*, https://www.gob.mx/diconsa/que-hacemos. Accessed 5 May 2020.

Dreiss, Maredith L. and Sharon Edgar Greenhill. *Chocolate: Pathway to the Gods*. Tucson: U of Arizona P, 2008.

Earle, Rebecca. "'If You Eat Their Food . . .': Diets and Bodies in Early Colonial Spanish America." *The American Historical Review*, vol. 115, no. 3, June 2010, pp. 688–713.

"'El antojito no es fast food Mexicana': José Iturriaga." *Sabores son Amores*, 3 September 2019, http://saboressonamores.com/el-antojito-no-es-fast-food-mexicana-jose-n-iturriaga/. Accessed 10 April 2020.

"Es la Rosca de Reyes parte de la cultura mexicana." *El Universal*, 6 January 2009, http://archivo.eluniversal.com.mx/articulos/51781.html. Accessed 29 December 2018.

Eyres, Noel. "Eat, Drink, and Be Sedentary: Obesity's Strain in Mexican Healthcare." *AXA*, 30 May 2018, https://www.axa.com/en/magazine/next-stop-mexico-part-2-obesity. Accessed 18 June 2020.

"40% de los mexicanos come fuera de su hogar al menos una vez a la semana o más a menudo." *Nielsen*, 17 November 2016, https://www.nielsen.com/mx/es/press-releases/2016/40-por-ciento-de-los-mexicanos-come-fuera

-de-su-hogar-al-menos-una-vez-a-la-semana-o-mas-a-menudo/. Accessed 12 November 2019.

García Rivas, Heriberto. *Cocina prehispánica mexicana. La comida de los antiguos mexicanos*. Mexico: Panorama Editorial, 2015.

Gerson, Fany. *My Sweet Mexico. Recipes for Authentic Pastries, Breads, Candies, and Frozen Treats*. Berkeley: Ten Speed Press, 2010.

Grubinger, Vern. "History of Strawberry." *University of Vermont*, June 2012, https://www.uvm.edu/vtvegandberry/factsheets/strawberryhistory.html. Accessed 19 December 2019.

Guedea, Virginia. "México en 1812: Control político y bebidas prohibidas." *Estudios de Historia Moderna y Contemporánea de México*, vol. 8, 1980, pp. 23–65.

Hoise, Rachel. "The Surprising Health Benefits of Tequila." *The Independent*, July 24 2018, https://www.independent.co.uk/life-style/health-and-families/tequila-health-benefits-national-day-2018-weight-loss-fitness-a8461211.html. Accessed on March 17, 2020.

Holtz, Deborah and Juan Carlos Mena. *Tacopedia*. New York: Phaidon Press, 2015.

Hoyer, Daniel. *Mayan Cuisine. Recipes from the Yucatán Region*. Salt Lake City: Gibbs Smith Publisher, 2008.

Juárez López, José Luis. *La lenta emergencia de la comida mexicana. Ambigüedades criollas, 1750–1800*. Mexico: Miguel Ángel Porrua, 2005.

Kennedy, Diana. *My Mexico. A Culinary Odyssey with More than 300 Recipes*. New York: Clarkson Publishers, 1998.

"La cocina Mexicana, un 'invento' del siglo XIX." *Instituto cultural de León*, 13 September 2020, http://institutoculturaldeleon.org.mx/icl/story/749/La-cocina-mexicana-un-invento-del-siglo-XIX#.XEYIyC3MxE5. Accessed 18 December 2019.

Landsel, David. "Meet the 10 Best Mexican Chefs in the United States Right Now." *Food & Wine*, 26 October 2017. https://www.foodandwine.com/travel/restaurants/meet-10-best-mexican-chefs-in-united-states-right-now. Accessed 17 March 2020.

"La obesidad infantil en México: una emergencia que requiere medidas inmediatas." *Noticias ONU*, 7 March 2020, https://news.un.org/es/story/2020/03/1470821. Accessed 20 June 2020.

Las crónicas del taco. Created by Pablo Cruz, Netflix, 2019.

López, Bricia. *Oaxaca. Home Cooking from the Heart of Mexico*. New York: Abrams, 2019.

López, Rick A. "The Noche Mexicana and the Exhuibition of Popular Arts: Two Ways of Exalting Indianess." *The Eagle and the Virgin. Nation and Cultural Revolution in Mexico, 1920–1940*, eds. Mary Kay Vaughan and Stepehen E. Lewis. Durham, NC: Duke UP, 2006. Pp. 22–42.

Lorenzo, José Luis. "Los orígenes mexicanos." *Historia General de Mexico. Tomo 1*. Mexico: El Colegio de Mexico, 1976.

Loyola Moreno, Tania, et al. "El conocimiento y percepción de riesgos for ingesta de alimentos fuera de instituciones no impacta positivamente." *Journal of Negative and No Positive Results*, vol. 2, no. 10, 2017, pp. 462–472.

Martínez, Zarela and Anne Mendelson. *Zarela's Veracruz*. New York: Houghton Mifflin, 2001.

Martínez Limón, Enrique, Carlos Monsiváis, and Michael Calderwood. *Tequila. Tradición y destino*. Mexico: Revimundo, 1999.

McGovern, Patrick. *Uncorking the Past. The Quest for Wine, Beer, and Other Alcoholic Beverages*. Berkeley and Los Angeles, U of California P, 2009.

Mensajero de la Salud. Mexico: Secretaría de Salud, n/d.

Mettler, Katie. "Three Dogs Played in a Pond. Toxic Algae Killed Them." *Washington Post*, 12 August 2019, https://www.washingtonpost.com/science/2019/08/12/three-dogs-played-pond-toxic-algae-killed-them/. Accessed 10 February 2019.

Miranda, Perla. "En México, 3 de cada 10 niños tiene diabetes: Secretaría de Salud." *El Universal*, 13 August 2018, https://www.eluniversal.com.mx/nacion/sociedad/en-mexico-3-de-cada-10-ninos-tienen-diabetes-secretaria-de-salud. Accessed 20 June 2020.

Moreno, Julio. *Yankee Don't Go Home. Mexican nationalism, American Business Culture, and The Shaping of Modern Mexico, 1920–1950*. Chapel Hill: U of North Carolina P, 2003.

Moskin, Julia. "This Mexican Chef Is Having a Very Good Year." *The New York Times*, 4 June 2019, https://www.nytimes.com/2019/06/04/dining/gabriela-camara-mexican-food.html. Accessed 30 March 2020.

Muñoz Zurita, Ricardo and Ignazio Urquiza. *Verde en la Cocina Mexicana*. Mexico City: Fundación Herdez, 1999.

Myers, Kathleen A. "A Glimpse of Family Life in Colonial Mexico: A Nun's Account." *Latin American Research Review*, vol. 28, no. 2, January 1993, pp. 63–87.

Nguyen, Tina. "Lady Chef Stampede: How Josefina Velázquez de León Unified Mexican Cuisine." *MediaIte*, March 14 2013, https://www.mediaite.com/food/lady-chef-stampede-josefina-velazquez-de-leon/. Accessed 10 February 2020.

Novo, Salvador. *Cocina mexicana o historia gastronómica de la ciudad de México*. Mexico: Editorial Porrúa, 1967.

Novo, Salvador. "Incursión gastronómica francesa en México." *Artes de México*, no. 43, 1998, pp. 46–8.

Pack, MM. "Got Milk? On the Trail of Pastel de Tres Leches." *The Austin Chronicle*, February 13 2004, https://www.austinchronicle.com/food/2004-02-13/196888/. Accessed February 25 2020.

Paz, Octavio. *Sor Juana or, the Traps of Faith*. Trans. Margaret Sayers Peden. Cambridge, MA: Belknap/Harvard UP, 1988.

Pett, Shaun. "A Second Act for Pujol, Mexico's World-Class Restaurant." *The New York Times*, 23 January 2017, https://www.nytimes.com/2017/01/23

/dining/pujol-move-mexico-city-enrique-olvera.html. Accessed 17 March 2020.
Prieto, Guillermo. *Versos Inéditos*. Mexico: Imprenta del Comercio de Dublan y Chavez, 1879.
Quintana, Patricia. *The Taste of Mexico*. New York: Stewart, Tabori & Chang, 1986.
Ramírez Coronel, Maribel. "El peso de la industria mexicana de alimentos procesados." *El Economista*, 9 June 2019, https://www.eleconomista.com.mx/opinion/El-peso-de-la-industria-mexicana-de-alimentos-procesados-20190609-0075.html. Accessed 20 June 2020.
Ramírez, Miriam. "El té se abre camino en tierra mexicana." *Milenio*, 23 April 2017, https://www.milenio.com/negocios/el-te-se-abre-camino-en-tierra-mexicana. Accessed 10 February 2020.
Rivas Pérez, Jorge F. "Domestic Display in the Spanish Overseas Territories." *Behind Closed Doors. Art in the Spanish American Home, 1492–1898*. Richard Aste, ed. The Monacelli Press/Brooklyn Museum, 2013.
Rogers, Kate. "Restaurant Spending Set to Hit High in 2019 as Consumers Spend More of Their Budget On Dining Out." *CNBC*, 19 August 2019, https://www.cnbc.com/2019/08/19/americans-putting-more-of-their-budget-toward-eating-out.html. Accessed 15 March 2020.
Rouquié, Alain. "Mexico y el TLCAN, veinte años después." *Foro Internacional*, vol. 55, no. 2, April-June 2015, pp. 433–453.
Russel, W. James. *Double Standard. Social Policy in Europe and the United States*. Lanham, Maryland: Rowman & Littlefield Publishers, 2011.
Ruy-Sanchez, Alberto and Margarita de Orellana, eds. *Tequila. A Traditional Art of Mexico*. Washington: Smithsonian Books, 2004.
Salazar, Estefani. "Así se ve el nuevo etiquetado de alimentos." *El Universal*, 30 July 2020, https://www.eluniversal.com.mx/menu/como-luce-el-nuevo-etiquetado-de-alimentos. Accessed 30 July 2020.
Sanchez, Ivonne. "Comer en la calle en México: entre orgullo y sentimiento de culpa." *Radio France International*, 1 November 2018, http://www.rfi.fr/es/salud/20180111-comer-en-la-calle-en-mexico-entre-orgullo-y-sentimiento-de-culpa-comida-mexicana-urba. Accessed 15 June 2020.
Satre, Lowell J. *Chocolate on Trial. Slavery, Politics, and the Ethics of Business*. Athens: Ohio UP, 2005.
Schneider, Deborah. *The Mexican Slow Cooker. Recipes for Mole, Enchiladas, Carnitas, Chile Verde Pork, and More Favorites*. Berkeley: Ten Speed Press, 2012.
Shaer, Matthew. "A Secret Tunnel Found in Mexico May Finally Solve the Mysteries of Teotihuacan." *Smithsonian Magazine*, June 2016, https://www.smithsonianmag.com/history/discovery-secret-tunnel-mexico-solve-mysteries—teotihuacan-180959070/. Accessed 6 November 2019.
Spurrier, Jeff. "Huauzontle, A Mexican Staple in L.A. Edible Gardens." *Los Angeles Times*, 10 July 2012, https://latimesblogs.latimes.com/home_blog/2012/07/huauzontle-.html. Accessed 20 December 2019.

"Starbucks Celebrates with 39% of Market." *Mexico News Daily*, 9 September 2017, https://mexiconewsdaily.com/news/starbucks-celebrates-with-39-of-market/. Accessed 10 January 2020.

Suárez Escobar, Marcela. "De viandas, lujos y sabores. La burguesía mexicana y sus delicias culinarias a finales del siglo XIX." *Caravelle*, no. 71, December 1988, pp. 37–523.

Synan, Mariel. "Cinnamon's Spicy History." *History*, 4 October 2013, https://www.history.com/news/cinnamons-spicy-history. Accessed 27 December 2019.

Taube, Karl. *Aztec and Maya Myths*. Avon: British Museum Press/University of Texas Press, 1993.

Téllez, Lesley. "The Forgotten Legacy of Mexico's Original Celebrity Chef." *Saveur*, 31 March 2016, https://www.saveur.com/josefina-velasquez-de-leon-original-mexican-celebrity-chef/. Accessed 28 February 2020.

"Todo lo que debes saber sobre el día del amor y la amistad." *Excelsior*, 14 February 2013, https://www.excelsior.com.mx/comunidad/2013/02/14/884146. Accessed 12 October 2019.

Townsend, Richard F. *The Aztecs*. New York: Thames and Hudson, 1992.

Valadez, Roberto. "En 2017 la comida callejera genrará más de 11 mil mdd." *Milenio*, 25 July 2015, https://www.milenio.com/negocios/2017-comida-callejera-generara-11-mil-mdd. Accessed 17 June 2020.

Vela, Laura. "Mexico tiene la peor dieta y esto es lo que nos cuesta a todos." *Excelsior*, 30 November 2016, https://www.excelsior.com.mx/nacional/2016/11/30/1131297. Accessed 26 June 2020.

Velázquez de León, Mauricio. "Mexican Food: Antojitos." *Lonely Planet*, 26 June 2012, https://www.lonelyplanet.com/mexico/travel-tips-and-articles/mexican-food-antojitos/40625c8c-8a11-5710-a052-1479d2771b9b. Accessed 28 December 2019.

Weis, Robert. "Las panaderías en la Ciudad de México de Porfirio Díaz: los empresarios vasco-navarros y la mobilización obrera." *Revista de Estudios Sociales*, no. 29, April 2008, pp. 70–85.

Whitmore, Alex. "Cacao Tejate: Ancient Chocolate Drink." *The Atlantic*, 28 April 2009, https://www.theatlantic.com/health/archive/2009/04/cacao-tejate-ancient-chocolate-drink/16609/. Accessed 10 January 2020.

Yadav, Deependra and SP Singh, "Mango: History, Origen, and Distribution." *Journal of Pharmacognosy and Phytochemistry*, vol. 6, no. 6, 2017, pp. 1257–1262.

Yunez-Naude, Antonio. "The Dismantling of CONASUPO, a Mexican State Trader in Agriculture." *The World Economy* vol. 26, no. 1, January 2003, pp. 97–122.

Zaslavsky, Nancy. *A Cook's Tour of Mexico. Authentic Recipes from the Countries Best Open-Air Markets, City Fondas, and Home Kitchen*. New York, St. Martin's Press, 1995.

Index

Acitrón. *See* Cactus
Agave, xi, 102, 109, 111, 112, 152, 177
Aguas frescas, 25, 106, 107, 114, 115, 153, 178; agua de alfalfa (alfalfa-flavored water), 118
Antojitos, 145, 193. *See also* Garnachas
Appetizers, xii, 41–53, 154, 176, 179
Arroz. See Rice
Atole, 12, 23, 25, 26, 28, 29, 30, 61, 62, 64, 74, 102, 105, 114, 122, 132, 145, 146, 155, 156, 197; atole de fresa (corn dough strawberry hot drink), 116; *champurrado,* 105, 146
Aztecs, xv, 2, 4, 5, 6, 7, 20, 21, 27, 28, 29, 84, 101, 104, 109, 130, 196

Barbacoa, 134, 135, 145, 151, 152, 158, 175
Beans, 2, 3, 7, 9, 26, 28, 29, 41, 42, 43, 45, 46, 48, 49, 50, 51, 52, 54, 62, 63, 64, 67, 68, 69, 71, 72, 124, 125, 129, 146, 147, 149, 191, 197, 198, 199; frijoles charros (Mexican cowboy beans), 60; frijoles de La Olla (beans in a pot), 16

Beef, 7, 10, 31, 45, 47, 49, 50, 52, 64, 65, 66, 67, 68, 71, 73, 129, 134, 135, 147, 148, 149, 150, 151, 152, 176, 179, 191, 192, 197; bistec en chile *pasilla* (beefsteak in pasilla sauce), 78
Beer, xvi, 41, 43, 47, 50, 53, 68, 102, 109, 113, 114, 121, 128, 135, 152, 167, 176, 177, 178
Beverages, 11, 101–115, 146, 158, 176; alcoholic, 95, 101, 102, 108, 109, 110, 111, 176; coffee, 28, 61, 62, 74, 84, 103–104, 105, 114, 145, 146, 147, 155, 168, 176, 189; nonalcoholic, 102–103, 175; ponche de navidad (Christmas punch), 144; water (*see Aguas frescas*)
Birria, 121, 134, 135, 158; birria tatemada estilo Jalisco (slow cooked beef Jalisco style), 142
Bolillo. See Bread
Bread, 8, 10, 23, 24, 25, 27, 29, 30, 32, 33, 43, 47, 61, 62, 64, 68, 74, 87, 88, 89, 90, 91, 92, 124, 125, 126, 130, 133, 146, 147, 156, 191, 198, 199; *bolillo,* 64, 199; bread crumbs, 47, 48, 67; garibaldis (Mexican cupcakes with apricot

preserve), 97; *pan de muerto*, 130, 155, 157; sweet bread, 64, 74, 81, 88, 90, 104, 105, 130, 146
Breakfast, 23, 32, 61, 62–64, 81, 89, 93, 103, 105, 107, 127, 131, 145, 146, 147, 152, 153, 156, 165, 168; traditional, 62
Buñuelos, 12, 81, 91, 133, 134, 155

Cacao, 3, 102, 104, 105, 110
Cactus, xi, 22, 43, 62, 73, 82, 95, 110, 112, 122, 124, 125, 151; *acitrón*, 82, 122; *biznaga*, 122; ensalada de nopalitos (cactus salad), 18; *nopal*, 25, 64, 95, 110, 151; nopalitos navegantes (cactus soup), 36
Cake, 5, 19, 23, 25, 27, 81, 82, 90, 91, 92, 93, 104, 105, 122, 127, 131, 134, 135, 154, 177; rosca de camote (sweet potato bundt cake), 100; rosca de reyes (three kings' cake), 137
Calabacitas, 19, 20, 32, 44, 45, 73; calabacitas rellenas (stuffed squash), 57; crema de calabacitas (cream of squash), 38
Calabaza. *See* Pumpkin
Camotes. *See* Sweet potatoes
Candied fruits, 30, 81, 82, 83, 87, 90, 122, 134
Candy, 24, 27, 81, 82, 83, 84, 85, 88, 122, 127, 132, 155, 156, 165
Capirotada, 87, 88, 92, 125, 126
Carnitas, 134, 135, 145, 146, 151, 152
Cena. *See* Dinner
Central Mexico, xv, 1, 2, 4, 5, 25, 28, 31, 32, 42–45, 64, 66, 71, 73, 82, 83, 89, 93, 109, 124, 129, 157
Ceviche, 53, 72, 123, 130, 174, 176, 178; ceviche Contramar, 186
Champurrado. *See* Atole

Chayote, 21, 43, 45, 47, 48, 52, 76, 91; chayote con queso (*chayote with cheese*), 59
Cheese, 6, 7, 20, 21, 22, 30, 32, 33, 42, 43, 44, 45, 46, 47, 48, 49, 50, 51, 52, 53, 62, 63, 64, 67, 69, 70, 73, 74, 85, 87, 88, 89, 92, 94, 125, 126, 129, 130, 131, 134, 147, 148, 151, 154, 155, 166, 171, 196, 197, 198, 199
Chicken, 4, 21, 22, 30, 31, 42, 44, 45, 46, 47, 52, 53, 64, 65, 66, 68, 69, 70, 71, 73, 88, 89, 124, 126, 129, 131, 133, 134, 135, 147, 148, 149, 152, 166, 168, 176, 177, 179, 191, 197; pollo a la crema de chipotle (chicken in creamy chipotle sauce), 77; pollo al oregano (chicken with oregano), 187
Chile (dish), 65, 66, 67, 68, 124. *See also* Chili peppers
Chili peppers, 2, 3, 7, 21, 22, 26, 27, 43, 44, 47, 48, 49, 50, 51, 52, 53, 54, 63, 65, 66, 67, 68, 69, 71, 82, 104, 105, 125, 129, 132, 136, 192, 197, 198; chiles curados (pickled chili peppers), 17; chiles rellenos (stuffed poblano peppers), 37
Chocolate, xvi, 7, 12, 22, 28, 61, 62, 64, 74, 81, 88, 89, 91, 93, 94, 102, 104, 105, 107, 122, 126, 127, 131, 134, 136, 154, 156, 157, 191, 197, 199
Cilantro, 22, 27, 43, 44, 50, 51, 52, 53, 54, 65, 67, 68, 72, 124, 150, 151
Coastal areas, 42, 49, 53–54, 72, 129, 152
Cocinas, 61, 86, 106, 145, 148, 151, 152, 165, 167
Cocoa, 89, 92, 110
Codorniz a La Espinaca (quails with spinach), 188
Coffee, 28, 61, 62, 74, 84, 103, 104, 105, 114, 145, 146, 147, 155, 168, 176, 189

Index

Comida, 41, 61, 62, 64, 66, 69, 72, 73, 74, 81, 103, 106, 127, 134, 148, 149, 150, 202. *See also* Lunch
Compotes, xii, 24, 25, 81
Corn, xi, xv, 2, 3, 7, 9, 21, 22, 29, 46, 49, 51, 74, 89, 91, 102, 105, 109, 110, 122, 127, 148, 154, 155, 157, 174, 178, 192, 197, 199, 212, 213; *elotes*, 128, 154, 155, 156, 176; *esquites*, 21, 154, 155, 156, 176; esquites (street corn kernels; recipe), 159
Cortés, Hernán, xv, xvi, 6, 30, 66, 146
Crystalized fruits, 23, 24, 25, 122

Desayuno. See Breakfast
Desserts, xii, 19, 23, 24, 25, 26, 27, 28, 29, 30, 33, 81, 82, 83, 85, 86, 87, 89, 91, 93, 94, 95, 97, 99, 131, 133, 134, 157, 179, 181, 182; carlota de limón (lime and cookies dessert), 203; jericalla (Mexican crème brulé), 96
Díaz Porfirio, 10, 104, 166, 189
Dietary concerns, 189–201
Dining out, 9, 165–183
Dinner, 10, 32, 41, 61, 74, 81, 82, 83, 93, 103, 104, 121, 122, 126, 127, 132, 133, 134, 145, 148, 150, 153, 168, 169, 173, 177, 180, 182
Dorilocos (Mexican Frito pie), 205
Dried fruits, 30, 84, 85, 87, 90, 125, 133, 191
Dulces. See Candy; Sweets

Eggs, 32, 49, 62, 63, 64, 84, 85, 88, 91, 93, 107, 125, 126, 147, 148, 152, 168, 191; huevos divorciados (eggs in two sauces), 75
Elotes. See Corn
Enchiladas, xi, 11, 22, 32, 70, 125, 146, 157, 158, 168, 177; enchiladas suizas (enchiladas in a creamy sauce), 184
Epazote, 27, 45, 46, 47, 48, 52, 64, 65, 67, 124, 154
Esquites. See Corn

Fava beans, 26, 44, 50, 52, 54, 124, 147; caldo de habas (fava bean soup), 56
Fish, 2, 5, 6, 30, 31, 46, 47, 50, 51, 52, 53, 54, 65, 71–73, 89, 123, 126, 129, 130, 133, 135, 151, 152, 170, 175, 178, 179, 181, 182, 197; *blanco de Pátzcuaro*, 31; charales, 31, 124; *huachinango*, 31, 71; huachinango a la veracruzana (red snapper Veracruz style), 185; *pejelagarto*, 46, 72
Flan, 68, 85, 86, 134; flan de naranja (orange-flavored flan), 98
Food history: colonial Mexico, 7–8; independent Mexico, 8–10; indigenous civilizations 1–7; modern Mexico, 10–13
Food safety, 192, 193, 195, 196
Frijoles. See Beans
Fruits, 2, 4, 5, 6, 7, 10, 22–26, 30, 41, 47, 50, 54, 82, 83, 84, 85, 87, 89, 90, 92, 93, 101, 102, 105, 106, 108, 109, 110, 113, 114, 122, 125, 130, 131, 132, 133, 134, 137, 138, 153, 155, 156, 191, 192, 193, 194, 197, 199; cocktail de frutas de mercado (fruit salad market style), 162; fruta de la calle (street fruit salad), 160; higos en almíbar (figs in syrup), 207

Garnachas, 147
Goat, 50, 51, 65, 133, 134, 146, 151, 152, 182
Guacamole, xi, 19, 21, 22, 68, 149, 177; guacamole taquero (green sauce with avocado), 34

Guajolota (sandwich), 64, 146; guajolota (*tamal* sandwich), 204
Guajolote. See Turkey

Habas. See Fava beans
Habsburg, Maximilian of, xvii, 8, 9, 113, 166, 171
Helados. See Ice cream
Holidays and special occasions, xiii, 41, 42, 61, 62, 64, 68, 69, 81, 82, 89, 91, 93, 105, 121–143, 145, 155, 156
Horchata, 29, 107, 117
Huauzontle, 20, 73, 125, 175, 177
Huevos, 61, 63, 168

Ice cream, 19, 23, 87, 94, 95, 157, 171
Influential ingredients: beans, 19; dairy products, 32–33; fruits, 22–26; grains, 28–29; herbs and spices, 26–28; meats and fish, 30–31; nuts and seeds, 29–30; vegetables, 19–22

Jícama, 21, 24, 43, 47, 50, 51, 130, 132, 133, 134, 155, 160, 205; ensalada de jicama (jicama salad), 35
Jugos, 145, 147, 152, 153

Lentejas. See Lentils
Lentils, 26, 124; sopa de lentejas (lentil soup), 39
León, Josefina Velázquez de, 70, 86, 90, 91
Licuados, 23, 25, 107, 147, 152, 153; licuado de plátano (banana smoothie), 119
Lunch, 23, 73, 107, 127, 145, 148,153, 165, 168, 173, 177

Main dishes: beef, 66–68; breakfast 62–64, *cena*, 73–74; *comida*, 64–73; fish and seafood, 71–723; pork, 65–66; poultry, 68–70; vegetables, 72–73
Maya, xv, 2, 3, 4, 7, 21, 24, 29, 46, 51, 101, 104, 130, 152, 196
Mezcal, 95, 102, 111, 112, 113, 121, 130, 146, 158, 177
Moctezuma: Aztec emperor, 5, 6; brewery, 114
Mole, 7, 10, 22, 23, 26, 27, 28, 29, 30, 31, 65, 66, 67, 68, 69, 94, 125, 131, 134, 135, 136, 146, 149, 157, 174, 175, 176, 177, 178, 180, 182; mole de olla (spicy beef soup), 76

Nieves, 94, 95, 154
Nopales. See Cactus
North America Free Trade Agreement (NAFTA), xviii, 190–191, 196, 198–199
Northern Mexico, 32, 33, 42, 49–51, 63, 65, 66, 67, 68, 82, 112, 113, 124, 151

Obesity, xiii, 196, 199, 200, 201
Oregano, 20, 27, 28, 45, 48, 63, 66, 70, 71, 72, 73, 129, 130

Pan de muerto. See Bread
Pavo. See Turkey
Pepián. See Pipián
Piloncillo, 84, 85, 87, 105, 107, 108, 110, 125, 126, 131, 132, 134, 146, 148, 155
Piña. See Pineapple
Pineapple, 3, 10, 23, 24, 43, 47, 67, 82, 83, 84, 85, 86, 89, 91, 95, 105, 106, 107, 108, 109, 111, 114, 115, 124, 149, 153, 197
Pipián, 21, 30, 69, 171, 175, 177
Pork, 6, 7, 20, 21, 22, 30, 31, 42, 43, 45, 46, 47, 49, 50, 52, 64, 65, 66, 68, 69, 71, 88, 89, 129, 133, 134,

Index

135, 147, 148, 149, 151, 152, 153, 182, 191, 192, 197
Potatoes, 2, 22, 44, 47, 48, 49, 50, 52, 53, 54, 65, 66, 67, 69, 73, 85, 123, 125, 131, 132, 133, 148, 155; papas con rajas (potatoes and poblano peppers), 58; tortitas de papa (potato patties), 79
Pozole, 129, 133, 134, 158, 197; pozole de camarón (shrimp *pozole*), 140
Prickly pear, 22, 25, 82, 83, 110, 158
Pulque, 10, 30, 95, 102, 104, 108, 109, 110, 111, 113, 146, 158
Pumpkin, 21, 30, 51, 65, 69, 82, 83, 84, 91, 93, 131, 136, 149, 155, 178

Quesadillas, xi, 20, 32, 42, 45, 49, 51, 64, 108, 125, 127, 128, 145, 147, 148, 155, 156, 158, 165, 176, 177, 180, 197; quesadillas de la esquina (street corner quesadillas), 163
Queso. See Cheese

Refrescos. See Soft drinks
Restaurants, xi, xiii, 9, 10, 13, 61, 71, 86, 89, 93, 94, 104, 113, 114, 122, 123, 126, 128, 150, 151, 154, 157, 165, 166, 167, 168, 168, 169, 170, 171, 172, 173, 174, 175, 176, 177, 178, 179, 180, 181, 182, 195, 196
Rice, 29, 41, 44, 48, 49, 50, 52, 54, 57, 64, 66, 67, 69, 70, 71, 72, 85, 96, 105, 107, 117, 136, 149, 175, 188, 191, 192, 197; arroz con leche (rice pudding), 99; horchata (rice drink), 117

Salsa, xi, 19, 21, 22, 27, 30, 33, 41, 42, 43, 45, 49, 50, 51, 53, 68, 73, 124, 129, 130, 147, 149, 150, 151, 194, 199; salsa de molcajete, 15

Salsa de molcajete, 15
Seafood, 31, 48, 53, 54, 65, 71, 123, 126, 129, 158, 170, 174, 177, 179, 181
Side dishes, 26, 30, 41–53, 68, 70, 72, 74, 132, 133
Snacks, 21, 29, 30, 42, 81, 123, 127, 128, 145, 153, 154
Soda, 113, 114, 115, 176, 177, 178, 196, 199, 201
Soft drinks, 114, 178, 196. *See also* Soda
Sopes, 19, 22, 32, 42, 45, 64, 108, 145, 147, 155, 156, 158, 179, 180, 194; *sopes* (little corn cakes; recipe), 55
Southern Mexico, 1, 2, 3, 33, 42, 45–49, 64, 83, 110, 113
Spirits, xviii, 84, 94, 108, 111, 112, 113, 158
Street food, xiii, 22, 42, 64, 74, 88, 89, 95, 106, 108, 123, 128, 129, 132, 145–157, 165, 176, 177, 193, 194, 195, 197
Sweet potatoes, 2, 54, 82, 83, 84, 85, 91, 131, 155
Sweets, 10, 26, 27, 81, 82, 84, 88, 94, 123, 127, 131, 132, 134, 153, 154, 156

Tacos, xi, 20, 21, 22, 24, 31, 43, 47, 49, 50, 51, 69, 71, 73, 108, 123, 127, 128, 129, 145, 148, 149, 150, 151, 165, 174, 175, 176, 177, 179, 180, 182, 194
Tamales, 5, 10, 11, 23, 28, 29, 46, 49, 53, 64, 88, 89, 105, 122, 128, 129, 131, 132, 145, 146, 155, 156, 157; tamales de dulce (sweet tamales), 139; tamales de Gansito (tamales with Gansito cake), 206; tamales verdes (green tamales), 161
Tepache, 107, 108, 113

Tequila, xvi, xviii, 29, 95, 102, 111, 112, 121, 130, 132, 146, 158, 177; José Cuervo, xvi; paloma de Troy (Troy's paloma, cocktail), 120

Tomatoes, xvi, 7, 20, 22, 28, 43, 47, 49, 50, 51, 52, 53, 54, 62, 63, 64, 65, 66, 67, 68, 69, 70, 71, 72, 73, 82, 87, 124, 125, 126, 129, 133, 192, 196, 197

Torta, 64, 146, 156, 157

Tortillas, xi, 4, 5, 8, 10, 29, 32, 41, 42, 43, 44, 45, 46, 47, 49, 50, 52, 53, 62, 63, 67, 68, 69, 70, 73, 123, 124, 125, 133, 136, 147, 148, 149, 151, 174, 196, 197; tortillas caseras (homemade tortillas), 14

Tortitas, 20, 43, 73, 125

Tostadas, 19, 22, 33, 53, 69, 127, 129, 130, 179

Tuna. See Prickly pear

Turkey, xvi, 2, 4, 19, 31, 52, 68, 69, 131, 132, 136, 146

Vanilla, 25, 27, 28, 81, 85, 86, 87, 89, 91, 92, 94, 105, 107, 147, 153

Verdolagas, 20, 45, 65

Yucatán Peninsula, 3, 42, 45, 51–52, 66, 100, 123, 151

ABOUT THE AUTHOR

R. Hernandez-Rodriguez is a professor of Spanish at Southern Connecticut State University. His articles on Mexican and Latin American literature and culture have appeared in various books and major academic journals. He has published *Splendors of Latin Cinema* (ABC-CLIO, 2010) and *Una poética de la despreocupación* (2003), and he is the co-editor of *¡Agítese bien! A New Look at the Hispanic Avant-Gardes* (2002).

www.ingramcontent.com/pod-product-compliance
Lightning Source LLC
Chambersburg PA
CBHW070337240426
43665CB00045B/2123